Understanding
The Call of the Wild

The Greenwood Press "Literature in Context" Series
Student Casebooks to Issues, Sources, and Historical Documents

UNDERSTANDING
The Call of the Wild

A STUDENT CASEBOOK TO ISSUES, SOURCES, AND HISTORICAL DOCUMENTS

Claudia Durst Johnson

The Greenwood Press
"Literature in Context" Series

GREENWOOD PRESS
Westport, Connecticut • London

Library of Congress Cataloging-in-Publication Data

Johnson, Claudia D.
    Understanding The call of the wild : a student casebook to issues,
    sources, and historical documents / Claudia Durst Johnson.
        p.   cm.—(The Greenwood Press "Literature in context" series,
    ISSN 1074–598X)
    Includes bibliographical references and index.
    ISBN 0–313–30882–9 (alk. paper)
        1. London, Jack, 1876–1916. Call of the wild.   2. Gold mines
    and mining—Klondike River Valley (Yukon)—History—Sources.
    3. Klondike River Valley (Yukon)—Gold discoveries—Sources.   4. Klondike
    River Valley (Yukon)—In literature.   5. Gold mines and
    mining in literature.   6. Wolves in literature.   7. Dogs in literature.
    I. Title.   II. Series.
    PS3523.O46C3834   2000
    813'.52—dc21   99–046038

British Library Cataloguing in Publication Data is available.

Library of Congress Catalog Card Number: 99–046038
ISBN: 0–313–30882–9
ISSN: 1074–598X

First published in 2000

Greenwood Press, 88 Post Road West, Westport, CT 06881
An imprint of Greenwood Publishing Group, Inc.
www.greenwood.com

Printed in the United States of America

∞™

The paper used in this book complies with the
Permanent Paper Standard issued by the National
Information Standards Organization (Z39.48–1984).

10 9 8 7 6 5 4 3 2 1

Copyright Acknowledgments

The author and publisher gratefully acknowledge permission for the use of the following
material:

Excerpts from A DOG-PUNCHER ON THE YUKON by Arthur T. Walden. Copyright © 1928
by Arthur T. Walden. Copyright © renewed 1956 by Walden L. Ainsworth. Reprinted by
permission of Houghton Mifflin Company. All rights reserved.

PETA mission statement from its Web site <www.peta-online.org/about/index>. Reprinted
by permission of PETA.

"Nome Dogs Battle Blizzard." *San Francisco Chronicle*, Monday, February 2, 1925, pp. 1,
2. Reprinted by permission of the Associated Press.

To Dr. Verna Wittrock,
Dog Lover,
Teacher, Scholar, and Pioneer Champion of
Rights for Academic Women,
for
Her Indispensable Help with This Project
and Her Unwavering Forty-Year Friendship

Contents

Preface

Jack London, an illegitimate child born in San Francisco in 1876 and reared in poverty across the bay in Oakland, California, had become the highest-paid, most widely read, and best-known writer in America by the time he was thirty-seven years old. In part, London achieved such tremendous popularity because he was the quintessential American adventurer, a westerner living in a country that culturally thrived on and was identified with exploration of unknown territory. He lived an adventurous life and then used events from his own life as fodder for his profession as a writer. At the early age of fifteen, he bought a small boat and embarked on an illegal and dangerous career as an "oyster pirate," raiding other men's lucrative oyster beds in San Francisco Bay. Then he joined the other side of the law in an equally hazardous job, helping the California Fish Patrol capture commercial fishermen plying their trade illegally in the bay. At seventeen, he signed on as an able-bodied seaman for a perilous seven-month seal-hunting expedition in the Pacific Ocean, a journey that took him to Hawaii, Siberian Russia, and Japan, where he and the rest of the crew almost lost their lives in a treacherous typhoon. In 1894, at eighteen, he hoboed across the country, on foot and in boxcars, as part of a social protest by a group of unemployed men who called themselves "Kelly's Army." Passing through Erie County, Ohio, on this trek, he was arrested for vagrancy and served time in a penitentiary. After his release, he made his way up the east coast and then returned to California across Canada by coal car and down from Vancouver by ship, earning his way by stoking coal.

Two years later, in 1897, at the age of twenty-one, he set sail for Juneau, Alaska, to join the great rush for gold in the Yukon, a journey that required climbs over jagged, icy peaks and down treacherous rapids just to reach the gold fields. After enduring a bitter subarctic winter there digging for instant wealth, in late spring, while suffering from scurvy, he rafted down the Yukon River on his way back home to California. These adventures, especially his Yukon experience, narrated to the public in his writings, made him an international hero whose escapades were often newspaper headlines.

The publication that first brought Jack London worldwide fame and continues to be his best-known work is a short novel whose main character is a Yukon sled dog named Buck. That work, begun in December 1902 and published in 1903, was entitled *The Call of the Wild*.

London had earlier written a short story entitled "Bâtard," in which a demonic dog kills his equally demonic owner. London originally saw the story of the noble, sympathetic Buck as his apology for having written "Bâtard." He planned it as a 4,000-word short story for a magazine. But the project soon overtook him, as he described it. In the two months it took him to write it, it grew to a 27,000-word novel. The result was an indisputable classic.

The success of this novel, which appeared serially in the *Saturday Evening Post* and was published as a book by the Macmillan Company, has been nothing short of phenomenal. On July 1, 1903, the day of its publication, 10,000 copies were sold. Within the first forty-three years of its publication, 6 million copies were sold in the United States alone. Furthermore, the book was even more widely read and acclaimed in countries outside the United States. At the end of the twentieth century, it has been translated into some ninety foreign languages. The novel has sold better and has gone through more printings in France and Germany than in the United States, is one of the most popular American books read in China and Japan, and is the most widely read American book in Russia. The total sales throughout the world, counted in the tens of millions, have made it an international best-seller of all time.

Like Louisa May Alcott's *Little Women* and Harper Lee's *To Kill
a Mockingbird*, Jack London's *The Call of the Wild* is one of those
books that is usually encountered in youth and has a profound,
lifelong effect on its readers. It has been called an adventure story,
a romance, a realistic nature story, a dog story, a historical or cultural treatise, and an allegory or myth. It holds special appeal for
those who know and love dogs and for those who know and love
nature and the wilderness. It also appeals to those who yearn for
a special kind of freedom that can only be found outside of society's constraints. The adventurer in its readers respond to the
novel whether the unknown land they would explore is an icy
wilderness near the Arctic Circle or some compelling psychological
and mythic frontier within human beings themselves.

The following study is intended to provide greater understanding of *The Call of the Wild* by placing it in the context of the events
and ideas of the era of its setting and by examining the abiding
issues that it raises. The first chapter, a literary analysis, is intended
to help the reader achieve a firm grasp of the novel's structure and
meaning. The remainder of the volume is devoted to inquiring into
the context against which the novel was written and the issues it
raises. Few novels have been so decidedly shaped by the geography
in which they occur—in this case the Alaskan Panhandle and the
Yukon Territory, which determine the course of Buck's life. The
second chapter explores that subarctic land, utterly unknown to
most readers in 1903. The third chapter is devoted to the event
that shapes the novel—the Klondike gold rush of 1897–98. The
fourth chapter focuses on the species to which the main character
of the novel belongs—the dog. Special attention is given to the
sled dog that predominated in the Yukon during the gold rush.
The fifth chapter examines one of the issues raised by the novel:
the brutality of the sled dog's life and cruelty to animals in general
at the time of the novel's setting. The sixth and final chapter studies a creature central to the novel—the wolf. Moreover, this discussion of the wolf and all he represents raises the ongoing issue
of the environment and mankind's foolish attempt to pursue comfort and riches by decimating the wilderness.

Among the contextual materials included on the Yukon itself are
reports of nineteenth-century explorations documenting its brutal
climate and terrain. In the third chapter, the gold rush is illuminated by newspaper accounts, advertisements, guidebooks, poetry,

and memoirs of those who were on the spot. The chapter on the
sled dog contains an excerpt from a history of dogs, descriptions
of breeds important to the novel, memoirs of those who traveled
by dogsled, and a newspaper report of the great diphtheria run of
1925. Chapter Five, on the issue of cruelty to animals, includes
excerpts from the Bible, memoirs of Yukoners recalling the cruelty
there to dogs and horses, a brief selection from the famous animal
novel *Black Beauty*, and the mission statement of People for the
Ethical Treatment of Animals (PETA), a current society for the prevention of cruelty to animals. The final chapter, on the wolf, contains excerpts from colonial laws setting up bounties for wolves, a
passage showing attitudes toward wolves, and deliberations in the
U.S. Congress on the endangered wolf.

Page numbers in parentheses for quotations from *The Call of
the Wild* refer to the 1990 Thrift Edition (New York: Dover
Publications).

1

Literary Analysis: Adventure and Myth

In August 1896, a group of prospectors in the Yukon Territory hit what would prove to be the richest lode of gold in the world. This discovery soon drew hundreds of thousands of people to a gold rush in the frozen north. Eleven months later, in July 1897, Jack London, then a poor twenty-one-year-old with literary ambitions, left his home in Oakland, California, to join the hordes seeking fortune and adventure on the Klondike River. The Yukon in those days was filled not only with fortune hunters, but with dogs, for dogs were the only means of transportation over the ice and snow. London and his party camped near the Yukon city of Dawson, at the center of gold-rush fever, and frequently visited with the Bond brothers, friends from northern California who had also come to mine for gold. London took a special liking to a big dog named Jack, a cross between a St. Bernard and a shepherd, owned by Marshall Bond. Five years after he had returned from the Yukon and had launched his career as a writer, he published his most popular work, *The Call of the Wild*, about a dog named Buck inspired by his friend's dog, Jack.

AMBIGUITIES

The Call of the Wild is a clear, straightforward narrative of the travails of the dog Buck, whose buried ancestral song leads him to

Jack London. Photo Collections, The Bancroft Library.

return to uncivilized nature to join an arctic wolf pack. Yet the direct, forthright narrative conceals a multilayered message, its complexity reaching to self-contradiction at times. For example, the novel is decidedly naturalistic in its unflinching descriptions of the raw and bloody brutality of nature, in scenes that are painful to read: the vicious beating of Buck by a man in red; the deaths of Curly, a naive and friendly Newfoundland killed by vicious huskies, and Spitz, the untrustworthy lead dog killed by his own team; the attack on the dog team by starved huskies; and the beating of Buck by Hal, one of the incompetents who buys the dog team— to cite a few of many such episodes. At the same time, as London critics Earle Labor and Jacqueline Tavernier-Courbin have observed,[1] the book can be classified as a romance, in that running through it is an affirmation of the spiritual center of all nature. An anthropomorphic (humanlike) Buck, for example, listens to the ancestral voices of a long-dead but lingering past, calls that arise from spirit and from instinct. The romantic, that is to say, spiritual dimension of the novel is also evident in the ascending and ultimately dominant quality of myth, concluding at last in Buck's transformation into "the Ghost Dog" as he fuses with the invisible ancestral past.

On a more mundane level, the naturalistic story shows people and creatures ineluctably caught in the grip of forces over which they have no control: natural law, economic imperatives, and deep-seated psychological drives. At the same time, we also see Buck acting as if he is in control, a creature of strength, as when he cunningly resists the French-Canadians' efforts to deny him a place at the head of the team, thus illustrating the rise of the strong, the clever, "the fittest" in the primordial wild. Later, he seems instinctively to understand John Thornton's words urging him to pull out the heavy sled frozen to the ice for no reason except to settle a wager.

Further ambivalence is shown in the thematic celebration of rugged individualism, at one extreme, and the team, where individualism is submerged into that of the group, at the other extreme. The dog Buck himself is something of a contradiction in terms. He is both heroic and demonic, viciously running down and wounding the treacherous lead dog Spitz before offering him to the pack to be killed, but later heroically risking his own life to save his master John Thornton in treacherous river rapids. He quickly learns to dispense with civilization's moral law. Still, he continues to exhibit qualities of heroism, love, and self-sacrifice, things that transcend moral law, issuing, as they do, from within himself rather than from civilized institutions.

In Buck, civilization itself comes to be suspect. The ultimate comforts and the good life of civilization with all its attendant pleasures are shown in the life of the dog on Judge Miller's ranch. Yet Buck, feeling the slow, insinuating appeal of the brutal world of nature, comes at last to reject all civilization.

London said that he wrote the book simply as the story of an admirable dog who returns to the wild, but later acknowledged the validity of multiple layers of meaning that readers discovered in his account and that literary scholars have explored repeatedly over the years. In attempting to understand *The Call of the Wild*, one needs to look at these several stories on various levels in the novel. The first is clearly a gripping nature or dog story. The second is an allegory of human psychology and behavior. Finally, there is the mythic story of the archetypical hero. These three overlapping levels can be labeled, in increasing order of complexity, as animal, human, and myth.

THE SETTING

The setting for the main action, the Yukon Territory of Canada and Alaska in 1897, a wild, largely unexplored, and uncivilized world of raw nature, places the novel, on one level, in the category of nature book. The geography is as precise and accurate as that of a travel book and can be easily plotted on a map of the region. The action begins on a ranch in Santa Clara, California, forty-four miles south of San Francisco, near the city of San Jose. From there, Buck is taken by railroad to San Francisco. After one night in a wharfside saloon in the city, he is taken by ferry across the Bay of San Francisco to Oakland and then north parallel to San Pablo Bay. A ferry takes him across the Carquinez Strait, where he again is placed on a railway car to Seattle, Washington. From Washington State, he is taken in the ship *Narwhal* across the northern Pacific Ocean and up Queen Charlotte Sound to the port of Dyea, just across from Skagway, Alaska.

The runs that Buck makes with the dogsled teams are between Skagway and Dawson, a journey that takes him out of Alaska into the Yukon Territory. Many of the place names between Skagway and Dawson can be located on detailed maps of the Northwest Territories. These include, more notably, the Chilkoot Divide, Lake Bennett, Lake Laberge, Thirty Mile River, Houtalingua, the Big Salmon and Little Salmon rivers, the White River, Five Fingers, the Pelly River, and the Yukon River.

After two runs between Skagway and Dawson, Buck is bought by three characters in Skagway who take the team as far north as the mouth of the White River. Here ownership of Buck transfers to John Thornton, who takes him to Dawson and areas north of Dawson. Finally, he travels in Thornton's party seventy miles up the Yukon River and then up the Stewart River to McQuestion and Mayo lakes in uncharted northwest territories far east of Dawson.

A DOG'S STORY

On a fundamental level, London wrote (and many readers enjoy) *The Call of the Wild* as a dog story: a tale about an extraordinary dog, Buck, who meets many challenges and undergoes changes as a result of his adventures. Buck is a massive, strong, regal dog with a rich coat of fur. He is intelligent, courageous, self-confident, and even-tempered except when pushed too far. Then he is as fierce as any wolf in the wild. He is sparing with his affection, but protective of his weaker team members and capable of great loyalty. The chief theme of the novel is his growth through adversity. Not only is Buck the central character of the novel, but the story is told primarily from his point of view.

The number of dog characters in the novel equals the number of human characters. At the beginning of the story, the reader meets two small house dogs and miscellaneous hunting dogs on Judge Miller's ranch in Santa Clara; and at the end, among John Thornton's dogs are two who are favored pets, killed by a group of Indians called the Yeehats. In between, eleven dogs with distinct personalities are introduced: the naive and friendly Newfoundland, Curly, who is slaughtered by a pack of dogs in the port city of Dyea upon their arrival in Alaska; Spitz, the lead dog and Buck's bitter rival; Dave, the old dog who wants to be left alone and who tries to insist on working even while he is dying; Billee, the friendly appeaser; the bad-tempered Joe; old, one-eyed, angry Sol-leks; Dolly, who goes mad; Pike, the shirker; Dub, the thief; and Koona and Teek, the two dogs who join the team just in time to perish beneath the ice.

The seven chapters of the novel are divided into four parts: first, Buck's life on the ranch and his kidnapping and travel to Alaska; second, his runs with the French-Canadians and Scotsman; third, his ordeal with the incompetents; and fourth, his stay with John Thornton and his return to the wild. Structurally, the novel contains a conventional plot structure: an initial exposition (the beginning situation); an initiating circumstance that starts the whole string of events; and then, in the tradition of the animal novel, a series of alarming episodes, each of which presents a challenge to Buck and most of which involve death or wounding.

The exposition or initial scenes of Buck's life as a dog on Judge Miller's ranch make his subsequent trials all the more formidable, even horrifying, by comparison. Here, in California, he is the valued pet, the animal king "ruling" over his "realm" in a "sun-kissed" climate. He spends his days leisurely, as a companion rather than a work dog. He escorts the young ladies and hunts with the young gentlemen. The nature that he knows here is simple, one-dimensional, and benign. With its lawns and cultivated fields, nature here is as tamed by man as Buck is himself.

The event that starts a chain of harsh episodes in Buck's life is an act of betrayal by a friend, Manuel, who sells him to his tormentors. This propels him into one hardship after another, a series of trials that test his ability to adapt and that profoundly change him. He is first introduced to adversity by the rope and the cage. Under the burden of these tools and symbols of enslavement, common sense overcomes his natural pride because he quickly realizes that despite his fear and pain, it is safer to ignore his tormentors, for raging at them only encourages them to further cruelties.

His next trial is the most important defining experience of his existence. A man in a red sweater releases him from his cage and beats him into submission with a club. From this moment on, Buck will always be aware that it is self-defeating to defy a man with a club. Many miles and months later, the memory of this beating continues to modify Buck's behavior. Ironically, this savage beating at the beginning of his adventures enables him to survive later.

As Buck is taken north, the implicit tragedy is his irrevocable removal from home. For most domesticated animals, as Buck was, there is no pull quite so strong as the bonds of home and master.

Many are the instances of dogs and cats who travel long distances to return to the place they knew as home. But Buck's passage over the waters of the northern Pacific Ocean into the Northland prevents any possibility of returning home.

Everything in his new surroundings is the opposite of the comforting familiarity of home. Indeed, much of his hardship is caused by his encounters with the unfamiliar in nature and culture. For example, although his St. Bernard ancestors flourished in a snowy climate, the dog raised in California is terrified by his first introduction to snow on the shores of Dyea. He is diminished when his antics are met with raucous laughter by those around him.

He has a similar experience his first night in camp, growing almost frantic in realizing that, surrounded by snow, he has nowhere to sleep. The men refuse to allow him in the tent, and the other dogs have disappeared without informing him of what he is to do.

The intricate work of the sled dog is also unfamiliar to a dog who has never had to work. Even his soft feet are unaccustomed to the work of pulling in the traces for miles and miles in arctic weather. Once he had been the regal master of all he surveyed, but now in his first weeks in Alaska and the Yukon, he is ignorant, inexperienced, and even, as when he first encounters snow, an object of ridicule.

He also becomes disturbed and disoriented by the unfamiliar in the cruel culture of his own species in the Northland. In a pivotal scene, Buck witnesses the slaughter of the good-natured dog Curly, not by men, but by a pack of dogs. The horrifying scene of dogs circling and tearing apart a wounded dog foreshadows and parallels a similar scene later in which Buck is not the distressed observer, but a participant in the death of another dog, Spitz. A comparison of Buck's behavior in the parallel scenes indicates just how markedly he has changed in the interval.

Shortly after he watches Curly's death, another scene of canine cruelty out on the trail leaves Buck terrified and off balance. A pack of starving huskies charges the sled dogs and rips into them viciously. Taking strength from the instinct to survive and from the team of which he has now become a member, Buck meets this challenge by going for the jugular of one of the marauders. At this moment, another startling act of canine cruelty of an entirely different order occurs. Spitz, the leader of Buck's team, slashes Buck's throat while Buck is fighting one of the huskies, their common

enemy, and in the general melee tries to throw Buck down so that
the huskies can finish him off. Instantly Buck realizes that he is in
a death struggle, not with a man, but with another dog.

From this experience, Buck senses for a time that his most dangerous enemy is no longer man, who has kidnapped him, clubbed
him senseless, and cursed him with work; his enemy is one of his
own species, a member of his own team. Spitz is the one with
experience and the unscrupulousness of harshest nature, but from
the moment of Buck's enlightenment, when Spitz tries to deliver
Buck to be torn apart by the pack of wild dogs, Buck takes the
upper hand with his patience, cunning, and imagination. He will
take his time bringing Spitz down, but from this moment Buck is
the unofficial lead dog. For self-preservation and in revenge for
Spitz's callous enjoyment of Curly's painful death in Dyea, Buck
first undermines Spitz's authority and then breaks his leg, leaving
him to be butchered by the team, which Buck has turned against
Spitz. Violence and death are now the way of Buck's world. But
Dave's slow and painful dying from disease is as horrible as any
vicious killing.

A reversal in the nature of Buck's adversaries occurs when the
three incompetents buy the dog team in Skagway. From the time
he is taken over by the incompetents to the end of his story, his
enemy is once again man, as it was after his kidnapping. Buck has
learned to defend himself against attacks by other creatures, but
he is helpless in the face of clubbings and starvation by men.

Under the control of Hal, Charles, and Mercedes, most of the
dogs die from overwork, starvation, and beatings. Buck has learned
long ago that it is useless to fight a man with a club in his hand,
but at John Thornton's camp he decides that even a clubbing will
not get him on his feet, and Thornton intervenes, leaving the rest
of the men and dogs to die beneath the ice.

The challenges that Buck faces in the company of John Thornton
are almost effortless because they come from love of his new master. These tests include his attack on Burton, a man who threatens
Thornton; his winning of a bet for Thornton; and his saving of
Thornton's life in the rapids at Forty Mile Creek.

But he also willingly accepts the challenges presented by wildest
nature. He sets out to hunt faster and faster animals, larger and
larger animals, as if to prove his own ability to survive, his own

mastery over his environment. His game includes salmon and squirrels and rabbits, a bear, and a moose.

His final excruciating challenge is presented by the Yeehat Indians who have just murdered every human and dog in Thornton's camp. This time it is too late to help his master. Simultaneously he faces the challenge of being accepted by the wolf pack and later taking leadership of the pack.

Throughout these tests and adversities, Buck has been undergoing the changes reflected in the four poetic lines that open the novel. Hardship makes him stronger and awakens "old longings" (1) that gradually move him closer to nature unaltered by man. The beating by the man in the red sweater introduces him to the "reign of primitive law" (6); it releases the primitive in him and frees him from the moral code of the judge's world. All the dogs and men he subsequently encounters in the Northland have already left behind the kind of civilization he knew on Judge Miller's ranch. The primitive rises in him again when he wakes confused and seemingly trapped beneath the snow. It is "the fear of the wild thing for the trap" (11). Out on the ice, his domestication is replaced by the primitive; buried instincts are kindled; and he feels his connection with the ancient days of his wolflike ancestor. The howling of nearly wild dogs also raises the primitive in Buck, returning him to the "howling ages."

At the time the team members all madly chase the rabbit, the call of the wild is aroused by the "joy to kill" (22), for all the dogs feel most alive in the face of danger and the kill. When Buck enables the dogs to kill Spitz, memories of ancient times rise in him again.

After having survived much violence and hardship, when he is in the darkness around the Scotch half-breed's fire, he feels his ancient heredity clearly. In a recurrent dream, he beholds the caveman who worked beside his ancestors.

Ironically, it is after he develops a love for a man, John Thornton, that the call of the primitive becomes strong. Protected and loved by Thornton now, he feels the old law of "kill or be killed, eat or be eaten" (44). Visions of cavemen become more persistent, and he hears the primitive call him from the forest. He finally has an encounter with the wild in the form of a timber wolf. He spends more time hunting in the wild, bringing down larger and larger prey—the bear, the moose, and eventually man, "the noblest game of all" (60). Without Thornton as a connection to civilization, he gives himself up completely to the wild. The transformation that forms the spine of the dog story is complete.

AN ALLEGORY OF MAN

The Call of the Wild is not only a story of a dog's adventurous transformation; it is also a story in which a dog's life reflects truths about the human condition. In this sense, the novel bears some resemblance to the literary form known as the beast fable, which gives human characteristics to an animal in order to illustrate or satirize human society and human nature. The familiar story of the race between the tortoise and the hare, for example, illustrates the folly of human arrogance and the value of human persistence.

The other dogs are largely one-dimensional fable types who can be described with adjectives usually given to humans. Dave is old and wants to be left alone. Joe is testy and mean tempered. Buck, on the other hand, is a more complex humanized animal than those found in fables. Even the first sentence states that if he could read, he would know that dogs were being kidnapped for service in the Yukon. Throughout, in human fashion, he observes and draws conclusions. At first he has moral scruples, and he always seems to understand human language. John Thornton says to Buck, "God! you can all but speak!" (43).

On an individual level, Buck seems to parallel Jack London himself. Like Buck, London was born and grew up in northern California. After leaving home, he traveled deeper and deeper into the heart of darkness, as Buck does, observing the depths to which human beings can sink in their treatment of each other and the savagery of nature itself. As a young man, London began to experience the violence and hardship caused by nature and man in the jobs he took on for survival: working on ranches, farms, and canneries in California, where living and working conditions were abominable. He got his glimpse of human hardship in the sweatshops operating around San Francisco. His search for adventure brought him into contact with the violence of nature during a seal-hunting expedition in Hawaii, where he was also shocked by what man had done to man. He also got a glimpse of human degradation during his march across the country in what was known as

"Kelly's Army" to protest economic conditions and the plight of the poor. For the portrait of Buck, who was caged and chained after his kidnapping, London seemed to draw on his own experience during the march: his imprisonment for vagrancy in Erie County, Ohio. Like Buck, he was aghast at seeing nature in the raw in the Klondike during the gold rush. Even this, however, was not as appalling as what he witnessed in London, England, shortly after he returned from the Klondike and while he was composing *The Call of the Wild*. His letters reveal that he could scarcely take in the extent of human suffering among the lower classes in a country so wealthy and "civilized." This experience strengthened his commitment to socialism, for he saw what civilization, specifically capitalism and governmental incompetence, had done to those on the bottom of the economic ladder.

London captures something of this in the novel he was composing at the time. The dogs, Buck included, like the humans he saw in London, are forced to serve human greed. The Klondike gold is part and parcel of capitalism, the system that suppressed the English poor. The desire for money in both cases leads strong creatures to enslave weaker ones. It is the rage for gold that leads to Buck's kidnapping, clubbings, starvation, and killing labor and to the deaths of other dogs. Economics puts the whole narrative in motion, for Manuel sells Buck to cover the gambling debts he has incurred to make enough money to live on because his salary does not cover the needs of his family.

Incompetence, coupled with greed, produces the greatest suffering for those forcibly enlisted in the search for gold, whether it is in a London factory or on a Klondike sled team. The ignorance of Hal, Mercedes, and Charles, the bungling newcomers, results in the death of all the dogs they take on except for Buck. They overload the sled, allow Mercedes to add her weight to the load by riding, take more dogs than they can carry food for, and travel over melting ice.

Capitalistic society's equally incompetent measures fail to take into account the needs of the workers it depends on to flourish. Similarly, the incompetents starve the very dogs they depend on for survival. Such actions, according to socialists, are suicidal and counterproductive and will eventually leave the business world without either a cooperative labor force or a market for its goods. The attack by the starving huskies is a reminder that society's lack of care for its workers can lead to desperation and revolution. Like the incompetent newcomers, capitalism is driving a heavy sled on thin ice.

Nature, even at its most savage, is preferable to such a brutal society. London, England, with its long tradition of refinement in literature and government, might well have been regarded as the pinnacle of Western-world culture at the time Jack London was writing *The Call of the Wild*. After observing conditions there, however, he was ready to put this high level of civilization behind him, much as Buck is ready to join the wolves after his experiences with the incompetents and the murder of John Thornton. London returned to "nature's nation," as the United States has been called, which, compared with England and Europe, was more closely connected to the natural world.

Ralph Waldo Emerson, America's great nineteenth-century philosopher, divided human beings into two groups: those who belonged to the Party of Civilization and those who belonged to the Party of Nature. Members of the Party of Civilization affirm that human institutions, such as the church and the government with their ethical laws and social rules, save humankind from the chaos and "tooth-and-claw" savagery of nature. Conversely, members of the Party of Nature believe that it is society that corrupts nature, rather than vice versa. Buck's return to the wild is also London's decision to align himself, as Emerson did, with the Party of Nature, despite the savagery that he acknowledges there.

To the same ideological ends, London's novel is a pointed study of personal freedom as a concept cherished by both man and beast. He uses the tale of Buck's progress from a tame pet to a wild beast to explore the relationship of freedom to civilization. Buck's story enlarges on the value we place on freedom—on owning ourselves rather than, for example, relinquishing some of our freedom so that we can be taken care of by someone else. One cannot assume that being free is without its problems. Given benevolent owners, the dogs or the people who must (or are willing to) lose their freedom may have fewer worries in life: someone else provides their food and other necessities, protects them from danger, and takes on difficult decisions for them. This was the argument advanced by slave owners in the nineteenth century. It is the life of perpetual childhood. Yet Buck and most of the slaves in the American South were willing to give up being "taken care of" in order to own themselves.

Buck's story also reminds us that we cannot automatically assume that personal freedom is sustained by what are understood to be high levels of civilization. The primitive dog in *The Call of the Wild* is free. Characteristics of Buck's distant ancestors emerge in him (a condition called atavism), and he experiences in a dream the ancient relationship with man. But these memories are of living side by side with man, not being owned by him. Yet in the civilized world, the idea of property is fully developed, and man owns the dog and uses him as a tool. History bears out the relationship between slavery and civilization portrayed in London's novel, for it teaches us that slavery has been a cornerstone of the most advanced civilizations on earth. One need look no farther than the Egyptians, whose art and engineering are unsurpassed, and the Athenians and Romans of the classical world, whose philosophy, literature, and science placed them at the height of Western civilization. The nineteenth-century English and Europeans, who ushered in the modern age, also developed a flourishing slave trade. The American planters of the nineteenth century freely argued that the social refinements indicative of their high level of civilization were made possible only by the slave labor they fought to sustain.

The theme of slavery and freedom in the story is illuminated in the parallels one finds between Buck's story and *Uncle Tom's Cabin*, the world-renowned story of the slave Uncle Tom, written fifty years earlier by Harriet Beecher Stowe. In both stories, economics lies behind the slavery they depict. Slavery is perpetuated by greed. Maintaining huge profits from cotton farming and lavish lifestyles is only possible in the American South through the use of slave labor. Similarly, the structure required in the mad rush for Klondike gold rests on the brutalizing labor of dogs.

One finds further parallels in that both the story of Uncle Tom and the story of Buck begin in conditions of benevolent ownership that end with betrayals. Uncle Tom is wrenched from his wife and children and placed in the hands of a brutal slave trader. Buck also is taken from his home and sold to a dog trader. London's novel is a mirror image of Stowe's in that Buck is taken to the harsh life of the far north, while Tom is sold into the "Deep South," where conditions are far more cruel than in his native Virginia.

What follows the betrayals in both cases is great suffering and hardship told in somewhat episodic fashion. Both Tom and Buck, sometimes chained or tied, experience the worst of slavery: brutal beatings, killing toil, and starvation. Not only do they suffer themselves, but they witness the effects of slavery on their fellow creatures. While both of them know cruel owners, they also have kindhearted ones. For a time, Tom's life is made easier in the St. Clare household, just as Buck has a reprieve from harsh work and abuse while he is owned by John Thornton.

Yet in both cases, despite the kindness of certain owners, benevolence cannot endure in a system in which freedom is abridged. If one is owned by someone else, then his or her life is inevitably tied to what happens to the owner. Tom's owner, St. Clare, and Buck's owner, John Thornton, both die, leaving Tom and Buck unprotected within a brutal system. Tom, of course, has no choice, but Buck escapes the system by leaving for the wild.

Acknowledging the parallels between Buck and the human slave solves one puzzle in the narrative. The question sometimes raised is: why, after such a positive experience with a master, John Thornton, would Buck reject the dog-human relationship of the civilized world and join a wild life closer to the world of the primitive Yeehats who murdered Thornton? One answer is that, like the slaves of the American South, what Buck is choosing is freedom. Even though for some and in many ways, a free life may be more difficult, self-ownership is finally to be preferred over being owned by someone else.

London was not the first author to comment on human slavery and freedom through the means of an animal story. Anna Sewell, a Quaker who had been a passionate foe of slavery, wrote a horse story in 1877 entitled *Black Beauty* that had a similar narrative. Perhaps so her readers would be sure to get the point, the then president of the humane society, George Thorndike Angell, gave Sewell's story its subtitle of *The "Uncle Tom's Cabin" of the Horse*. Whether or not London was as intentional as was Sewell in his parallels with *Uncle Tom's Cabin*, specifically, the narrative pattern was common to many true and fictional accounts of human slavery and enlarged on the inevitable exploitation of man and beast in the rapacious pursuit of material wealth. The horse Beauty, like Buck and the slaves in Stowe's novel, is sold away from his family, is coarsely and intrusively examined by his buyers, is gentle enough to be trusted with children and young women, has knowledge of floggings, and comes to long for freedom: "What more could I want? Why, liberty!" (24). If *Black Beauty* was the *Uncle Tom's Cabin* of the horse, Margaret Marshall Saunders's *Beautiful Joe*, another nineteenth-century story written to diminish cruelty to animals, was the *Black Beauty* of the dog, in the introductory paragraphs making reference to *Black Beauty* and linking the canine narrator to a slave named Cupid.

THE MYTH

As well as being both a nature story and an exploration of the human condition, *The Call of the Wild* also operates on the level of myth. It takes on a religious tone through Buck, its mythic hero. To explore this idea, we first need to define myth: it is a legendary story, having no precise beginning or known author, that arises in a culture. Although each culture has its own myths, identical myths arise in many different cultures as well. These stories express universal truths that defy straightforward explanations, for example, the creation of the world or the renewability of the human spirit that parallels the earth's renewal in spring.

The journey of the hero recounted in *The Call of the Wild* encompasses several universal myths that sometimes overlap: the loss of happiness (as told in the myth of the Garden of Eden); the myth of initiation (as embodied in the series of tests a boy must complete before he becomes a man); the descent into hell (as in the myths of Ulysses, Aeneas, and Dante); and the myth of resurrection. While even the ordinary human being can make such a transforming journey, it is usually represented by the progress of a creature of extraordinary proportions.

Buck is recognized as such an extraordinary supercreature even from the beginning of his story. On the judge's ranch, he "rules" as a "king" (2). He is an "aristocrat" who carries himself in "right royal fashion" (2). One of the French-Canadians, Perrault, recognizes him as "one in ten t'ousand" (7). François, the other, predicts that Buck will one day vanquish the lead dog, Spitz. When Buck does defeat Spitz, he insists on the lead and performs his job in rare fashion. As John Thornton's dog, his legendary status grows when he breaks the sled out of the ice. At the end, he has become the Ghost Dog. He is no longer just a dog, but a supernatural being.

The Myth of Lost Happiness

The story of the Garden of Eden very well illustrates the myth of lost happiness and innocence. According to legend, Eden was a protected place where nature was benign. All creatures, man included, lived together harmoniously. The lion and the lamb could lie down together. There were no diseases, and there was no brutal weather. Furthermore, every requirement of humankind was met in the Garden. There was no concept of work, starvation, change, suffering, or death.

But a crime changed all that. In this case, Adam and Eve ate the fruit of a tree that was forbidden them, and this caused their expulsion from the Garden into a world where nature is cruel and inharmonious and where humans must suffer, toil, grow old, and die.

Buck's kidnapping from the Miller ranch is an interpretation of the Garden myth. The ranch is a garden, of course, with its lawns and crops. Dogs of several kinds get along without major disagreements. Their physical activity is play rather than work. Judge Miller presides over it all like a benevolent deity. Like Adam and Eve in the Garden of Eden, Buck has had no reason to distrust any animal or human, including Manuel.

The separation from the garden happens when a crime is committed. Manuel sells Buck, a dog that is not his to sell. For Buck, this is the end of innocence, the last of the garden, and the beginning of his life in a fallen world. From now on, he will encounter suffering, backbreaking toil, death, and the brutality of nature.

Initiation

In initiation rites, young men undergo trials and tests, usually under the tutelage of more experienced guides. While the guide offers direction and advice, in the final analysis the initiate is on his own and has to meet a challenge to prove that he is a man.

Each of the episodes that follow Buck's expulsion is a step in his initiation into the cruel world outside the garden. Each is a test that brings him closer to the reality of the world and his own true nature and potential. His experiences characteristic of the initiation myth include his learning to work in the traces as a sled dog under the guidance of François and Perrault, his awareness of deep love and respect under the mentorship of John Thornton, and his initiation into the untamed wilderness and into the wolf pack by the lone wolf he meets near Thornton's camp.

For much of his initiation, Buck has no guide but tribal memory and instinct. He learns to kill his food like one born to the wilderness, eventually spending four days stalking the bull moose he has singled out. Each encounter brings him closer to a sense of his own truth: that is, his power as a sled dog at first and later his primitive nature and ability to survive as an animal in the wild.

Descent into Hell

The descent into hell is one of the most powerful and persistent myths in human culture. It is central to such classical stories as those of Ulysses, the mythic Greek heroic warrior; Aeneas, a mythic Trojan warrior whose descendants founded Rome; and Dante, the Italian poet, who wrote of his trip to hell. The stories from different cultures have many common threads. A man, usually of heroic stature, who finds himself confused, deluded, and directionless is afforded a trip to hell or a similar underworld. There he undergoes psychological or spiritual suffering and encounters older characters who open his eyes and provide him with wisdom and direction. In Dante's *Inferno*, the hero encounters many different kinds of sinners. The worst of these have been traitors and are punished by being entrapped in ice at the center of hell. If the hero is lucky, he is able to emerge from hell, knowing now who he is and what direction his life must take. After Ulysses' trip to the underworld, he finally heads his ship directly for home rather than traveling here and there in search of risky adventures. Aeneas, on his trip to hell, gets explicit instructions about locating the place where his descendants will found a new city—in this case, Rome.

Buck also finds himself in a frigid icy hell of darkness, a place of death and treachery completely opposite to the paradise he knew in California. He had been a king, but now an evil man (a devil) in a red sweater (a color appropriate for a devil) shows him his limitations. He can be beaten and controlled. The traditional way of entering the classical underworld was to be ferried over the river Styx. Buck enters the white horror of the Northland in a similar way: by boat he reaches the shore of Dyea. Once he is there, hellish horrors continually confront him: the tribal murder of Curly on his first day in Dyea, the persistent treachery of Spitz, who is called a devil, the nightmare attack by the maddened huskies, the madness of the dog Dolly, the slow death of Dave, the starvation of the entire team, the fall beneath the ice of the three humans and the remaining dogs, and finally the diabolical slaughter of John Thornton and his entire camp.

Moreover, as with others who visit a psychological hell, he learns of his own capacity for brutality, chiefly in his manipulation of the team and the defeat of Spitz. He too, as the French-Canadians attest, is a devil. The horrors he sees and his own brutal capacity for survival that develops because of them lead him to follow the ancient inner song to enter the wild.

The Resurrection Story

Stories of death and resurrection are present in many cultures. One such story, from Egypt, tells of Osiris, the god of the Nile River. Osiris was killed and dismembered by Set, the god of darkness and death, but Osiris's sister and his wife brought him back from the dead. Osiris's death and resurrection have multiple levels of meaning. The story represents the annual, destructive flooding of the Nile River (death), which, when it recedes, leaves fertile soil for the cultivation of crops (resurrection). Thus, as in this case, resurrection and rebirth can only happen if death happens.

Such stories are echoed in the natural cycle of the earth, which dies in winter and comes back to life every spring. Baptism by immersion is a ritual representing the myth of spiritual resurrection. The old person dies, an act symbolized by his or her being lowered under the water. Then the raising of the person out of the water represents the emergence of a new spirit, a resurrection. Only if the child dies can the adult in him or her come forth.

A symbolic prefiguring of Buck's rebirth occurs after his first night in the Northland when he has buried himself beneath the snow. He wakes, enclosed on all sides, as if in a coffin. Then he leaps up through the snow into the bright light of day. Symbolically, he has been baptized in snow rather than water.

Buck is also reborn in love, revived by John Thornton after being nearly starved, beaten, and worked to death by the three incompetents. As Hal beats him with a club, "the spark of life within flickered and went down. It was nearly out" (40). Only Thornton's intervention, at the risk of being knifed by Hal, brings Buck back to life. Love, though it does not last forever, becomes the redeeming force, powerful enough to resurrect the dead. At the end, Buck has become more than animal, more than humanized dog; as the Ghost Dog, he transcends nature and passes into myth.

THE PROBLEMS

The Call of the Wild defies the simple label of "dog story." Its vision of man, of nature, and of civilization is enigmatic. Look at one example: it has been called the most spiritual, even religious, of books. At the same time, it is claimed that the book naturalistically negates the possibility of a god. Furthermore, it seems to affirm the greatness of individual strength and determination, but at the same time, it places individuals at the mercy of many forces outside themselves. Various forces, including the law of nature, determine Buck's actions. Still, there are moments when Buck seems to be deliberative and in control. One can see that he rationally plans the undermining of Spitz; he maneuvers to get in a leadership position in the traces after Spitz; and for no apparent imperative except to please John Thornton, he breaks the heavy sled out of the ice.

The novel embodies another perplexing issue when the narrator says that the hero abandons the morality of the world he has known. Buck loses any compunction he had earlier against stealing, for example, and has no moral reservation about undermining Spitz and leaving him wounded for the other dogs to kill. (This is similar to a scene in another dog novel by Alfred Ollivant called *Bob, Son of Battle*, in which a group of sheep dogs circles and kills a villainous dog named Red Wull who is found to be a sheep killer.) On the other hand, heroism, love, self-sacrifice, and empathy form the basis of the novel. One can argue that Buck's own moral law rises above his old world's codes, for his actions proceed, not from the rules of judgmental civilized institutions, but from the heart.

Still, while it is true that the vision of the world the novel presents is complex, nevertheless, there can be no question that the lives of creatures, man included, are largely determined by forces beyond their control. A prime example is the disappearance of Buck's comparatively kind drivers, François and Perrault, from the scene. They leave, not because they make a conscious decision to make a change, but because official orders arrive directing their actions.

Yet no humanlike deity is discernible working behind the scenes to direct the course of the characters' lives. Instead, these forces reside in economic law, natural law, or creature consciousness, rather than in God. Economic forces, for instance, determine the lives of both men and animals in the novel. Manuel is helpless in the face of poverty and his inability to care for his family with his meager wages. This leads him to the original sin of selling—betraying—Buck. Gold glitters throughout the novel, and greed for gold sends great hordes of people racing to the Yukon and by any means possible acquiring the great numbers of dogs needed to travel on the frozen terrain of the North. The narrator implies that an economic imperative is really behind or determines everything that happens in the novel:

> Thus, as token of what a puppet thing life is, the ancient song surged through him and he came into his own again; and he came because men had found a yellow metal in the North, and because Manuel was a gardener's helper whose wages did not lap over the needs of his wife and divers small copies of himself. (14)

In Buck's individual actions, of course, the forces that drive him are instinct, tribal memory, and the laws of nature. Despite his immense prowess and intelligence, these forces, vague and indistinct and beyond his control, are primarily what determine his life in the presence of a club, another threatening dog, or the wolf pack that he joins.

Jack London, like Ralph Waldo Emerson, the American philosopher who believed that spiritual truths were reflected in nature, belongs to the "Party of Nature," as Emerson called it. But London's perception of nature bears little resemblance to Emerson's vision of it. Emerson's version of nature was represented by tranquil New England landscapes and rhododendron blossoms. For Jack London, nature was "tooth and claw"—the hard killing ice and the desperate cry of a rabbit attacked by dogs. Nevertheless, on a sphere above the arctic ice and the Emersonian flower, we might find a meeting of the minds, for, like Emerson, London seems to say in *The Call of the Wild* that nature points us to higher, spiritual truths.

NOTE

1. Jacqueline Tavernier-Courbin, *The Call of the Wild: A Naturalistic Romance* (New York: Twayne Publishers, 1994); and Earle Labor and Jeanne Campbell Reesman, *Jack London* (New York: Twayne Publishers, 1994).

PROJECTS FOR ORAL OR WRITTEN EXPLORATION

1. Why do you think that London chose a dog story to explore the human condition? Why did he not just make the hero a man?

2. Conduct a debate on the subject of how the novel should be classified. Is it best described as naturalistic or religious?

3. From research, construct a careful definition of determinism. Where in the novel do you find evidence that humans or dogs rise above determinism?

4. Write a careful analysis of the meaning of snow in the novel. Research the traditional symbolism of snow. To what extent has London adopted or varied from this tradition?

5. In what ways has London made Buck anthropomorphic, or human-like?

6. Can you make a strong connection between London's socialism (the belief that capital and land belong to all a community's citizens in common) and *The Call of the Wild*?

7. Define morality and explore references to morality in the novel. Is this an amoral novel?

8. Can Buck's brutal behavior be rationalized? Explain why or why not.

9. Contrast the early scene in Santa Clara with the scenes of John Thornton. How exactly are they alike, and how are they different?

10. The novel has been touted as a story of rugged American individualism, yet most of the action takes place while Buck is a member of a sled team or a member of Thornton's camp, and the novel ends with his becoming a member of a wolf pack. Discuss the attitude toward individualism and the group that emerges in the novel.

11. Define myth using the *Oxford English Dictionary* and do some research on the hero in myth. What characteristics of the mythic hero does Buck have?

SUGGESTIONS FOR FURTHER READING

Other Northland works by Jack London:
   Children of the Forest. New York: The Macmillan Co., 1902.
   A Daughter of the Snows. Philadelphia: J. B. Lippincott, 1902.
   The Faith of Men and Other Stories. New York: Macmillan, 1904.
   The God of His Fathers and Other Stories. New York: McClure, Phillips, 1904.

The Son of the Wolf: Tales of the Far North. Boston: Houghton, Mifflin, 1900.

White Fang. New York: Macmillan, 1906.

Garber, Marjorie. *Dog Love*. New York: Simon & Schuster, 1996.

Labor, Earle, and Jeanne Campbell Reesman. *Jack London*. Rev. ed. New York: Twayne Publishers, 1994.

Nuernberg, Susan M., ed. *The Critical Response to Jack London*. Westport, CT: Greenwood Press, 1995.

Ownbey, Ray Wilson, ed. *Jack London: Essays in Criticism*. Santa Barbara, CA: Peregrine Smith, 1978.

Pizer, Donald. *Realism and Naturalism in Nineteenth-Century American Literature*. Rev. ed. Carbondale: Southern Illinois University Press, 1984.

Saunders, Margaret Marshall. *Beautiful Joe: An Autobiography*. Philadelphia: C. H. Barnes, 1896.

Sewell, Anna. *Black Beauty*. New York: H. M. Caldwell Co., 1894.

Tavernier-Courbin, Jacqueline. *The Call of the Wild: A Naturalistic Romance*. New York: Twayne Publishers, 1994.

———, ed. *Critical Essays on Jack London*. Boston: G. K. Hall, 1983.

Walcutt, Charles Child, ed. *Seven Novelists in the American Naturalist Tradition: An Introduction*. Minneapolis: University of Minnesota Press, 1974.

Walker, Franklin Dickerson. *Jack London and the Klondike: The Genesis of an American Writer*. San Marino, CA: Huntington Library, 1966.

Watson, Charles N. *The Novels of Jack London: A Reappraisal*. Madison: University of Wisconsin Press, 1983.

Wilcox, Earl J., ed. *The Call of the Wild by Jack London: A Casebook with Text, Background Sources, Reviews, Critical Essays, and Bibliography*. Chicago: Nelson-Hall, 1980.

2

The Alaskan Panhandle and the Yukon Territory

The Alaskan Panhandle and the Yukon Territory form an appropriate backdrop for a noble dog's decision to turn his back on civilization. In few literary works does the setting itself have such profound importance. Compelling scenes permeate the narrative: the snow-covered beach at Dyea; the bitter cold that bites into Buck's wounded shoulder his first night in the Northwest; the snow that he must learn to sleep in; the run "across glaciers and snowdrifts hundreds of feet deep" (12); the precipitous Chilkoot Divide; the threat of a flood from the spring breakup of ice; ice that forms between his toes; ice that covers his drinking water; wind "that cut like a white-hot knife" (15); the attack by starving huskies; his own constant hunger; the fifty-below-zero weather; the falls through the ice; the cliffs that have to be scaled and the long, steep descents on the other side; the "rotten" ice that swallows up Hal's dog team; the dangerous rapids of Forty Mile Creek.

One might even argue persuasively that the far Northwest assumes the importance in the novel of a major character. Consequently, to fully understand Buck's story in *The Call of the Wild*, it is imperative to know something about this incredible area of North America, which was unknown to most of the world at the turn of the twentieth century and even today, one hundred years later, is still remote and sparsely inhabited. The Yukon Territory and Alaska, so inaccessible and isolated, so brutally frigid, and with a terrain so perilous, were places where all creatures, man included, suffered and died from the brutality of nature and where nature was cruelly misused by man at his most rapacious.

Long before the Klondike gold rush, the icy shorelines of the Alaskan Panhandle and the Aleutian Islands were soaked in the blood of millions of animals, especially seals, clubbed and shot for their furs and oil. By the time Jack London went to the Yukon, the sea otter, the beaver, the bison, and the whale had been hunted close to extinction. After the gold rush began, the valleys, mountains, and frigid expanses of the Yukon Territory were littered with the bones of horses and dogs that had been driven mercilessly in man's greedy scramble for gold. In both endeavors, the hunts for furs and precious metals, the point was not just to make a living, but to make a killing. Buck's experiences and his final decision to join nature become understandable in light of the history of the area because even though the nature he returned to was incredibly difficult, it was not as cruel as man's attempts to conquer nature.

The primary areas pertinent to Buck's story are two: the Panhandle of Alaska, now a part of the United States, and the Yukon Territory, once a part of the great Northwest and now a separate territory of Canada. By consulting a map, one can see that Alaska is an immense area of land with two southernmost "legs"—one a string of islands and a peninsula curving down to the west, and one a strip of land with border islands curving down to the east. Russians made their way into the area through the southwestern strip, which includes the Aleutian Islands, Unalaska, and the Alaskan Peninsula. From there they moved to the southeastern strip, the area where Buck lands to begin his work as a sled dog.

This southeastern strip, called the Alaskan Panhandle, is composed of islands and peninsulas. A strip of Canada's British Columbia borders it at the northeast, and above this lies the Yukon Territory, also part of Canada. North of Skagway, Alaska, British Columbia, and the Yukon Territory come together in a triangle. Dyea, once a lively, if inadequate, port, and Skagway are both located in the Panhandle. Buck lands at Dyea, located on the coast in the general vicinity of Skagway, and the southernmost terminus of the dog team's sled run is Skagway. The dog team's northern destination is the town of Dawson in the Klondike area of the Yukon Territory.

CLIMATE

The weather in both the Alaskan Panhandle and the Yukon Territory defies easy habitation. The Panhandle is buffeted by heavy, cold winds that come down the glacial canyons. For all but two months out of the year, the area struggles with blinding fogs and constant rain, making any landings there dangerous. On top of the brutal weather, the area is subject to earthquakes.

In the Yukon Territory, which lies partially inside the Arctic Circle, hard winter prevails for all but two months of the year, with temperatures that in some places reach lows of seventy degrees below zero. The average January temperature for Dawson is twenty-two degrees below zero, though the temperature often goes down to fifty degrees below zero. At such low temperatures, even kerosene, gasoline, and oils freeze. Human flesh can become a block of ice in only a brief exposure in such cold, and even dogs with heavy coats of fur have been known to freeze solid.

In "The Story of Jees Uck," London described the mercury freezing in the thermometer and the spirit thermometer registering 90 degrees below zero for two weeks. In "The One Thousand Dozen," London paints a landscape in which he again has the temperature reach brutal levels of sixty or more degrees below zero. A person who makes the mistake of breathing through his mouth in such cold could easily injure his lungs, he claims. The moisture that one breathed out in such cold would, he writes in "To Build a Fire," create ice—small glaciers—on the face. Because of this, many people in the Yukon wore nose straps to protect their nose and cheeks from becoming frostbitten.

Explorers of the area knew how imperative it was to warm and dry one's feet if they got wet, because they would freeze in an instant, and death was a sure result. Shorthaired dogs, foolishly taken to the Yukon, almost invariably froze to death. Even in the warmer valleys, there is only an average of two months of frost-free weather, and often much less. Forty percent of the Yukon Territory is too cold to sustain trees. Mountains are covered by glaciers, and much of the other areas is ice fields for ten months of the year. The Yukon contains the largest nonpolar ice fields in North America. Most of the area, including the lowlands, is covered by permafrost—constantly frozen ground just beneath the surface layer. This presents terrible problems resulting from instability

when construction or sudden rises in temperature thaw the permafrost temporarily. At such times, buildings and modes of transportation end up sinking into water. A similar problem, mentioned
in *The Call of the Wild*, occurs when the ice beneath the snow
melts. Whole dog teams can vanish into freezing water when their
drivers are not aware of "rotting ice," as it was called, beneath the
snow.

London describes a similar problem in "To Build a Fire." In a
stream, the bottom layer would be hard ice. But springs, which
never froze, would create a six-to-eight-inch layer of water above
the bottom layer of ice. A thin layer of ice would form on top of
this water, and another layer (about six inches) of water would
form on top of that, topped with a third thin layer of ice and then
snow. None but the most experienced traveler would know what
the smooth snow concealed. If one traveled on this seemingly
harmless snow, he would inevitably break through the thin layers
of ice and fall into the freezing water, drenching himself. If he did
not immediately build a fire and dry his feet and legs, they would
freeze, and he would die. The man to whom this happens in "To
Build a Fire" encounters further problems when he tries to start a
fire to thaw himself out because his fingers get too frozen and stiff
for him to strike a match. Finally he has to use his wrists to light
the match and then actually burn his fingers in order to thaw them
out so that he can use them.

Another danger came when ice broke up in the spring, often
causing jams in the rivers. In "At the Rainbow's End," London describes the terrifying flood that occurs when a jam develops down-
stream and another jam is loosened above it in the same stream.
Every man and dog just disappears.

TERRAIN

Coupled with the brutal weather, the formidable terrain of the
Yukon Territory rendered most of it uninhabitable. It is crossed by
deep valleys, some one to two thousand feet deep. Most of its
canyons are overhung with glaciers and subject to horrendous
landslides. The Yukon's mountains, the highest in Canada, are covered with permanent ice caps. The extremely high mountains and
deep valleys are crisscrossed with rivers and streams that rage
down the landscape in perilous rapids.

One example of the rough terrain, the notorious Chilkoot Pass, over which Buck, in *The Call of the Wild*, and Jack London had to travel, is twenty-five miles steep. Part of the slope is at a forty-five-degree incline. In winter, it is solid ice, and in summer, it is surfaced with sharp boulders and mud holes in which horses and dogs could get trapped forever.

London writes about the terrain in the Yukon in a story called "An Odyssey of the North." Naass, an Indian chief, tells a group around the campfire about his horrifying adventures in driving sled dogs into the eastern Yukon, an area in which John Thornton set up his camp in *The Call of the Wild*. He talks of ice forming on the surface and of treacherous rivers beneath the ice. In such a place, he says, the ice broke and the dogs and supplies disappeared beneath the rapids hidden underneath. To reach their destination, they had to navigate a huge ice-covered mountain that jutted up from the landscape so sharply that they had to cut steps in the ice to cross it. They finally reached a snow- and ice-covered valley that seemed to extend forever. At last, they found themselves at the edge of an abyss so deep and dark that they called it the mouth of hell, but into this hell they had to descend.

THE FIRST INHABITANTS

Native peoples of Alaska and the Yukon also play a part in Buck's story. The dog team passes an Indian village on its way to Dawson, and Indians called Yeehats who live in the eastern Yukon Territory kill Thornton and all his camp. As was the case in all of the Americas, native tribes populated the northwest areas of Alaska and the Yukon long before Europeans arrived on the scene. In Alaska, the Aleuts living in the Aleutian Islands, southwest of the Alaskan mainland, successfully hunted seals up and down the southern shoreline of Alaska. An aggressive tribe known as the Tlingits had strongholds in the whole of the Alaskan Panhandle. Although they made their main home in the Panhandle, London probably patterned the Yeehats in the eastern area of the Yukon after the warlike Tlingits. The Athapaskan tribes occupied the Alaskan mainland and the Yukon Territory. The native settlement that Buck's team passes is likely Athapaskan. The Athapaskans were a very poor, nomadic tribe so starved at times that they reportedly became cannibalistic.

The impact of European settlements on all these native populations was devastating. The first and most widespread casualties
were caused by diseases brought by Europeans. Native peoples had
no immunity to European diseases, and epidemics wiped out
much of the population. As Europeans moved west, so did disease
and death. The indigenous peoples of the Yukon were hit hardest
in the mid-nineteenth century. The Haida Indians, who lived on
Queen Charlotte Island, off the Alaskan Panhandle, went from
eight thousand in the early nineteenth century to eight hundred
by the end of the century. Some of the tribes in Alaska and the
Yukon Territory lost 90 percent of their populations by the end of
the nineteenth century. London writes of this situation in "The
League of Old Men," in which he describes Indians dying of small-
pox and measles.

After the Europeans were firmly established, the natives starved
because they had been encouraged to become dependent on outside goods for survival, goods that subsequently became unavailable. This London also describes in "The League of Old Men":

> So we grew to hunger for the things the white men brought in trade.
> . . . One winter we sold our meat for clocks that would not go, and
> watches with broken guts, and files worn smooth, and pistols with-
> out cartridges and worthless. And then came famine, and we were
> without meat, and two score died ere the break of spring. (164)

Animals needed by the Indians for survival were decimated from
overhunting by whites; and finally, Indian lands were confiscated
by the U.S. and Canadian governments. It has been estimated that
there were about 1 million Indians living in the Yukon Territory
when whites first arrived. By 1867, this number had dropped to
100,000. The Hudson's Bay Company, which made inroads in the
Yukon, brought devastating cultural change by insisting that the
Athapaskans change from wearing furs to wearing totally inadequate Western clothing made of cotton and wool so that the company could collect more furs for profit.

The natives most people identify with the Northland—the Eskimos of Alaska and the Inuits of the Yukon Territory—lived beyond
the areas involved in the Klondike gold rush. Eskimos lived in the
northern and western parts of the Alaskan mainland, and Inuits
lived in the arctic Yukon, considerably north of Dawson.

Between 1850 and 1929, the people of European descent began signing treaties with many of Canada's native peoples. But in the Northwest and the Yukon Territory, no treaties were signed at all. With or without treaties, however, the result was the same: these nomadic peoples who had followed game across great stretches of territory in order to feed themselves were placed on reserves beginning in the nineteenth century, and government promises to provide them with education and agricultural assistance and to restore their hunting rights were largely ignored.

WHITE EXPLORERS, BUSINESSMEN, AND SETTLERS

Alaskan Panhandle

The Europeans who came to the Alaskan Panhandle and the Yukon Territory in the beginning of the nineteenth century were drawn by furs rather than precious metals. By 1745, Russians, eager for seal furs, had established themselves on Alaska's Aleutian Islands. They set about immediately to rid themselves of as many Aleut Indians as possible, killing as many as three thousand men at a time. This period in Alaskan history is described by Jack London in "Lost Face." Of the Russians he writes, "Through the savages of the new world they had cut a path of blood" (341).

The Russians shortly discovered, however, that they were ill equipped to collect seal furs without the skilled help of the Aleuts and pragmatically decided to pay the Indians to kill seals for them rather than themselves trying to kill both Indians and seals at the same time. Encouraged by rich fur harvests, made possible with the help of the Aleuts, the Russians made their way eastward to the Alaskan Panhandle and then south. In 1799, under the command of Alexander Baranov, the first governor and manager for merchant Grigori Shelekov, they formally established a settlement named St. Michaels on a peninsula in the southern Panhandle about two hundred miles south of the present Skagway (not to be confused with St. Michaels on the Yukon River). Unfortunately for them, the Tlingit Indians controlled the Alaskan Panhandle and had their own headquarters in a nearby settlement named Sitka. In 1802, the Tlingits captured St. Michaels and killed most of the inhabitants, but with the help of a battleship, in 1804 the Russians under Baranov, in turn, captured the Tlingit town of Sitka. Sitka shortly became not merely the Russian headquarters for the fur trade, but also a settlement flourishing with Russian culture and the arts. The Russians, who continued to be dependent on the native peoples in their seal hunting, intermarried with the Aleuts and Athapaskans, brought their families to Sitka from Russia, and managed to lessen the threat posed by the Tlingits.

Although other businesses began to flourish in Russian Alaska, the exportation of seal pelts to Europe continued to be at the core of the economy. The harvesting or killing of these creatures was done with cold-blooded exactitude. At dawn on the day of the kill, seals who had perched on the coast were driven inland for a mile or two to the killing grounds. Very old and very young seals whose fur was considered unsuitable were culled out and sent back to sea. At the foreman's signal—the call of "Strike!"—hunters moved in to bludgeon them over the head with hickory clubs. Before the last seal was killed, other men were skinning the first killed. However, the Russians, along with their Aleut hunters, were so successful at seal hunting that they were rapidly eliminating the animal on which they depended for their fortunes, so in 1834, seal killing was greatly restricted. New techniques in processing the fur meant that many more seals could be harvested, and renegade hunters began trying to shoot seals underwater. The hunt became indiscriminate, pregnant cows being shot along with young and old males. Moreover, at least half of the seals shot in this manner sank to the bottom of the ocean and were never harvested. In 1904, Henry W. Elliott, an artist and official with the Smithsonian Institution, testified before a special committee of the House of Representatives about the danger to seals in the Northland. Elliott argued that the Russians had been aware as early as 1834 of the danger of eliminating seals through overhunting. In that year, the Russians called a halt to all seal hunting for a period of twelve years.

Financial reverses in Russia necessitated the sale of Alaska, and in 1867 a treaty was drawn up for its sale to the United States for a sum of 7.2 million dollars. By the time the United States bought Alaska, there were 4,500,000 seals in Alaska, but the Russians had again begun killing them at a rate of 50,000 a year. The Russians informed those involved in drawing up the treaty that the territory included around 4,000,000 seals for the taking. But the seal population was melting away, so in 1870, the United States limited the annual take to 100,000 pelts and declared any shooting of seals at sea to be illegal. Little was done to enforce any laws in Alaska, however, and by 1911, when new limitations were enforced, the number of seals in Alaska had dropped from 4,000,000 to 110,000.

With the arrival of the U.S. Army in Sitka, many Russians left, but some, especially those who had intermarried with the native population, stayed and prospered. The undisciplined and unruly American army spent most of its time making and drinking alcoholic concoctions. People of many professions and interests began flooding into Sitka and the rest of Alaska to strike it rich in some way: mining prospectors, businessmen, entertainers, and gamblers. Many among them were former "forty-niners" who had come west to seek gold in California. In 1877, the army was pulled out of Sitka to fight in the more urgent wars of the western plains, leaving little law enforcement behind. In fact, no system of law operated in Alaska, and when order had to be enforced on occasion to protect the citizenry, it was done by gunboats sent into the harbor by the United States. Finally, in 1884, Alaska was placed under the civil and criminal laws of Oregon.

The Yukon Territory

Outsiders in search of furs had come to the northernmost part of North America as early as the seventeenth century, but white men came to the heart of the Yukon much later than they did to what is now the Alaskan Panhandle. The Hudson's Bay Company is inextricably linked to the history of the Yukon before the gold strike of 1896. This was an English company chartered by Charles II of England in 1670 to develop fur trade in the New World and to find a Northwest Passage to the Pacific Ocean. After the conquest of Canada by the British in 1763, the company, which from the beginning had almost unlimited powers (for example, to make peace or war with the Indians and to make and enforce laws), grew by leaps and bounds. With few exceptions, the Hudson's Bay Company operated as a virtual monopoly in the Yukon, with rights to any furs available there.

The first explorer in the Yukon was Sir John Franklin, an Englishman, who reached the Arctic Ocean shore in the northwest corner of the Yukon in 1825. His findings led the Hudson's Bay Company to send another explorer, John Bell, to the area to establish a trading post for the acquisition of furs, but it was not until 1839 that Bell accomplished his journey and established Fort McPherson for the company. It was Bell who discovered the great Yukon River, making possible the establishment of another key outpost called Fort Yukon.

In 1838, the Hudson's Bay Company's monopoly was formalized legally, giving it sole rights in the territory. In 1842, a third explorer, Robert Campbell, was the first white man to reach the southern part of the Yukon, where he discovered another key river and named it the Pelly. For ten years, the most central and most active Hudson's Bay Company outpost in the Yukon Territory was Fort Selkirk, which lay where the Lewes and Pelly rivers joined, south of Dawson. Like the Russians in the Aleutian Islands and the Panhandle of Alaska, explorers in the Yukon went there for furs. Unlike the Russians, however, they established no homes of their own on the frigid shores. They worked for the Northwest Company and Hudson's Bay Company, whose purpose was to acquire furs of all kinds to meet an always-ready market. As in Alaska, the Hudson's Bay Company, which eventually had a monopoly on furs in the Yukon, required the cooperation of native peoples. However, unsuccessful challenges to its monopoly continued until 1870, when its claim to all business in the Yukon was legally denied and the company closed most of its business in the area.

Nevertheless, the way having been paved by explorers and trappers of the Hudson's Bay Company, more and more individual fortune hunters came into the Yukon, primarily to search for precious metals, an enterprise that eventually overtook fur trading. In 1867, with the formation of the Dominion of Canada, the Yukon Territory came to be administered by Canada as part of the Northwest Territories. At the time of the gold rush, the Yukon was made a separate territory, with its capital in Dawson.

BRUTALITY OF MAN AND NATURE

Jack London himself is one of our best sources for information on the overwhelming challenges of the Yukon in the nineteenth century well before the gold rush began. One of the most graphic, painful illustrations of the brutality of man and nature in the Yukon occurs in London's short story "The Law of Life," which has as its setting the early days when the native inhabitants controlled the

territory. The brutal reality of human and animal behavior is related in the story of an old Indian, Koskoosh, who is, according to
the usual practice, abandoned in the snow by his tribesmen. He
shivers, trying to keep his flickering small fire alive and losing himself in memories of the great adventures of his life. Soon he is
startled from his daydreams by the sensation of a wolf's muzzle
against his cheek. In a reflex action, he shoos the wolf away, but
when he sees an entire circle of wolves waiting around him, he
drops his head on his knees to yield to the inevitable, knowing
that the law of life in the Yukon means that he will now be food
for wolves.

The constant theme for the native peoples, prospectors, and fur
traders in an immense, isolated, dangerous landscape that throws
up every impediment to travel is the hunger and starvation of both
dogs and men. For example, in London's story "Grit of Women,"
a character named Sitka Charley tells of a not-uncommon practice
of keeping some remnant of the dog team going by feeding the
weaker dogs to the stronger ones. In this situation, as elsewhere,
the dog-team drivers plan to eat the rest of the dogs themselves
when their supplies run out. Their plan goes awry, however, when
the dogs all hit rotten ice and are swallowed up by the water beneath the surface. The drivers are not the only hungry ones, however, for before the day is out, they encounter an Indian who has
been staying alive by eating pieces of his moccasins that he first
boils in a cup.

Buck's own history and ancestry are integral parts of his life in
the far north. Likewise, the primitive history of the hellish landscape to which he has been brought is part and parcel of his present life.

The documents that follow include a chart that enumerates the
seals killed in Alaska in the early nineteenth century that made the
Russian-America Company rich at the expense of the animals and
environment of the Alaskan Panhandle. An account of Hudson's
Bay Company employee H. M. Robinson shows how the Yukon
weather and terrain took their toll on those who were dispatched
to plunder furs in the nineteenth century. The last document in
this chapter is a humorous poem about the Yukon cold written by
Robert W. Service, known as the Yukon poet.

SEAL KILLING IN ALASKA

In *The Call of the Wild*, the unbridled capitalism that had bur-
geoned after the Civil War contributed to the exploitation of nature
in the mad rush to use any means whatsoever to acquire wealth.
The pursuit of nature's bounty in the Yukon resulted in the wholesale damage done to the wilderness. We see this exploitation in
the selling of Buck and in the beatings, starvation, and overwork
to which he is subject, especially at the hands of Hal and company.
Such abuse leads to his defection from civilization.

The pattern of exploitation of nature for profit began in the far
North long before Buck arrived there, when the Russian-America
Company and the North America Commercial Company in the
Alaskan Panhandle, where Buck lands, and the Hudson's Bay Company in the Yukon harvested animal furs to the verge of extinction
in many cases. The extent to which animals, especially seals, were
hunted in Alaska was brought to the attention of the U.S. Congress
in 1904. When the United States bought Alaska, there were
4,500,000 seals in Alaska, but the Russians, after a moratorium on
seal hunting, were again killing them at a rate of 50,000 a year.
Furthermore, another company, this one British, had also joined
the hunt and was indiscriminately killing male seals, practically
eliminating almost all breeding males and endangering the whole
species. The table generated by the Russians that was introduced
in evidence in Congress shows the decrease in the number of seals
in Alaska over a twenty-year period.

FROM *FUR SEALS OF ALASKA. HEARINGS BEFORE THE UNITED STATES COMMITTEE ON WAYS AND MEANS.* HOUSE OF REPRESENTATIVES, 58TH CONGRESS, 2ND SESSION (Washington, D.C.: U.S. Government Printing Office, 1904, 65)

Russian record of dimminution, 1817–1834.
[Table I, part 2.—Veniaminov's Zapieska, etc., St. Petersburg, 1842.]

| | Seals taken from— | | |
Year.	St. Paul Island.	St. George Island.	Total.
1817	47,860	12,328	60,188
1818	45,932	13,924	59,856
1819	40,300	11,925	52,225
1820	39,700	10,520	50,220
1821	35,750	9,245	44,995
1822	28,150	8,319	36,469
1823	24,100	5,773	29,873
1824	19,850	5,550	25,400
1825	24,600	5,500	30,100
1826	23,250	—	23,250
1827	17,750	1,950	19,700
1828	18,450	4,778	23,228
1829	17,150	3,661	20,811
1830	15,200	2,834	18,034
1831	12,950	3,084	16,034
1832	13,150	3,296	16,446
1833	13,200	3,212	16,412
1834	12,700	3,051	15,751
1835	[a]4,052	2,528	6,580
1836	[a]4,040	2,550	6,590
1837	[a]4,220	2,582	6,803
Total	464,259	114,665	578,924

[a]Only 100 yearlings and 3,952 "pups" (5 months old) in this total; same for 1836 and 1837.

HAZARDS OF YUKON WEATHER

Buck, the dog reared in sunny California, is stunned by the snow, ice, and bitter cold of the Yukon. He must learn techniques for survival in the harsh climate: how to bite the ice from his feet, how to burrow under the snow to sleep, and how to break the ice with his forelegs to get at drinking water.

H. M. Robinson, an employee of the Hudson's Bay Company in the mid-nineteenth century, when it maintained forts and trading posts throughout the Northwest, wrote in 1879 of a journey he undertook by dogsled that was made perilous by the subarctic cold. Robinson describes in some detail the precautions that one had to take to keep alive and the ways in which the extraordinarily cold temperatures affected the human body and mind. In this instance, he believes that he is close to death, and he notes the frightening psychological effects of the bitter cold, writing of his companion who has lost his mind and wandered away from camp and who, when brought back, has to be physically restrained from entering the fire. He mentions others who become delirious and strip off all their clothes in weather so cold that a person's exposed nose, cheeks, feet, and hands can freeze in the blink of an eye.

FROM H. M. ROBINSON, *THE GREAT FUR LAND; OR, SKETCHES OF LIFE IN THE HUDSON'S BAY TERRITORY*
(New York: G. P. Putnam's Sons, 1879)

On in the gray snow-light, with a fierce wind sweeping down the long reaches of the lake; nothing spoken, for such cold weather makes men silent, morose, and savage.

Lake-travel, though rapid, is exceedingly harassing on account of the high winds which perpetually sweep over the immense plain of their frozen surface, intensifying even moderate cold to a painful degree. The ice is always rough, coated with snow of varying thickness, or drifted into hillocks and ridges, alternating with spots of glass-like smoothness, which are constantly upsetting the sledges. And this same upsetting, a trifling matter enough on shore, is likely to prove a serious annoyance where the hardness of the ice nearly breaks one's bones. The same hardness, too, increases the fatigue of sledge-travel, which at its best may be likened to sitting on a thin board dragged quickly over a newly-macadamized road. Then, too, the pedestrian on a frozen lake labors under peculiar disadvantages. Where the snow lies deeply, the crust gives way at each step, precipitating the driver to the bottom with a sudden jar; where it lies thinly on the surface, or is drifted away, the hardness of the ice injures even the practiced *voyageurs*, causing swellings of the ankles and soles of the feet, and enlargement of the lower back sinews of the legs. Again, the winter traveler speedily discovers that very slight exercise induces copious perspiration, which in the most momentary halt, gets cold upon the skin, in fact, in a high wind, the exposed side will appear frozen over, while the rest of the body is comparatively warm and comfortable. Once cold in this way, it is almost impossible to get warm again without the heat of fire, or the severest exercise; and, should the latter be adopted, it must perforce be continued until a camping-place is reached. Moreover, to a strong man, there is something humiliating in being hauled about in a portable bed, like some feeble invalid, while the hardy *voyageurs* are maintaining their steady pace from hour to hour, day to day, or week to week; for fatigue seems with them an unknown word. (20–21)

• • •

When light showers of snow fall in minute particles, as if it were frozen dew, from a sky without a cloud, and the sun shining brightly, the winter traveler in the Fur Land knows just what degree of cold he may expect. He knows that masses of ice, the size of a man's fist, will form on his beard and mustache, from the moisture of his breath freezing as it passes through the hair; that his eye-lashes will have to be kept in rapid motion to prevent them from becoming permanently closed; that his hands can scarcely be exposed for a moment; that his bare fingers laid upon a gun-barrel will stick to it as if glued, from the instantaneous freezing of their moisture; that the snow will melt only close to the fire, which forms a trench for itself, in which it sinks slowly to the level of the ground; that the snow, light and powdery, will not melt beneath the warmth of his foot, and his moccasins will be as dry on the journey as if he had walked through sawdust; that a crust of ice will form over the tea in his tin-cup, as he sits within a yard of the roaring fire; that he will have a ravenous appetite for fat, and can swallow great lumps of hard grease—unmolded tallow candles—without bread or anything to modify it. So he dresses accordingly—that is, the white traveler.

He first puts on three or four flannel shirts, one of duffel, and over all a leather one, beaded and fringed to suit the taste; his hands are encased in mittaines, or large gloves of moose-skin, made without fingers, and extending well up toward the elbows; loose enough to be easily doffed on occasion, and carried slung by a band about the neck to prevent being lost; his feet are swathed in duffel, and covered with enormous moccasins; his legs are encased in thick duffel leggins, until they resemble a severe case of elephantiasis; his ears and neck are protected by a thick curtain of fur; and yet, with it all, he is hardly able to keep warm with the most active exercise. (228–29)

• • •

But the measureless spaces of the Fur Land have other dangers and discomforts than those of uncharted immensity. To any one who has not experienced the atmosphere of that hyperborean region the intensity of its coldness can scarcely be described. The sun, being so far southward, creates but little heat, and the major part of the time is hidden behind sombre and leaden clouds. Before you, in every direction, the eye meets an unbroken waste of snow. Far away, perhaps, as the eye can reach, a faint line of scattered tree-tops may barely be distinguished, appearing no higher than fern-bushes, marking the course of some prairie-stream crossing your path, or running parallel with it—not a thing of life or motion within the range of vision between the earth and sky, save the conveyance near you. The vastness and magnitude of the scene are overpowering. The immensity of the dead level is overwhelming. You are an atom in the gigantic panorama of frozen Nature about you.

Coming in from the rarefied atmosphere generated by sixty-seven degrees of frost, an extended and sentient forefinger, pointing in the direction of one's nose, instantly informs him of the frozen condition of that member. Then he recalls the fact that, fifteen minutes before, a slight pricking sensation was experienced in the end of the nose—momentary, and in the hurry of the instant scarcely noticed. It was at that particular moment that it had frozen. Had he looked out, or rather down, he would have seen the ghostly spectacle; for firmer, colder, whiter, and harder than hard hearts, stony eyes, marble foreheads, or any other silicious similitude, stands forth prominently a frozen nose.

Some theorist might make a study of frozen noses which would be interesting. Inference might be connected with inference in infinite duration. One might read an essay from it on the eternal fitness of things, and history viewed by the light of frozen noses might reveal new secrets. For example, the inability of the Roman nose to stand the rigors of an Arctic winter limits the boundaries of the Roman empire; the Esquimaux nose is admirably fitted by nature, on account of its limited extent, for the climate in which it breathes, hence its assignment to hyperborean latitudes. This, however, is by the way.

One's nose was frozen, say, in traversing at a rapid walk a distance of not more than one hundred yards; for it is a "poudre" day. Sixty-seven degrees of frost, unaccompanied by wind, is endurable if you are taking vigorous exercise, and are warmly dressed; but let the faintest possible wind arise—a gentle zephyr, a thing which just turns the smoke above the lodge-poles, or twists the feather detached from the wing of a passing bird—then look out, for the chances are that every person met will extend that forefinger to mark some frozen spot on your reddish-blue countenance. This, however, is the extent of the courtesy; they do not follow out the Russian plan of rubbing out the plague-spot with a handful of snow, probably out of deference to the limited amount of attrition most noses stand without peeling.

A poudre day, with the temperature in the thirties below, is a thing to be spoken of in a whisper. Not a soul leaves the fireside who can avoid it; to wander away from well-known landmarks is to run the risk of never returning. Every winter half a score of men walk off into the whirling particles of snow and drift, and the morning sun finds a calm and peaceful face turned up to the sky, with its life frozen out, and its form hard and unimpressible, as if carved from granite. The early morning of such a day may be clear and still; but upon close inspection the atmosphere will be found filled with crystal, scintillating, minute, almost imperceptible particles of snow, drifting on wings of air, impalpable and fleeting. Soon after daybreak the wind begins to rise. Off to the north rolls a little eddy of snow, a mere puff, not larger than one's hand. Another follows; miniature coils circle over the smooth surface of the snow, and sink back imperceptibly to the level again. Drifts of larger proportions roll over the expanse, until the atmosphere becomes thick with the frozen particles. All landmarks are lost, and the range of vision is limited to a few feet. The wind howls like a raging beast, and the merciless cold congeals the very heart's blood. It is the sirocco of the North!

On such days traveling is particularly toilsome and dangerous. The state of the atmosphere renders respiration difficult, increasing the action of the heart, and producing a slight but constant dizziness. All landmarks are obliterated, and unless one is thoroughly conversant with the country, he is liable to lose his way, and be caught at nightfall without shelter or fire. But the most dangerous phase of travel is the tendency toward inertia. Fatigued by the least effort, paralyzed by the cold, perhaps frostbitten in many places, despite every precaution, the traveler is likely to give up in despair. "I cannot" and "I will not" become synonymous terms. All effort is apparently useless; the attention is distracted by the necessity of fighting continually to keep face and hands free from frostbite; keeping the road in so blinding a tempest seems to be impossible; the animals one is driving face about in harness, and refuse to proceed; and so, beset on every hand, with an intellect benumbed and paralyzed by the intense cold, and a body overcome by physical inertia, one gives up all effort as only adding unnecessary pain, and sits down to be bound hand and foot by the final stupor. Five minutes' rest in some snowdrift on the plain is enough, in certain conditions of fatigue and temperature, to paralyze the energies of the strongest man, and make him welcome any fate if only let alone to take his ease. We recall more than one time when we would have given all we possessed simply to have been permitted to lie down in a snowbank for ten minutes; and left to ourselves, we should certainly have done so. Some of the best dog-drivers on the plains have related to us similar experiences, where the inertia of a poudre day on the prairie seemed too intense to be resisted. Persons who know the prairie only in summer or autumn have but little notion of its winter fierceness and desolation. To get a true conception of life in these solitudes they must go toward the close of November into the treeless waste; there, amid wreck and tempest and biting cold, and snowdrifts so dense that earth and heaven seem wrapped together in undistinguishable chaos, they will see a sight as different from their summer ideal as day is from night.

But, though not so dangerous, the still days are the coldest. There are every winter a dozen or more days so magically still that all the usual sounds of nature seem to be suspended; when the ice cracks miles away with a report like that of a cannon; when the breaking of a twig reaches one like the falling of a tree; when one's own footsteps, clad in soft moccasins, come back from the yielding snow like the crunching of an iron heel through gravel; when every artificial sound is exaggerated a hundred fold, and Nature seems to start at every break in the intense silence. The atmosphere is as clear as crystal, and the range of vision seems to be unlimited. Seen from a window, from the cosy limits of an almost hermetically-sealed room, the clear sunshine and crisp freshness of the day appear to invite one forth to enjoy its seeming mildness. But the native knows better than to venture out. A fifteen minutes' walk in that clear ether is a fifteen minutes' fight for existence. A sudden prick and one's nose is frozen; next go both cheeks; one raises his hand to rub away the ghastly white spots, only to add his fingers to the list of icy members. Rub as you will, run hard, swing your arms—all to no purpose; the little white spots increase in size, until the whole face is covered with the waxen leprosy. The breath congeals almost upon leaving the mouth, and the icy vapor falls instead of rising. Expectorate, and instantly there is a lump of ice where the spittle fell. Ah, it is cold beyond belief. The spirit registers a temperature away down in the forties. We have seen a stalwart man, after a few hours' exposure on such a day, walk into the room where every footfall clanked upon the floor like blocks of wood clapping together; his feet frozen solid as lumps of ice.

On such a day one may stand for hours in the snow with moccasined feet, and leave no trace of moisture behind. The snow is granulated like sand; there is no adhesiveness in it. It is as difficult to draw a sledge through it as through a bed of sand. Slipperiness has gone out of it. A horse gives out in a few minutes. And yet the aspect of all nature is calm, still, and equable as on a May day.

One of these still nights upon the prairie is unspeakably awful. The cold is measured by degrees as much below the freezing point as ordinary summer temperature is above it. Scraping away the snow, the blankets and robes are spread down. Then you dress for bed. Your heaviest coat is donned, and the hood carefully pulled up over the heavy fur cap upon your head; the largest moccasins and thickest socks are drawn on (common leather boots would freeze one's feet in a twinkling); huge leather mittens, extending to the elbows, and trebly lined, come next; you lie down and draw all the available robes and blankets about you. Then begins the cold. The frost comes out of the clear grey sky with still, silent rigor. The spirit in the thermometer placed by your head sinks down into the thirties and forties below zero. Just when the dawn begins to break in the east it will not infrequently be at fifty. You are tired, perhaps, and sleep comes by the mere force of fatigue. But never from your waking brain goes the consciousness of cold. You lie with tightly-folded arms and upgathered knees, and shiver beneath all your coverings, until forced to rise and seek safety by the fire. If you are a novice and have no fire, count your beads and say your prayers, for your sleep will be long. (295–301)

• • •

The effect of the interminable winter landscapes of the Fur Land upon the mind of the new-comer is melancholy in the extreme; more especially upon the still days, and where an occasional dwelling or tent is embraced in the desolate scene. No wind breaks the silence, or shakes the lumps of snow off the aspens or willows; and nothing is heard save the occasional cracking of the trees, as the severe frost acts upon the branches. The dwelling, if any, stands in a little hollow, where the willows and poplars are luxuriant enough to afford a shelter from the north wind. Just in front a small path leads to the river, of which an extended view is had through the opening, showing the fantastic outlines of huge blocks and mounds of ice relieved against the white snow. A huge chasm, partially filled with fallen trees and mounds of snow, yawns on the left of the house; and the ruddy sparks of fire which issue from its chimney-top throw this and the surrounding forest in deeper gloom. All around lies the unending plain, wrapped in funeral cerements of ghastly white, or dotted here and there with slender trees, which seem to bend and shiver as they stand with their feet in the snow.

With the advent of a "blizzard," however, all still life ends and chaos begins. A blizzard is the white squall of the prairies, the simoon of the plains. Like its brother of the Sahara, when it comes all animate nature bows before it. The traveler prostrates himself in the snow, if he is of the initiated, and, covering his head, waits until it passes by. To pursue a different course, and journey on is to be lost. Let me give you an instance which may serve to illustrate its power, and the dangers of travel in the Fur Land:

In the month of February, 1869, I was called by urgent business from my residence near the foot of Lake Winnipeg to an interior post, distant some two hundred and fifty miles. This call involved no ordinary journey. It meant a weary, exhaustive travel of ten or twelve days across an un-broken prairie, without shelter of any kind, without the probability of encountering a single human being throughout the entire route, and the almost certainty of being overtaken by some of the terrible storms prev-alent at that season. But the call was imperative, and I set about preparing for the journey. (303–4)

• • •

In the forward conveyance was placed provisions for ourselves and provender for the animals, while my own sledge was comfortably fur-nished with the huge bundle of robes and blankets requisite for our comfort and even safety in camp. Into this shoe-like sledge I fondly hoped to creep and glide smoothly to my journey's end. But the intensity of the cold soon disenchanted me of that illusion; for we had proceeded but a few miles when I was forced to take to my feet and run after the sledge to avoid being frozen. Even then the severity of the cold was such that, when jumping on the sledge for a momentary respite, on reaching the ground again my blood would seem frozen, the muscles refuse to act, and it would require a sharp trot of a mile or more before I could recover usual warmth. (304)

• • •

I awoke again, as near as I can judge, in about an hour and a half; this time from a general sensation of cold which enveloped me. I found both my companions awake, on speaking to them, and that Mr. Wheeler had been unable to sleep at all, owing to the cold, as he lay with his head to the wind, and could not prevent it from entering under the covering. It was blowing a perfect gale, and the air was so filled with whirling particles of snow that we could not distinguish our animals at the distance of a few yards. From that time forward it was impossible to sleep. We did every thing we could devise to ward off the cold, and the half-breed seemed especially anxious that I should not suffer; covered me with care, and shielded me as much as possible with his own person. But the chill seemed to have taken complete possession of me. I could not restrain my desire to shake and shiver, although knowing that it augmented the difficulty. For a time we conversed on the severity of the storm, and our error in not having built a fire, but gradually relapsed into silence; each one, evidently, engaged in endeavoring to protect himself, or moodily brooding over his own sufferings.

Real physical suffering it had now become. The skin on my arms and limbs felt quite cold to the touch, and my bones grew heavy and chill as bars of iron. Yet, I had no fear, or thought even, of freezing to death. On that point I simply expected to shiver until morning would give us light sufficient to build a fire. The mind, however, was unnaturally acute. Thought on every subject was very vivid and distinct. I remember to have received a better insight of several subjects which occurred to me than at any previous time, and was able to think more rapidly. This was, I suppose, owing to the increased and enforced vitality necessary to sustain life, and to the stimulated condition of the brain under the suffering arising from the cold. Every thing was clear and distinct. I thought over the business I was upon, and studied the minutest details of it, all with remarkable rapidity. Occasionally my companion spoke to me, or touched me gently with his arm, but neither served to break up the general current of thought.

All through this outer surface of thought, however, there ran an undertow of suffering. I was conscious of growing colder; my limbs, especially, felt more chill and heavy. I began also to experience a peculiar sensation, as if the flesh, for the depth of a quarter or half an inch, was frozen solid, and the congealment gradually extending to the bone. The bone itself at times felt like a red-hot bar. I noticed, further, an increased labor in the beating of the heart, and could distinguish the pulsations quite easily. At every throb I could feel the blood seemingly strike the end of the veins and arteries in the extremities. This after a time produced a slight dizziness in the head and a laborious respiration. As time went on, the sensation of the surface-freezing extended to the trunk of the body, and my thoughts grew less connected, changing frequently from subject to subject, and narrowing down to my own sufferings. I noticed, furthermore, that the half-breed spoke more frequently than before, and shook me occasionally. Still I had no thought of danger, and even laughed at Mr. Wheeler exclaiming, "Men, men, I believe I am freezing to death!"

However, during this whole period of two hours or more I could not prevent a continual shivering and shaking. I endeavored several times to control my nerves and remain quietly in one position, but without avail. At the end of that time I noticed that I was becoming quieter; but, while physically so, my mind was suffering more. My whole idea was to get warm. My body was cold all over—frozen in, I felt, to an equal depth in every place. I clung closer to my companion in the vain hope of producing more warmth. Oh, if I could only get warm again! I felt that I could willingly barter every earthly possession to be warm. I thought bitterly of our culpable carelessness in not building a fire the evening previous, and of the joy it would be to sit before such blazing fires as we had on nights now gone. If I could only get warm again! Was there not some way in which we could get to a fire? Could not the half-breed build one? If he would only try, I would give him anything; nothing was too dear if I could only feel warm. There was a particular room in my brother's house, with a large open fireplace in it. If it were only evening, and we were gathered about a bright, cheerful fire, how nice and warm I could get! One sometimes goes into an hotel sitting-room in winter, and they have a huge box-stove, made to take in cord-wood whole. What a genial warmth and heat there is! What a glow there is over the entire room! Oh, if I could only get warm like that!

I would be aroused at times out of thoughts like these by my companion, who now took to pushing me, and constantly warning me against falling asleep. Mr. Wheeler, also, was continually talking of his freezing, and assured us both that his ears were already frozen.

For the first time I really became conscious of the danger we were in. Strange to say, it had no effect upon me. I felt no alarm at the possibility of being overtaken by death, I was so cold—if I could only get warm again! This was the burden of my thought. Yet I was fully conscious of the danger. I knew, if death overtook me, in exactly what shape it would come. And I knew, furthermore, that I had already passed through the first stage, and was nearly through the second. Still, with this well-defined knowledge of what was before me, I was totally indifferent to the pangs of death. I only wanted to be warm; I felt that in some way I must get warm. I thought over the prospect of a speedy death indifferently. There was no trouble about the future at all—I did not think of it. The physical suffering and stupor were too great to admit of it.

Twice before in my life I had been in momentary expectation of death; and one experience of the horrors of dissolution was the same as this. That was a case of *dangue* fever. While perfectly conscious in the last moments—told they were my last, and asked if I was prepared to undergo them—I felt the same sensation as here; if I were only comfortable, I would willingly go. I knew a gentleman once who told me that, when in a similar situation—on the point of death—his only feeling was one of hunger; no thought or fear for the future at all, if only his appetite could be satisfied. But how different that other experience, when called upon to face death in full bodily vigor! The terrors which encompassed me are indescribable.

Continuing in the consciousness of danger, and yet thinking only of my suffering and desire to become warm, after the lapse of an hour, probably, I began to get warm—that is, the sensation was one of warmth and comfort, but was in reality, a species of numbness. I felt my flesh in several places, and it produced a prickly, numb feeling, similar to that experienced when a limb is asleep. I was comfortable and happy, because I was warm, and grew indignant with my companion for his unwearied thumps on my body, and the continual answers he required to his questions; I wanted to be let alone. Fully conscious that, if I went to sleep I would never awaken again, I was perfectly willing to go asleep. Even then I remember thinking of poor travelers, lost in the snow, being brought in by St. Bernard dogs.

But I was warm, and laughed silently at Mr. Wheeler's complaints of freezing. I paid no further attention to the shakings of my companion or his questions, but gathered myself up, and lay thinking how comfortable I was. Pretty soon I began to doze, then to awaken suddenly, when I received a more severe blow than usual. Then I awoke to see the half-breed sitting up and bending eagerly over my face, and hear a few muttered words to Wheeler—and then a sense of comfort and oblivion.

Now I was dead. Sensibility had left me. It was evident that I would suffer no more. In thirty or forty minutes, an hour at farthest, my body would die. Then what?

That I should awaken with a bright fire before me, and be wrapped in robes and blankets, seemed the most natural thing in the world to me. For the matter of that, it appeared to me that when I had fallen asleep I had anticipated just such a consummation of things, and it was fully half an hour before I began in the least to comprehend that any thing out of the ordinary channel had occurred. True, I knew in a vague and indistinct way that the half-breed was talking of Mr. Wheeler being lost, but the matter seemed to be no affair of mine, and created no surprise. I looked at him chafing my arms and legs, and simply felt that it was quite right and natural that it should be so.

Gradually, however, I regained consciousness sufficiently to understand that, finding me fast freezing, and impossible to arouse, he had gone, at the imminent risk of his own life, some three hundred yards farther down the stream, and finding a dry and partially rotten log, had built a fire; had then returned to find me totally unconscious, and to carry me, robes and all, to the fire. The few words he had addressed to Mr. Wheeler before leaving me showed that he, too, was fast lapsing into the same state, and, when I was carried in safety to the fire, had returned to find Mr. Wheeler gone—having, evidently, awakened from his stupor sufficiently to realize that he was alone, and to wander off, half frenzied, in search of us.

These facts being at last impressed upon my mind by the excited and voluble half-breed, I urged him to renew the seach [*sic*] for our lost companion; but he positively refused. He explained that, in doing what he had already done, he had jeopardized his own life, and had frozen both hands and feet considerably; that, while paid to care for me, he had nothing to do with Mr. Wheeler. He urged that, if he left the bank of the stream, he was likely to be lost, the snow at once obliterating all trace of his tracks. I ordered him to go, begged him to go, but without avail. An offer of five golden sovereigns met with a like refusal. At length, I told him that, if he would find Mr. Wheeler, dead or alive, I would give him a good horse. For this consideration he went. In twenty minutes he returned, leading the unfortunate man, badly frozen, whom he had found running wildly about in a circle on the prairie. He was kept from the fire with some difficulty, until his hands, feet, and face, were thawed out with water, but did not recover his mind until six hours after. From frequent personal observation, I am led to believe that nearly every one who freezes to death upon the prairies, or elsewhere, becomes insane before death.*

Having been thoroughly warmed and recruited by a steaming-hot breakfast, we followed the river to avoid losing our way, and in the afternoon reached a Hudson's Bay Company's post. Here we were informed that the temperature had fallen, during the previous night, to forty-five degrees below zero! We remained in that hospitable shelter for two days, during which the terrific storm raged with unabated fury. Some dozen Indians and half-breeds perished upon the route over which we had just passed.

After this lapse of time, I recall my thoughts and feelings with much more distinctness and accuracy than I could for some time immediately subsequent to the events related. No one who has passed through great danger realizes fully the extent of it at once. It requires time to impress the memory with all its circumstances. What my feelings were at this unexpected preservation from the dreadful fate which threatened me, it is impossible to express. (307–14)

*I have had five cases of freezing to death brought under my personal observation. In every instance the subject gave indubitable indications of insanity before death, and in every case exhibited it in the same way—by casting off his clothing and wandering away from it. One subject was entirely nude, and distant fully a mile from the last article of clothing he had discarded.

THE YUKON COLD

The poet known as the voice of the Yukon, Robert W. Service, had joined the many prospectors who went to the Yukon in 1897. One of Service's lighthearted testimonies to the Yukon weather is his famous poem "The Cremation of Sam McGee." The cold, he says, stabs through the fold in one's parka "like a driven nail." The humor and surprise ending are exaggerations of the infamous Yukon winter.

FROM ROBERT W. SERVICE, "THE CREMATION OF SAM MCGEE,"
IN *THE SPELL OF THE YUKON AND OTHER VERSES*
(New York: Barse & Hopkins Publishers, 1907)

There are strange things done in the midnight sun
  By the men who moil for gold;
The Arctic trails have their secret tales
  That would make your blood run cold;
The Northern Lights have seen queer sights,
  But the queerest they ever did see
Was that night on the marge of Lake Lebarge
  I cremated Sam McGee.

Now Sam McGee was from Tennessee, where the cotton blooms and blows.
Why he left his home in the South to roam 'round the Pole, God only knows.
He was always cold, but the land of gold seemed to hold him like a spell;
Though he'd often say in his homely way that "he'd sooner live in hell."

On a Christmas Day we were mushing our way over the Dawson trail.
Talk of your cold! through the parka's fold it stabbed like a driven nail.
If our eyes we'd close, then the lashes froze till sometimes we couldn't see;
It wasn't much fun, but the only one to whimper was Sam McGee.

And that very night, as we lay packed tight in our robes beneath
    the snow,
And the dogs were fed, and the stars o'erhead were dancing heel
    and toe,
He turned to me, and "Cap," says he, "I'll cash in this trip, I
    guess;
And if I do, I'm asking that you won't refuse my last request."

Well, he seemed so low that I couldn't say no; then he says with a
    sort of moan:
"It's the cursed cold, and it's got right hold till I'm chilled clean
    through to the bone.
Yet 'taint being dead—it's my awful dread of the icy grave that
    pains;
So I want you to swear that, foul or fair, you'll cremate my last
    remains."

A pal's last need is a thing to heed, so I swore I would not fail;
And we started on at the streak of dawn; but God! he looked
    ghastly pale.
He crouched on the sleigh, and he raved all day of his home in
    Tennessee;
And before nightfall a corpse was all that was left of Sam McGee.

There wasn't a breath in that land of death, and I hurried, horror-
    driven,
With a corpse half hid that I couldn't get rid, because of a
    promise given;
It was lashed to the sleigh, and it seemed to say: "You may tax
    your brawn and brains,
But you promised true, and it's up to you to cremate those last
    remains."

Now a promise made is a debt unpaid, and the trail has its own
    stern code.
In the days to come, though my lips were dumb, in my heart how
    I cursed that load.
In the long, long night, by the lone firelight, while the huskies,
    round in a ring,
Howled out their woes to the homeless snows—O God! how I
    loathed the thing.

And every day that quiet clay seemed to heavy and heavier grow;
And on I went, though the dogs were spent and the grub was
    getting low;
The trail was bad, and I felt half mad, but I swore I would not
    give in;

And I'd often sing to the hateful thing, and it hearkened with a
    grin.
Till I came to the marge of Lake Lebarge, and a derelict there lay;
It was jammed in the ice, but I saw in a trice it was called the
    "Alice May."
And I looked at it, and I thought a bit, and I looked at my frozen
    chum;
Then "Here," said I, with a sudden cry, "is my crema-tor-eum."

Some planks I tore from the cabin floor, and I lit the boiler fire;
Some coal I found that was lying around, and I heaped the fuel
    higher;
The flames just soared, and the furnace roared—such a blaze you
    seldom see;
And I burrowed a hole in the glowing coal, and I stuffed in Sam
    McGee.

Then I made a hike, for I didn't like to hear him sizzle so;
And the heavens scowled, and the huskies howled, and the wind
    began to blow.
It was icy cold, but the hot sweat rolled down my cheeks, and I
    don't know why;
And the greasy smoke in an inky cloak went streaking down the
    sky.

I do not know how long in the snow I wrestled with grisly fear;
But the stars came out and they danced about ere again I
    ventured near;
I was sick with dread, but I bravely said: "I'll just take a peep
    inside.
I guess he's cooked, and it's time I looked;" . . . then the door I
    opened wide.

And there sat Sam, looking cool and calm, in the heart of the
    furnace roar;
And he wore a smile you could see a mile, and he said: "Please
    close that door.
It's fine in here, but I greatly fear you'll let in the cold and
    storm—
Since I left Plumtree, down in Tennessee, it's the first time I've
    been warm."

There are strange things done in the midnight sun
    By the men who moil for gold;
The Arctic trails have their secret tales
    That would make your blood run cold;

The Northern Lights have seen queer sights,
  But the queerest they ever did see
Was that night on the marge of Lake Lebarge
  I cremated Sam McGee. (50–54)

PROJECTS FOR ORAL OR WRITTEN EXPLORATION

1. Some readers have claimed that the snow in *The Call of the Wild* represents purity. Others say that it chiefly embodies terror. How would you characterize the snow in the story? Write an essay on the subject, supporting your contention with specifics from the story.

2. As we can see after looking at excerpts from London's other Yukon stories, the tone and details are much more realistically harsh than they are in *The Call of the Wild*. For what reason has he made the depiction of the Yukon less brutal in this novel than in his other stories?

3. If you agree that the far Northwest is much like a character in the story, to what extent is it villainous and to what extent heroic?

4. Numerous conditions, not just the cold, make the Yukon a difficult place to travel. Write an essay on travel in the Yukon at the turn of the twentieth century.

5. Some of the writers represented in this chapter have made reference to the importance of having access to a fire in the bitter cold of the Yukon. Using excerpts provided here, refer to London's story "To Build a Fire" and write an essay on the necessity of having a fire and the difficulties in building one.

6. Choose a topic pertinent to this chapter and write a historical research paper on it. Possibilities include the Hudson's Bay Company, the Russian-American Company, seal hunting, the sale of Alaska to the United States, border disputes between Canada and the United States, and the fate of Native Americans in Canada and the Alaska Panhandle.

7. The hunting of the seal to extinction became an issue again in the mid-twentieth century. Write a research paper in which you place the more recent arguments regarding seal hunting in the historical context of seal hunting in Alaska in the nineteenth century.

SUGGESTIONS FOR FURTHER READING

Bennett, Gordon. *Yukon Transportation*. Ottawa: National Historic Parks and Sites Branch, Parks Canada, Indian and Northern Affairs, 1978.
Berger, Thomas. *Northern Frontier/Northern Homeland*. Ottawa: Department of Supply and Services, 1977.

Brody, Hugh. *Living Arctic*. Vancouver: Douglas & McIntyre, 1987.

Coates, K. S. *Canada's Colonies*. Toronto: James Lorimer, 1985.

Coates, K. S., and William R. Morrison. *Land of the Midnight Sun*. Edmonton: Hurtig, 1988.

Fagan, Brian M. *The Great Journey*. New York: Thames & Hudson, 1987.

Francis, Daniel. *Arctic Chase*. St. John's, Newfoundland: Breakwater Books, 1984.

————. *Discovery of the North*. Edmonton: Hurtig, 1986.

Hunt, William R. *North of 53 Degrees*. New York: Macmillan, 1974.

Karamanski, Theodore. *Fur Trade and Exploration*. Vancouver: University of British Columbia Press, 1983.

Minter, Roy. *The White Pass*. Fairbanks: University of Alaska Press, 1987.

Pierce, W. H. *Thirteen Years of Travel and Exploration in Alaska*. Anchorage: Alaska Northwest Publishing, 1977.

Wilson, Clifford. *Campbell of the Yukon*. Toronto: Macmillan of Canada, 1970.

Wright, A. A. *Prelude to Bonanza*. Sidney, B.C.: Gray's Pub., 1976.

Prospective miners on Chilkoot Pass, 1897. Special Collections, University of Washington Libraries. Neg. # Hegg 101.

The Yukon Gold Rush

THE GOLD RUSH AND BUCK'S STORY

The Yukon gold rush of 1897–98 is part and parcel of Buck's story. The second sentence of the novel refers to the "Arctic darkness," where men look for "a yellow metal" (1). The mania for gold in a part of the world where travel is feasible only by dogsled places a premium on all dogs and puts them all in jeopardy. Buck, because he is big and has a thick coat of fur, is a natural target. He is, as the expression goes, as good as gold. So it is the gold rush that hurls him out of paradise; the gold rush that drives men to subdue him with clubs; the gold rush that takes him so far from home that he can never return; the gold rush that turns him into a slave laborer.

Buck makes the journey from Dyea to Dawson and from Skagway to Dawson over the same track trod by the millions of prospectors seeking gold in the Yukon in 1897 and 1898. The landing at Dyea, the pull through Chilkoot Pass, the encounter with Indians and their huskies at Lake Laberge, the scenes in the saloons of Dawson, the rapids on Forty Mile Creek were all part of the gold rush experience.

Every person and every dog Buck meets in the Yukon is there as part of the great gold rush. He encounters men who make their living stealing dogs to sell to Yukon prospectors. As a result of the gold rush, the Canadian government needed to expand its messenger services and brought more dogs to draw the mail sleds driven (in this as in many other cases) by French-Canadians—"carrying word from the world to the men who sought gold under the shadow of the Pole" (27). Buck at one point is owned by three neophyte incompetents who have gone to the Yukon to get rich quick on gold, traveling by dogsled to the richest fields in the Klondike River Basin. They stumble on John Thornton, also a miner, who has set up camp at the mouth of the White River. Knowing the rottenness of the ice as they do not, he tells them that he would not risk going on the ice for "all the gold in Alaska" (40). Buck goes with Thornton, who is staking claims around the Dawson area. Here they meet other gold miners in the saloons of Dawson, including a "Klondike King"—someone who has struck it rich mining for gold. In Dawson, men use the gold they have mined to bet that Buck can or cannot perform the feat of breaking a sled out of ice. The 1,600 dollars that Buck wins allows Thornton and his partners to prospect for gold farther east, where other miners have not looked. As they travel into the greater unknown, they wash many pans of dirt looking for gold. Eventually they arrive at a valley where "gold showed like yellow butter across the bottom of the washing-pan" (52). Here they find "thousands of dollars in clean dust and nuggets" (53). In a last reference to the gold rush in *The Call of the Wild*, Thornton and his partners secure the gold they find in bags made of moose hide.

DISCOVERY OF GOLD IN THE YUKON

By 1840, a few miners had come to the Yukon looking for gold. Gradually the search for metals began to replace the hunt for furs in this area rich with natural resources. In 1886, a promising lode of gold was discovered in the Forty Mile Creek area (where Buck rescued Thornton from drowning). The discovery was a rehearsal for what happened ten years later in that hundreds of miners came to the Yukon at that time, hoping to strike it rich. But the great rush to the Yukon for gold was precipitated by a single event: the discovery on August 16, 1896, of a particularly rich find on Rabbit Creek (which came to be known as Bonanza Creek), a tributary of the Klondike River northeast of Dawson. On a tip by Robert Henderson, three men—George Carmack, Skookum Jim, and Tagish Charlie—investigated and found the area so rich in gold that it made many men rich and attracted many thousands more in the hope of getting rich. Thus began what is recognized as the world's greatest gold rush. Some two years later, 100,000 hopefuls had flooded the Yukon, a remote and treacherous place that had virtually none of the civilized means for survival.

The areas richest in gold were in the valleys where the Yukon and Klondike rivers came together. Immediately upon Carmack's discovery in August, the men already mining in the Yukon staked out the most promising claims along the tributaries there. By the time the actual gold rush by outsiders occurred almost a year later, the best land had already been claimed. Nevertheless, in the ten years that followed the initial discovery on Rabbit Creek, miners extracted over $100 million of gold in the Klondike-Yukon River area alone.

PREPARATION FOR THE YUKON

News of the find began to spread to the rest of the world outside the Yukon when some of the miners who had struck it rich—Klondike Kings, they were called—sailed into San Francisco on the *Excelsior* on July 15, 1897, and into Seattle on the *Portland* two days later, on July 17, 1897. The men lugged great sacks and crates of gold off the two ships. The newspapers of the day estimated that miners came off the *Portland* with two tons of pure gold.

In a country wracked by a devastating economic depression that left many people without jobs, housing, or food, the effect of this event was dramatic and immediate. People from all over the United States prepared to go to the Yukon at once. About 30 percent of those swept up in the rush were from the United States; a few were forty-niners who had come to California to look for gold in 1849. Thirty percent were from Canada and 15 percent from Britain, with a lesser number from Europe. Half of those who went were under forty years of age. Seventy-five percent were unmarried, and 99 percent were male. They were from all walks of life, all trades and professions. Every capable person in whole villages packed up to go. Sometimes one or two people would be financed by a group that stayed at home but would then expect to share in any gold that was found. Most of the prospectors worked in teams.

Part of the attraction was the prospect of striking it rich without an expensive outlay of equipment. One just needed, first of all, to get there by buying cheap passage, usually out of Seattle or San Francisco. All one needed for the mining process itself, they were told, was a gold-mining pan and axes, picks, and shovels. The rest of the provisions, though cumbersome, were not extremely expensive: food, tents, special clothing, and the money to pay multiple fees. A new form of literature immediately arose and was in great demand: guidebooks indicating how to get there, what to take, and what to expect. Still, many without sense or money tried to take advantage of the opportunity without adequate preparation. Some tried unsuccessfully to get to the Alaskan Panhandle in leaky boats secured in Seattle. Others, having been told that some form of transportation was imperative for travel in the Yukon, took whatever was available without expenditure: sick or aging horses or mules or small, shorthaired dogs that were bound to freeze to death. Other travelers were under the delusion that food could be purchased all along the Yukon trails. Only Canadian border guards, who refused to let miners enter British Columbia or the Yukon without a year's provisions, kept many from starving to death along the way. Still, many attempted to avoid having to pass through Canadian officials and pay the entry fees demanded by the Canadian government.

THE JOURNEY

There were several routes to the gold-rich area. One was across Canada from Edmonton through the Mackenzie Mountains. Rarely did anyone actually complete this journey. Some attempting to avoid Canadian checkpoints came by way of Valdez, Alaska. Those who were well heeled could take an all-water route to Dawson via northern Alaska and St. Michael to the Yukon River. However, most began their land journey in either Skagway or Dyea, as Buck did.

The trip from Seattle to the Dawson area of the Yukon took six months. The journey to Skagway or Dyea in the Alaskan Panhandle was sometimes tempestuous because of high winds, but it was also a time when miners could swap stories about what they had been told to expect. Often it was a time when alliances were formed to make the burden easier. Dyea was an especially difficult place to sail into. The winds were high, and the wharves were inadequate and rustic. For most of 1896 and 1897, the only building was a store, and newcomers had to sleep in their tents. Everything cost money. For example, a fee was charged to unload one's baggage onto the dock and to pitch a tent.

Skagway presented an additional problem. Few had anticipated the graft and crime in this port of entry where a notorious gang led by the infamous Soapy Smith created elaborate and effective schemes for cheating new arrivals. A favorite scam was to offer to send a telegram back home for a newcomer and to fetch him an answer if one was forthcoming. Most outsiders had no way of knowing that no telegraph lines came into Skagway.

WHITE PASS

Miners had a choice of two routes from the Panhandle to Lake Bennett, where the journey on inland water began. They could go from Skagway through the White Pass, or they could go from Dyea through the Chilkoot Pass. The White Pass was less steep, and it was theoretically possible to take pack animals on this route. But the way was so dangerous with mud holes and rotten ice and the miners were so ignorant of how to manage horses and mules in this terrain that few pack animals survived the journey—forty-five miles over bogs, mud holes, multiple rapidly flowing rivers, and soggy and steep hills between ten-foot-high boulders. At most points, the trail was only wide enough for one animal, and all the animals labored under impossibly heavy burdens. In 1897, three thousand horses began the journey on the White Pass. Almost every one of them died on the way, littering the trail with bodies from beginning to end. For this reason, it came to be known as Dead Horse Pass. Some trapped or wounded or starved animals were shot, but others were left to die horribly rather than wasting bullets on them. White Pass held another danger: the miners who took this route were at the mercy of bandits who ambushed and robbed them of everything they needed to survive and to mine gold in the Yukon.

It took about ninety days for miners to travel the forty-five miles over White Pass. Many men died along the way. Others passed by the unburied corpses with little or no notice. After days of dangerous travel at a snail's pace, some miners went mad, invariably taking out their frustrations on their animals. One man whose dogs could no longer move on the White Pass beat them until they were half dead and then pushed them one by one into a waterhole under the ice. Another whose oxen could no longer budge under the heavy load built a fire under them, burning them alive. Jack London describes the stupidity and brutality in his story "Which Make Men Remember":

> Freighting an outfit over the White Pass in '97 broke many a man's heart, for there was a world of reason when they gave that trail its name. The horses died like mosquitoes in the first frost, and from Skaguay to Bennett they rotted in heaps. They died at the Rocks, they were poisoned at the Summit, and they starved at the Lakes; they fell off the trail, what there was of it, or they went through it; in the river they drowned under their loads, or were smashed to pieces against the boulders; they snapped their legs in the crevices and broke their backs falling backwards with their packs; in the sloughs they sank from sight or smothered in the slime, and they were disembowelled in the bogs where the corduroy logs turned end up in the mud; men shot them, worked them to death, and when they were gone, went back to the beach and bought more. Some did not bother to shoot them,—stripping the saddles off and the shoes and leaving them where they fell. Their hearts turned to stone—those which did not break—and they became beasts, the men on Dead Horse Trail. ("Which Make Men Remember," *Complete Short Stories*, 321)

THE CHILKOOT PASS

The other choice was the notorious Chilkoot Pass, sometimes called the Klondike Gold Rush Trail, which an estimated twenty to thirty thousand people crossed in 1897 and 1898. The various stages along this route began with a six-mile trip by water. During most of this time, the travelers on land pulled canoes loaded with their gear. After this, they climbed eight miles up a canyon that brought them to Sheep Camp. Next they climbed some four miles on hands and feet to the summit. Traveling from the summit down to the next camp at Lake Lindeman took about eight days.

Packing the necessary equipment up this nightmarish pass to Lake Bennett took most men from one to three months, much of it traveling at a forty-five-degree angle. The Chilkoot Pass can best be described as a glacier-covered escarpment. The miners-to-be had to get anywhere from three hundred to a thousand pounds of gear over ice on a trail strewn with boulders and so steep that they were often climbing on hands and knees. With so much gear—food to last for months, tents, tools, and so on—no one could make the journey in one trip. Instead, a man might carry fifty to one hundred pounds over one leg of the climb, leave it, and go back for another load, until he had all his belongings. In some especially steep portions of the trail, they could go no more than two miles in two days. The last incredibly steep part of the climb was described as trying to climb the walls of a house. In the middle of winter, they hacked steps into the ice to aid in the climb. Eventually, fifteen hundred steps were carved out of the ice on that last ascent of the Chilkoot Pass. Imagine the length of a football field. Now imagine walking the length of a football field three and a half times. It took the miners six hours to go that far at the top of Chilkoot Pass.

For a thousand dollars, one could hire Indian packers to take belongings over the pass. Not many could afford such a luxury. Some miners, badly in need of money, not only made many trips hauling their own gear over the ice, but hired themselves out as packers for other people.

In addition to the hard work of climbing with their packs, the travelers were also in constant danger, for in some places the trail was only a foot or two wide, and if one stumbled under the heavy loads and stepped off the path, he might well plunge off and be buried under loose snow. In addition, slides and avalanches constantly tore down through the pass. In April 1898, a thirty-foot mountain of snow stormed down the pass, carrying along huge boulders. Seventy-three prospective miners died, most buried alive under thousands of pounds of snow. Sometimes one might survive such a slide, but lose all one's gear. Horrific storms sometimes halted all progress on the trail, the snow falling so thick and blowing so hard that men were smothered in their tents.

The travelers often needed to cross rivers where the bridges were little more than ropes. Many who went across these precarious bridges with fifty to one hundred pounds of gear on their backs met their deaths when they plunged into the icy, swiftly flowing water below. It is no wonder that many turned back here before they even reached the gold fields, or that some took their own lives on the way.

THE TRIP BY WATER TO THE GOLD FIELDS

The dangers and hardships were not over for those who had mastered the Chilkoot Pass, for the rest of the trip, though downhill, was by waterways fraught with raging, life-threatening rapids over boulders, seen and unseen, whirlpools that could overturn small boats and entrap men until they drowned, and concealed holes in the ice through which men, dogs, and supplies could disappear. The rapids also splintered so many oars and boats on the hidden rocks that the whole complex system of waterways from Lake Bennett to Dawson was strewn with the wreckage. Often the only safe way to proceed was to get out of the boat and walk to the bottom of the rapids.

The trail to Dawson led through five lakes. In his short story "Trust," London describes how excruciating and dangerous it was to travel on one of these lakes, Lake Tagish, in the middle of an icy gale:

> They fought the gale up to their waists in the icy water, often up to their necks, often over their heads and buried by the big, crested waves. There was no rest, never a moment's pause from the cheerless, heart-breaking battle. That night, at the head of Tagish Lake, in the thick of a driving snow-squall, they overhauled the *Flora*. . . . Churchill looked like a wild man. His clothes barely clung to him. His face was iced up and swollen from the protracted effort of twenty-four hours, while his hands were so swollen that he could not close the fingers. As for his feet, it was an agony to stand on them. ("Trust," *Complete Short Stories*, 1337)

One of the lakes, Lake Laberge, was reputed to be one of the coldest spots in the Yukon, made especially bitter by high winds. Once one had weathered Lake Laberge, however, most of the rapids that remained were relatively minor compared with those between Lake Laberge and the Chilkoot Pass.

DAWSON

The goal was Dawson, a village at the center of gold-mining activity, a sparsely inhabited settlement before the Carmack find. Before the summer of 1897, it was composed only of tents and log huts, but within a year, it mushroomed into a town of 30,000 people with churches, hospitals, schools, theaters, and, of course, the ever-present saloons. The theaters produced the ever-popular *Uncle Tom's Cabin*. In most productions, the big scene was a pack of bloodhounds chasing Eliza, the young runaway slave, across a frozen river. In the Dawson production, the bloodhounds were represented by a single yelping puppy who was pulled across the stage by a wire. Civilized institutions there were, but all were built on mud that often reached above the first-story windows.

Everything was for sale in Dawson and for a very high price. Trees did not grow in Dawson's subarctic climate, so logs brought from areas farther south were extremely valuable. Entrepreneurs packed everything imaginable to Dawson to make money. For example, eggs sold for eighteen dollars a dozen. Jack London wrote a story about a man who risked life and limb to bring one thousand eggs to sell in Dawson only to discover at the last that they had all rotted. In historical accounts is found the story of a man who brought several hundred cats and kittens to Dawson to sell. Most of his fellow travelers regarded the whole enterprise as deranged, but he sold them all immediately for several hundred dollars each.

Dawson was important to the miners because it was here that they had to come to secure their claims and pay the requisite fees that enabled them to mine for gold. Here they could exchange gold dust for needed food and supplies. Here they found jobs to keep them alive—bartending, cooking, chopping wood, washing clothes, or building boats, for example. In Dawson they also found ways of communicating with each other and with the outside world in public gatherings where rare newspapers were read aloud.

In 1898, a typhoid epidemic broke out in Dawson as a result of an influx of mosquitoes and drinking water tainted by sewage. Records show that several hundred people died of typhoid or scurvy. In addition, a famine developed in the area in the spring of 1898, leaving both those in the village and those in remote camps without enough food to stay alive.

DISCOURAGEMENTS UPON ARRIVAL

Most learned with a shock upon arrival in the gold-mining district that almost all the land had already been staked. Many would stake some land and then travel to Dawson to secure their claims, only to learn that the land had already been staked previously. Some found out the hard way about claim jumping when their stakes were pulled out in their absence.

THE YUKON MINING OPERATION

The soil richest in gold lay near the banks of rivers and creeks, some forty to sixty feet below the surface. Thus a miner never really knew for sure the worth of the claim he had staked until many months and much work later. The material from the surface on down to the gold was frozen solid and was as hard as marble. To get to the forty or so feet below the surface where the gold lay, miners needed to thaw their way down with constant fires, driving shafts into the ground until they could throw up the dirt into huge mountainous piles on the surface. Much of the work was done by lantern light because there were never more than seven hours of daylight to work in. Because everything froze instantly, however, there was no way to wash the dirt in troughs or gold pans to discover if it contained any gold. For one thing, the dirt itself immediately became rock hard when it was thrown up out of the hole. For another, water, which would ordinarily be used for rinsing the dirt, also froze instantly. Thus the process of mining could not be completed until the spring thaw. At that time, if all went well, water would be used to pan the mountains of dirt that had been piled up all winter. If all did not go well, huge explosive walls of water would burst over the camp, carrying away everything that had been accumulated for months.

It is scarcely surprising that of all the thousands who went to the Klondike to search for gold, only a handful came home with profits. By 1899, the gold rush to the Yukon had ended with news of even more promising fields across the border in Alaska.

JACK LONDON'S TRIP TO THE YUKON

Jack London's trip to the Yukon followed the typical pattern. On July 15, 1897, some of the Klondike Kings, loaded down with gold, landed in San Francisco on the *Excelsior*, bringing news and tangible evidence of the possibility of striking it rich in the Yukon. Jack London, with no professional or family responsibilities and as eager for adventure as for gold, immediately made plans to go to the Yukon, as did thousands of other people. His brother-in-law J. H. Shepard decided to advance London the cash to go and, moreover, to join him on the trip as well. Ten days later, on July 25, London and Shepard boarded a boat, the *Umatilla*, in San Francisco for a fee of $25 each and were on their way to the Yukon. It took eight days to get to Dyea. On the way, like so many others, they met three men with whom they teamed up.

Jack London's landing in Dyea was rife with problems. His party found no wharves, no shelters, and unbearably high winds. Anxious to get to the Yukon before winter set in, they made the decision to leave Dyea as soon as possible. Not only did they decline the paid services of Indian packers, London even hired himself out as a packer at various points on their journey. Stripped down to his long johns, London often made as many as four trips over portions of the Chilkoot Pass, carrying 150 pounds each time. Before they reached the summit, Shepard, who had a history of heart trouble, decided to return home, as did many other would-be miners. After reaching the summit of the pass, London and his party descended to Lake Lindeman, a trip of eight days. There they spent two weeks building a boat for the rest of the journey to Dawson, downhill and by water.

The problem now was the rapids, which London, as an experienced sailor, was skilled in navigating. He got their own boat through, not without risks, and took the boats of other miners through. Lake Laberge, one of five lakes on their way to Dawson, was especially difficult for London because of the north wind and icy water. It took his party two months and two days from the time they landed at Dyea to reach the Stewart River, eighty miles south of Dawson. Although they had planned to winter on the Stewart River, they eventually moved on north to Henderson Creek. After they staked their claims, London was sent as their representative to Dawson, where the claims had to be filed officially. Here he stayed for six weeks, taking care of business, until the weather allowed him to return.

London returned to work the claim with his partners and visited other miners in the area, including Marshall Bond, also from California, whose magnificent dog Jack he so greatly admired. In May, the spring thaw and subsequent flooding created new dangers for London and his party. The island where they had staked their claim was flooded by water, and their cabin was destroyed. Out of the wood of their torn-down cabin they made a raft to take them to Dawson. Once they were there, they were able to sell the logs for a good price.

By this time, scurvy—the disease that hit many miners—had struck Jack London. He spent three weeks in May and June getting proper food and medical treatment in Dawson. On June 8, 1898, in a simple sailboat, he left Dawson for home. In August, a little over a year after he had left for the Klondike, he was back at home in California.

London's sense of the Yukon gold rush as he wrote about it in *The Call of the Wild* and other stories is corroborated by the various documents detailing the Yukon gold rush that follow. These include a firsthand memoir of the discovery that began the gold rush; newspaper articles published in San Francisco and Oakland, California, after miners came into town with their fortunes in gold; advice about going to the Yukon; advertisements of those seeking to make money from the gold rush; firsthand accounts of crossing Chilkoot Pass; firsthand accounts of navigating the lakes and rapids on the way to Dawson; a copy of a form to be completed in filing claims; and poems about gold-rush fever.

THE INITIAL DISCOVERY OF GOLD IN THE KLONDIKE

Scattered miners had been prospecting in the Yukon for several decades before George Carmack (sometimes spelled Cormack) and his associates discovered the spectacularly rich source of gold on Rabbit Creek. The first document is a record of that discovery written by a man who was at the site within two weeks of Carmack's find. In 1897, M.H.E. Hayne, a member of the Northwest Territories' Mounted Police, found a ready audience for his story about his two years in the Yukon. In that year, the frenzied possibility of getting rich quick provoked Buck's kidnapping. Those who were considering a trip to pan for gold there or an investment in gold mining there were eager for any available information on what was then an unknown and mysterious area.

Hayne describes the initial skepticism of other miners toward Carmack's find and then, after they became convinced that a new area rich in gold had indeed been discovered, their mad rush to the Yukon-Klondike basin to stake their claims. He also describes the relatively few miners who were digging great fortunes from the earth before news of the discovery reached the rest of the world.

FROM M.H.E. HAYNE AND H. WEST TAYLOR, *THE PIONEERS OF THE KLONDYKE*
(London: Sampson Low, Marston & Co., 1897)

[W]e ourselves had no notion of the existence of the gold until, on August 20, 1896, a couple of men dropped down the Yukon in a canoe and landed at Forty Mile town, then almost deserted in favour of Circle City. These two men were an Indian and a white man, who had been travelling round hunting with the Indians for the past ten or eleven years, George Carmack by name. He had never had any luck before, and he was one whose statements were received with a certain amount of doubt; for he would never acknowledge himself beaten, and always endeavored to present his fortunes in the most advantageous light. This time, however, he had struck it rich, and had no need to exaggerate. He took a few favored friends into his confidence in Forty Mile, and came across to us next day, bearing a sample of the gold he had found. He then duly re-

corded and registered his claim with us, producing his sample, and stat-
ing on oath that he had found it on the particular creek whose locality
he described. This, with the payment of a $15 fee, legalized his claim,
and entitled him to stake off 500 feet along the edge of the creek. Creek
and river-claims in the Yukon district are all 500 feet long, and extend in
width from base to base of the hill or beach on each side. In addition to
this, by the laws which govern such things, he was further entitled to
stake out a second 500 feet claim, as the owner and recorder of the
"Discovery" claim on a hitherto unexploited creek. This, as it turned out,
made him the fortunate possessor of over 300 yards of the richest gold-
bearing gravel yet discovered in the world. A fitting recompense for
eleven years' perseverance!

The claim he had staked out was on a tributary of the Klondyke river,
which in its turn enters the Yukon about fifty miles above Forty Mile. It
was known as "The Bonanza." It is a fair-sized creek, about twenty miles
long, with plenty of water all the year round, though it is too shallow for
boats. The supply of water, in fact, is almost too abundant for mining
purposes in the spring and summer. The view of it which I reproduce
was a "bird's-eye" taken from a height above.

Even after Carmack had registered his claim and returned to work it,
there was a certain amount of scepticism as to the real truth of the new
discovery. Experienced miners, however, who examined the sample, soon
began to believe that it must be true, and for this reason. If you show an
experienced man a nugget or a small quantity of gold-dust, he is immediately able to tell you the particular neighborhood from which it has
been taken. This he does by the general size of the sample, and by looking closely to see how much it has been washed. Now this piece that
Carmack had brought in was unlike any they had seen before, though
the uninitiated would not have been able to detect any difference between this and any other piece of virgin gold. Consequently they were
unable to locate it to any of the creeks already being worked. This inclined them to the belief that a new streak had been discovered, and that
consequently Carmack's statement was a true one.

Meanwhile those to whom Carmack had imparted his news were
crowding out of Forty Mile, waiting till night had closed in so as to get
away unseen if possible, and each one trying to get well away without
any one else knowing he had gone. When I crossed over to the town on
the morning of the 21st, I was surprised to find it empty, and secretly
marvelled at the credulity shown by these men, all of whom were already
in possession of good paying claims, in crowding away on the mere
chance of getting something better. It was thoroughly characteristic of
the ceaseless unrest that always prevails in mining communities, where
every man, however successful, is frantically jealous of being "cut out" by

his neighbors, and cannot endure the thought of being left out in the cold when some good new thing is being started.

From this time forward, right away through the subsequent winter, there was a ceaseless rush up the Yukon to the mouth of the Klondyke. No one, of course, knew anything of the extent of the new gold-bearing district, and so expectation ran high as to whether each new arrival would be able to find a claim for himself, or earn good wages by working another man's claim for him. Lucky miners! The whole population for miles around could be counted by hundreds, and only about 350 claims were recorded that winter. There was more than room for everybody, though everybody went in, and there were not enough men to do the work! And to crown it all, they had nearly a year's start over all the rest of the world! Little wonder then that fortunes were made that winter which will enable their owners to live in affluence for the rest of their lives, and bequeath a comfortable inheritance to their children. This, I think, is what makes the whole story so unique and so romantic. The idea of these few men— the whole available population of the country—digging out the gold in shovelfuls, secure in the knowledge that no outsiders could arrive to contest it with them for a good nine months, is unparalleled, so far as I know, in the whole annals of gold-mining, and will always constitute one of the most noteworthy features in connection with the latest discovery. (134–38)

· · ·

The extent of the rush will be shown by the fact that, although I reached Bonanza Creek on September 1, less than a fortnight after Carmack's arrival at Forty Mile with the news of his strike, all the claims below "discovery" were staked out, and not only so, but I had to tramp a long way up the creek before I came to the last claim, and was able to stake out one for myself—quite up in the head-waters of the creek. (144)

· · ·

I remember one man in particular of those who asked me about the distance they would have to go before they could stake out on the Main Creek. He had been a bar-tender in Forty Mile, and had joined the general exodus that followed Carmack's registry of his claim. This man, as I say, staked on one of these "pups" on the same day as I had staked high up on the Bonanza. In the following spring, as a result of his "laziness," he came out with me on the steamer *Portland*, carrying with him $132,000 in gold-dust, which he had taken out of his "pup" stake! And this did not represent more than a fraction of his fortune. He had purchased the adjoining claim for another $100,000, all taken from his original claim, and left a partner in charge of these two claims, which were still his undisputed possession, to look after his interest during his absence. If that is not putting a premium on indolence I don't know what is. It was his intention to return this fall, or early next spring, and take out another fortune. I have since heard, though whether it be more than one of the many rumors which have got about I cannot say, that he has sold out to a New York syndicate for $2,000,000 (£400,000)! (146–47)

NEWS OF THE YUKON GOLD REACHES SAN FRANCISCO AND SEATTLE

The impact of the news of gold in the Yukon is indicated by an issue of the *San Francisco Call* on July 18, 1897, the day after successful gold miners had arrived with their loot in Seattle, Washington. The news swept virtually every major story off the pages of this substantial daily newspaper. Pages one, two, and three are devoted to news about the Klondike (sometimes, as here, spelled "Klondyke") find. At the top of page one is a one-inch headline: "STREAM OF GOLD FROM KLONDYKE." Enormous subheadlines blast across the page: "Steamship Portland Reached Seattle Laden With Yellow Dust," and underneath that: "MINERS RETURN ENRICHED BY THEIR FINDS." Still another enormous headline is carried beneath that: "Declare, That the Reports From the New Diggings Have Not Been Exaggerated—The Cargo Worth $800,000."

The fever that gripped the world at the time of Buck's kidnapping is clearly in evidence in the excerpt from the article that follows. The story was filed by a *Call* reporter who had been dispatched to Seattle to cover the *Portland*'s landing. This ship was loaded with sixty-eight passengers and their fortunes in gold. The scene in Seattle was a wild one. Crowds had gathered around the ship and around the hotel where many of the miners were depositing their gold in the safe.

The story conveyed to its readers, deep in the economic depression, proof positive that some people could get rich quick with inconsiderable initial investment: these miners who disembarked from the *Portland* had made their fortunes within three or four months of Carmack's find. The reporter describes the Yukon as a river of gold. The impact of the story is heightened by the reporter's interviews with the men and women as they leave the ship and his inclusion of several letters received by Seattle residents from Yukon prospectors. The article contains several hints that might have given any prospector pause about jumping on the next ship to the Yukon: rumors of a famine in the impending winter, which, although its possibility was denied emphatically by one of the returning passengers, did indeed occur; the suggestion that most of the rich areas had already been claimed; and the wide outside investments in the area by rich men and companies, leading one commentator to say that very few except those who were already rich made money in the Yukon.

FROM "STREAM OF GOLD FROM KLONDYKE"
(*San Francisco Call*, July 18, 1897)

SEATTLE, WASH., July 17—When the North American Trading and Transportation Company's gold laden ship Portland, from St. Michaels, Alaska, steamed into the harbor of Seattle this morning at 7 o'clock, it had besides sixty-eight souls in the nature of human freight, a yellow metal cargo conservatively estimated at $800,000. All save five or six of the passengers were miners who had from $5000 to $135,000 each. They had taken these snug sums from the famous Klondyke.

The dust and nuggets were scraped together and dug out since last August, in which month the widely heralded district was discovered. It is safe, therefore, to say that no one of the number worked to exceed nine months in the actual acquirement of his golden possessions. In truth, most of the wealth was taken out during the three or four winter months. . . . [T]he Portland must have brought down far in excess of $1,000,000.

The express companies refused point-blank to disclose the amount of their gold shipments, yet inquiry elicited the information that about two-thirds of the gold expressed to-day was consigned to the San Francisco Mint. The Helena Mint got a good share, and smaller amounts were expressed to other points. Many of the miners were loth to give any information as to the extent of their possessions.

Some of the larger amounts taken from the Klondyke were: Clarence Berry, Fresno, Cal., $135,000; William Stanley, Seattle, $93,000; Henry Anderson, a resident of this State, $65,000; Frank Keller, $50,000; J. J. Clement, Los Angeles, $50,000; T. J. Kelley, California, $33,000; William Sloane, formerly of Nanaimo, interests in five claims. He has employed a manager at $400 a month to look after his interests and keep men at work during the winter.

• • •

P. Coteland—I had a claim and sold it for $600. The parties who bought it were offered $10,000, but refused to take it. I have been working for Wilkinson & Sloan, and have not brought out very much money.

R. H. Blake—I was in the Yukon three years, but have not been mining. I have come home on business, but will go back in the spring, for it is too good a country to stay away from.

Inspector Strickland of the Canadian mounted police came back with Sergeant M. H. E. Hayne and five men, whose enlistments will expire in August. Inspector Strickland and Mrs. Strickland, Mr. and Mrs. Clarence J. Berry and Mrs. Eli A. Gage all arrived on the Portland and are at the Hotel Butler. Inspector Strickland is very reticent about the money he brought out, and one story has it that the amount is $180,000. Another is that it is $96,000. Sergeant Hayne, who is at the Northern, said:

"I had claim 73, above Discovery, on Bonanza Creek, and I sold it. I had it in charge of a man at $15 a day. I will not say how much money any of us brought out, but all of the police have good money."

The others of the police who returned are P. C. Engle, H. N. Jenkins, E. Newbrook, and E. Tedford. Mrs. Gaze is a guest at the Hotel Butler. She is a daughter-in-law of Secretary of the Treasury Gage and went north on the steamer Portland and returned on it from St. Michaels, Mr. Gage having gone up the river.

"Mr. Gage told me that he would come out this fall," said Mrs. Gage, "but I learned from other sources that he may not. He told a friend of ours that he would probably stay, and that is how I found it out. Of course he is going on business for the Northwest Transportation and Trading Company, but he will look after a little private business, too. Some very wealthy men came back with the steamer. One has $96,000. Hardly any have less than $15,000. The country is enormously rich. The present gold diggings are only a very small part of it and there is little doubt but there are millions upon millions in gold that is only waiting for the miners to come and dig it out.

"The reports from the Klondyke are not much exaggerated, for I have talked with people whom I know to be truthful. Do I think there is a danger of a famine this winter? Such a thing as a famine cannot occur in Alaska. Everybody has plenty of money and the company has taken a much larger amount of provisions in than it did last year, and so has the Alaska Commercial Company. Many have gone over the divide who have taken their 'grub' with them. I am going to telegraph right away to my father-in-law and tell him all about it."

Mrs. Gage met her brother, Mr. Weare, at St. Michaels. He returned with Mr. Gage to Forty Mile.

J. E. Boucher of Wisconsin was seen in his stateroom on board the Portland.

"Are you one of the lucky ones?" he was asked.

The Wisconsin man made a dive under the bunk for a blanket, and replied en route, "We were all lucky; every man on the boat was lucky."

"How much have all of you brought out?"

"None at all," replied the miner, as he rolled three double blankets into a heap.

"None at all? Why, I thought you said you were all lucky."

"None at all in comparison to what is there"—and never a grin at the sarcasm in the remark.

• • •

"Did you bring out much?"

"Only a little—just enough to go home the winter. I am going back next spring."

"How much do you call 'only a little?' "

"I brought out about $6000. I invested in a lot up there. I am going home to Wisconsin for the winter."

"Are you going to take a lot of Wisconsin men back with you?"

"No. Every one who goes in that country should go on his own responsibility. He must go well outfitted and prepared for hard work. I don't want any man to go on my say-so." And the man who had brought out "only a little to go home for the winter" scooted down the gangplank with his blankets.

The Canadian mounted police appear to have fared extremely well in the Northwest Territory, which they were directed by the British North American Government to protect. The five of the twenty original guards returned on the Portland with gold amounting to $225,000. Mrs. Gage evidently alluded to Inspector Strickland when she spoke of one passenger having in his possession $96,000. The remaining fifteen Canadian police are engaged in mining. They went up for two years' service and were relieved a few months ago by a detachment that went in over the range from Sitka. The guardsmen were handicapped in not being able to do their own work and made their money in mining speculation.

They staked out claims and with the spring rush sold them for large amounts. They also employed men to work claims they held. The five guards who came down on the Portland will go to their headquarters in the Northwest Territory and receive their discharges.

R. W. Barto of this city received via the Portland the following self-explanatory letter from a former resident of Seattle:

> SKOOKUM GULCH, Bonanza District,
> May 25, 1897.

To. R. W. Barto, Seattle: DEAR SIR—I have been expecting to hear from you for some time. I had the hardest trip of my life last winter, but I think I will make some money. We have a claim each on Skookum Gulch, a tributary of Bonanza. I dare say these are the richest diggings in the world.

You have heard something about it no doubt, but no half what it really is. I will not say much about it to you, as I don't want to excite you. The richest thing I know of is No. 30, on the El Dorado Creek, a tributary of Bonanza. Three men shoveled in eighty-five pounds weight of gold dust in seven hours. That is considered good ground here. Living has been very plain and expensive here this winter. Flour is $1.80 a pound, or 85¢ a sack. Dried fruit is $1.25 a pound, and bacon the same. I will close, hoping to hear from you soon. Yours,

JOE GOLDSMITH.

Police Officer Payton Brown received a Klondyke letter via the Portland today from W. R. Good, a well-known reputable citizen, reading in part as follows:

"You requested me to inform you all I could on the country. I will tell you of it as it really is. We have been out and seen all the mines. There are miners who have taken out $150,000 last winter in 150 feet of their claims. It is hard to believe, but when you see coal-oil cans with more than you can lift in them, baking-powder cans and pickle jars full of gold, you will begin to believe it.

Work is not plentiful now, as it is all winter diggings. The wages are $10 a day in Dawson City and $15 out at the mines. They say work will be plenty this next winter. Three steam-boats have been up this spring, so there are lots of provisions here now. Dawson City is growing fast, although it is all tents yet. Lots sell from $100 to $8000. If too many hands come in it will cut wages, but it is all right now. There is lot of prospecting going on this summer. Men are striking out in every direction.

The four very rich creeks in the Klondyke district are El Dorado, Bonanza, Baer and Gold Bottom. On this the miners are generally agreed, though some big fortunes have already been taken from Indian Creek, which is comparatively unprospected. Of the 160 creeks, big and little, El Dorado is the richest. It is a veritable gold stream.

The Canadian Government, THE CALL correspondent learns from a trustworthy source, has had experts in the Klondyke for five or six months, and, according to their report, El Dorado Creek alone contains $25,000,000. The creek is located to the extent of forty-six claims, and so rich is the dirt that it is estimated that it will run $1000 to the lineal foot.

These figures are practically verified by William Stanley and Wooden, his partner. They have four claims on El Dorado Creek and have only worked one, and that only to the extent of eighty feet, from which $120,000 has been taken.

Charles F. Wilson, first officer of the Portland, says the miners regard one claim on El Dorado about as good as another. There is little or no difference, being simply a question of development. The combined wealth of the four creeks—according to semi-official estimates, is

$60,000,000. Three-fourths of the claims are reported to have been located or are controlled by about 250 men. Discussing the Klondyke, Officer Wilson says:

"Out of the strike made last winter the records show that about 160 became wealthy. I should say that the Klondyke has yielded $5,000,000 easily since last October. Over $2,000,000 has been brought out and the rest is stored in the district or is being used in the purchase and development of claims. I am confident that the Portland brought out this trip much more than $1,000,000. By no means was all of the treasure stored in the ship's safes. Some of the men were willing to take chances and simply put their dust into bags and valises and wrapped them in their blankets. So you see it was hard to keep account of treasure handled in this way.

"Only nineteen claims were developed on El Dorado Creek during the winter. One or two claims on this creek have sold for as high as $300,000 each. In short I think the Klondyke is the greatest gold district that God ever opened up for the people."

Wilson says a great deal of money is being spent recklessly around Dawson City; that it is a common thing for some miners to spend $7000 or $8000 in the saloons and among dissolute women and gamblers in a single night.

Michael Kelly, an old-time resident of Seattle, was a passenger down from the Klondyke, where he left his son, Phil Kelly. Their earnings since last November, including the sale of one claim, amount to about $25,000. Of the famed diggings, Kelly said:

"So far as the reports as to Bonanza and El Dorado are concerned they have not been exaggerated, but people must take into consideration that all claims there are taken up. There are plenty of men there now to work the claims this winter. . . .

"Hunter Creek showed some good prospects, but had not been followed up enough to show when I left, and the same is true of Gold Bottom and Bear creeks. Just as I was leaving reports of finds being made on Dominion Creek, which is really the left fork of Indian Creek, were current. The finds ran from 10 cents to $1.25 a pan.

"On Henderson Creek, two and a half miles below the mouth of Stewart River, finds were reported. Some of the boys who went in with me stopped there. They had not gone down to bedrock, but got as high as 25 cents to a pan in the gravel.

"My advice to people going in would be to go next spring by Dyea, take a nice little outfit, leave about the middle of March, get used to the hardships, and if they are able to prospect for themselves they can prospect from the foot of Marsh or Mud Lake even before they get to the canyon. Finds may be made as good as any yet reported being as the country has never been prospected much."

Ex-County Clerk H. T. Hannon, writing from Dawson City under date of June 2, says:

> Mines of the Klondyke are all right. No such placer mines have ever been discovered before. My men have cleaned up hundreds of thousands of dollars during the winter, and a great many more lesser amounts. Everybody is wild with excitement. Provisions are very scarce and dear. I sold to-day eighteen pounds of bacon that was about to spoil for $18. Many miners have lived for the last two months on beans only. Moreover, the boat came in to-day from Circle City with provisions, and I suppose they will be much cheaper now. We have a good eight months' supply, so we have no fears.

M. J. Strickland, inspector of the Canadian police on the Klondyke and Yukon, in expatiating to a crowd in the Butler Hotel to-night on the richness of the new district, said:

"Nowhere on the face of the globe, in point of richness, has there been discovered anything like the Klondyke. California, Australia, none of them compare with it.

"But it should be borne in mind," the inspector continued, "that we are hearing just now only of those who have succeeded or are succeeding. Those who fail should not be lost sight of, especially when one contemplates going in. Next spring from 10,000 to 15,000 people, and possibly 20,000, will in my opinion go into the Yukon and Klondyke. If so many go it will be a matter of impossibility to feed them. The two transportation companies are having hard work now to supply the demand."

It would be difficult to portray the excitement the Portland and Excelsior reports from the Klondyke has generated in Seattle, some of whose citizens had the good fortune to gather in a very respectable percentage of the gold yield. Men have been standing on the streets in knots of four and five eagerly discussing the news since early morning. Others are busily engaged in making preparations to depart on the steamship Al-Ki, which sails to-morrow, or the Portland, returning to St. Michaels on Tuesday or Wednesday. The supply stores are doing a great business. Three-fourths of those going are being grub-staked.

The amount advanced varies from $3000 to $5000. Many clubs, composed principally of clerks and men of small means, are being formed for the purpose of "outfitting" some ambitious would-be Klondyker.

The excitement was intense around the express offices, where the gold dust was weighed and prepared for shipment. Great crowds blocked the streets before the Northern Pacific, Great Northern and Wells-Fargo offices. A special detail of police had to be placed on guard at each.

Clarence J. Berry showed THE CALL correspondent in the safe of the Butler Hotel to-night a Northern Pacific Company receipt for $84,000. A half hour later Mr. Berry deposited two bags of nuggets with the clerk of the hotel. The money sent by the Northern Pacific Express was consigned to Berry and Frank Phiscator at San Francisco. Phiscator is a Chicagoan and has considerable interest in the dust.

Berry states that he took out $130,000 during the winter. He and his brothers own five claims in the Klondyke diggings. He considers each a fortune. Three are located on the famous El Dorado, one on Indian Creek and one on Bonanza. The brothers are still at the diggings looking out for the joint interests. Only two of the claims are being worked.

There is none of the boast and braggadocio about Berry. He is a conservative man, both in statement and business transaction, and he reluctantly consented to talk.

"Three new creeks have been discovered in the Klondyke district by the crowd that went in this spring," Berry began. "They have not been prospected much; and of course I cannot tell how rich they are. I make it a rule to buy a claim on every new creek. As a rule you can get one on a new creek for a small amount of money. . . .

"There are some places where the ground will yield $3000 a lineal foot. On El Dorado there are single claims that one could not buy for $300,000—in fact for half a million."

Berry leaves for San Francisco to-morrow night. He is accompanied by Mrs. Berry, who has been with him at the diggings.

PEOPLE PREPARE TO LEAVE FOR THE KLONDIKE

Of interest to the reader of *The Call of the Wild* is the following story on page one of the *Oakland Times* about some of the local people who were joining the stampede to the Yukon. Paragraph four mentions Jack London and his brother-in-law J. H. Shepard, who had left for the Yukon on July 25.

With tongue in cheek, the *Oakland Times* reports in the same article news that the great gold discovery had inspired a local Oakland minister to start out suddenly to the Yukon as a missionary, while, he admitted, hunting for gold at the same time. The *Times* reporter obliquely brings up an interesting problem: how is the minister going to inspire people to follow Holy Scripture, which says, "Lay not up for yourselves treasures on earth," while at the same time he lays up treasures on earth of Yukon gold? It is the abuses that derive from such materialism gone mad that lead Buck to abandon human society.

FROM "MORE WANT TO GO"
(*Oakland Times*, July 30, 1897)

MORE WANT TO GO.

Oaklanders Anxious to Brave the Alaska Climate.

The Interest in the Quest For Gold Continues.

A Minister From This City to go to the New Field
to Carry on Missionary Work.

The Klondyke country is still the object of interest with many Oakland people and despite the hardships of an Alaska winter there are more people who are anxious to go.

Several parties stand ready to start if men with means will "grub stake" them.

The Navarro party will leave on the 10th inst and the steamer is being gotten ready. She will take about 100 people; and already thirty-five have been booked in San Francisco. There has been some inquiry at the Oakland office by parties from this city who want to embark for the gold fields.

Mr. Chester Crandall, the well known merchant tailor of Twenty-third avenue, will be one of the next company bound for the great gold fields of Alaska. Others are Jack London, Mr. Shepard and Rev. Holt, for some time the supply at the Twenty-fourth Avenue M. E. Church. Mr. Holt will go as a missionary, and will at the same time seek for the hidden treasures of the earth, as well as induce men to lay up treasures in heaven. He has been outfitted by some benevolent gentleman and will proceed at once to the far north, where he will locate and endeavor to spread a little of the atmosphere of religion about him. He is prepared to brave all the hardships that that [*sic*] he may encounter on the way to his field of duty.

Prominent among those who are going to try their fortunes in the Klondyke are the McGee boys of Fruitvale, who left Wednesday, and Sawyer Burnett of East Sixteenth street and Fourth avenue, who will leave on the next steamer.

Alex Lambert of Lorin will shortly leave for Juneau to join his brother Cash. (1)

TRANSPORTATION TO THE YUKON

On July 18, 1897, the day the Yukon story exploded onto the pages of the *Call*, the Alaska Commercial Company was already making the most of the gold discovery with a big advertisement for its steamer the *Excelsior*, in which passage was available to the Northwest. Note that the *Excelsior* took passengers on the expensive allwater route across the Bering Sea to St. Michael on the west coast of Alaska and from there up the Yukon River across Alaska into the Yukon, where it meets the Klondike River. Note also that throughout these documents, many used the name "Alaska" to apply to what was actually the Yukon Territory.

STEAMER ADVERTISEMENT
(*San Francisco Call*, July 18, 1897)

EQUIPMENT FOR PROSPECTORS

Other entrepreneurs were making money outfitting prospectors. Nothing was more important than packing well for the trip to the Klondike. Knowing what gear to take and how to pack it is a major topic of discussion in *The Call of the Wild* when Mercedes, Hal, and Charles, the incompetents, enter the picture. The inability of the dogs to move the overpacked sled leads to "the inexorable elimination of the superfluous" when blankets and clothes and other supplies have to be dumped. Still the sled is too heavy, and they make the mistake of adding more dogs than they can pack food for. This is stupidity and greed combined, the dual theme of unbridled capitalism. It leads to the misuse, starvation, and death of the dogs and eventually to the death of the three people as well.

On one hand, prospectors had to make sure that they had enough food, medicine, and supplies to last a very long time in a place where all supplies had to be shipped in. Clothing suitable for this particular climate and sufficient gear to get them through the various passes and rapids also had to be packed. On the other hand, since they had to carry their gear, often on their backs, over rough and dangerous terrain, they needed to make sure that they were not packing one ounce more than they absolutely needed. Indeed, most men familiar with the territory advised against packing firearms, like the gun pictured here, for, they argued, there was not any large game to shoot here, and firearms would just add weight and get a miner in trouble.

The company that issued this advertisement was a British one that undoubtedly found its customers in British Canada as well as in England. Even at this time, British adventurers had an interest in arctic and antarctic exploration.

GUIDES FOR PROSPECTORS

Another English entrepreneur who saw an opportunity to make money from the gold rush was A. E. Ironmonger Sola, an adventurer with connections to the Mining and Geographical Institute in London, England. Based on his three-and-one-half-year exploration of the Yukon, Sola not only marketed a book of information about the Yukon for prospectors, but also offered his services as a guide to those with money to go first-class.

ADVERTISEMENT FOR A GUIDE IN A. E. IRONMONGER SOLA, *KLONDYKE: TRUTH AND FACTS OF THE NEW EL DORADO* (London: Mining and Geographical Institute, 1897, 103)

Mr. A. E. IRONMONGER SOLA is returning to the Klondyke in the Spring of 1898, in charge of an expedition. Application should be made at once by parties wishing to join, as only a limited number can be taken. This will be found the cheapest and easiest way of getting into the country, as Mr. Sola has had years of experience, and knows exactly how to go and what to do. For a given sum everything is found, fares 1st class, and a guarantee to land parties at Dawson City, and provide them with one year's complete outfit.

APPLY—

THE MINING AND GEOGRAPHICAL INSTITUTE,

BROAD STREET HOUSE,

LONDON, E.C.

GUIDEBOOKS FOR PROSPECTORS

Would-be miners had to gather all the information they could get to be ready for Yukon travel. In 1897, dozens of guidebooks on travel and mining in the gold territory appeared. One such book was written by L. A. Coolidge, once chief of the Alaskan Boundary Expedition. Coolidge provided his readers with all manner of practical information, including the supplies needed to sustain one person for one month in the Yukon.

Some who relied on the following lists provided by Coolidge may have found themselves in difficulty, for a month's supply was rarely enough to last from Dyea to Dawson, a trip that usually took much longer than a month. Furthermore, Canadian border police often turned back miners who had only a month's worth of provisions.

FROM L. A. COOLIDGE, *KLONDIKE AND THE YUKON COUNTRY*
(Philadelphia: Henry Altemus, 1897)

SEEKING THE POT OF GOLD.

The first requirement for one seeking the gold fields is a hardy constitution; the second is capital. For the Yukon is not, as some other gold countries have been, a poor man's paradise. Gold is there in Aladdin-like profusion, but it is not to be had for the asking. It comes only as the fruit of wearisome and perilous travel, of desperate combat with the rigors of an Arctic climate, of deadly waiting for Arctic winters to unloose their icy hands. For the privilege of a few months of toil the prospecting miner must endure many months of unremunerative delay, during which he must pay extortionately for the mere privilege of living. For the season of placer mining lasts only during June, July and August.

Before beginning even to hunt for gold the aspiring miner must prepare himself for the long and tedious trip to the fields, and this is a task that will tax the endurance and nerve of the most hardy. It means, according to one who has made the trip, "packing provisions over pathless mountains, towing a heavy boat against a five to an eight-mile current, over battered boulders, digging in the bottomless frost, sleeping where night overtakes, fighting gnats and mosquitoes by the millions, shooting seething canyons and rapids and enduring for seven long months a relentless cold which never rises above zero and frequently falls to 80 below."

Any man who is physically able to endure all this, who will go to the gold fields for a few years, can, by strict attention to business, make a good strike, with the possibilities of a fortune.

But he must have money to start with. All who have been to the gold fields agree in saying that no man should undertake the journey with less than $400 in capital. And he had better have $1000. The expense of reaching the mines is considerable. One hundred and fifty dollars is a modest figure for the journey from Seattle, and when once in the gold region the expense of living is enormous. The prices of even the most ordinary provisions are fabulous, and the companies doing business there refuse to give credit, as they can sell all their goods and more for ready cash. Provisions are almost unobtainable at any price. An officer of the U. S. Geological Survey, who has traveled through this country, has assured the author of this book that if he were looking for certain profit and had the necessary capital he would never think of hunting for gold, but would invest everything in provisions and groceries, which would yield enormous profits should they be got into the Yukon region.

If the traveler contemplates the overland trip his outfit should be bought in Juneau, the metropolis of Southeastern Alaska, the last outpost of civilization in the path of the voyager for gold. The needs of the traveler can be gauged there better than anywhere else, nearer the centre of population and wealth. Experienced men have found that the provisions a man ought to lay by before starting on the overland journey from Juneau make a formidable list. The articles required for one man for one month are somewhat as follows:

Twenty pounds of flour, with baking powder.

12 pounds of bacon.

6 pounds of beans.

5 pounds of dried fruits.

3 pounds of dessicated vegetables.

4 pounds of butter.

5 pounds of sugar.

4 cans of milk.

1 pound of tea.

3 pounds of coffee.

2 pounds of salt.

Five pounds of corn meal.

Pepper.

Matches.

Mustard.

Cooking utensils and dishes.

Frying pan.

Water kettle.

Tent.

Yukon stove.

Two pairs good blankets.

One rubber blanket.

Bean pot.

Two plates.

Drinking cup.

Tea pot.

Knife and fork.

Large cooking pan.

Small cooking pan.

These are simply for sustenance. In addition the traveler will find it necessary to build his own boat with which to thread the chain of lakes and rivers leading to the gold basin. He will need the following tools:

Jack plane.

Whip saw.

Hand saw.

Rip saw.

Draw knife.

Ax.

Hatchet.

Pocket rule.

Six pounds of assorted nails.

Three pounds of oakum.

Five pounds of pitch.

Five pounds of five-eighths rope.

He will also find that he must have some protection against the deadly assaults of gnats and mosquitos, which fill the air throughout Alaska; that he will have to be provided for mountain climbing and for protection against snow blindness, which is one of the most demoralizing afflictions that can befall the traveler over the snow-covered passes. So he will need:

Mosquito netting.

One pair crag-proof hip boots.

Snow glasses.

Medicines.

These are the provisions necessary for a miner for a single month, and whether he will need more for his journey depends somewhat upon the manner in which he travels. In the first place nobody should undertake to travel alone. The trip should be made in parties of two or more, which will conduce to safety and also lightness of the individual's load. It is possible for parties to attend to their own transportation over the divide between Juneau and the lakes. In that case they should start before the first of April so as to catch the snows and ice. They can use sleighs over the summit of Chilkoot Pass and along the lakes down to the place of junction with the river. By the time the river is reached the ice will have begun to break away and the rest of the journey can be managed by boat. By this arrangement the gold fields can be reached four weeks earlier than by waiting for the opening of the summer season before starting from Juneau. Should the start be deferred till after April 30, Indians will have to be employed to do the packing across the pass. The Indians charge $14 per hundred for this service, and each is accustomed to carry about a hundred weight.

Before making a start the wise traveler will consider the cost of living in the diggings and provide himself accordingly. Following are a few of the average prices of provisions and articles of common use:

Cost of shirts	$5.00
Boots, per pair	10.00
Rubber boots, per pair	25.00
Caribou hams, each	40.00
Flour, per fifty pounds	20.00
Beef, per pound (fresh)	.50
Bacon, per pound	.75
Coffee, per pound	1.00
Sugar, per pound	.50
Eggs, per dozen	2.00
Condensed milk, per can	1.00
Live dogs, per pound	2.00
Picks, each	15.00
Shovels, each	15.00

Wages, per day	15.00
Lumber, per 1000 feet	150.00

When the miners left Dawson City the following prices were in vogue:

Flour, per 100 lbs.	$12.00
Moose ham, per lb.	1.00
Caribou meat, per lb.	.65
Beans, per lb.	.10
Rice, per lb.	.25
Sugar, per lb.	.25
Bacon, per lb.	.40
Butter, per roll	1.50
Eggs, per dozen	1.50
Better eggs, per dozen	2.00
Salmon, each	$1 to 1.50
Potatoes, per lb.	.25
Turnips, per lb.	.15
Tea, per lb.	1.00
Coffee, per lb.	.50
Dried fruits, per lb.	.35
Canned fruits	.50
Canned meats	.75
Lemons, each	.20
Oranges, each	.50
Tobacco, per lb.	1.50
Liquors, per drink	.50
Shovels	2.50
Picks	5.00
Coal oil, per gallon	1.00
Overalls	1.50
Underwear, per suit	$5 to 7.50
Shoes	5.00
Rubber boots	$10 to 15.00

The tourist from the Atlantic seaboard will find in the following table information concerning the expenses of travel according to his means and inclination:

Fare from New York to Seattle via Northern Pacific, $81.50.

Fee for Pullman sleeper, $20.50.

Fee for tourist sleeper, run only west of St. Paulu, $5.

Meals served in dining car for entire trip, $16.

Meals are served at stations along the route a la carte. (37–45)

TRAVEL DISTANCES TO THE GOLD FIELD

Among those cashing in on the selling of information about this little-known region was Joseph Ladue, a pioneer and explorer of the Yukon who laid claim to being the "founder of Dawson City." Dawson was the settlement nearest the gold discovery. Its population soared from a couple of hundred in 1896 to about 30,000 in the course of a year.

Among the information in Ladue's book is an essential list of the miles one has to travel to reach the rich gold fields. From this, one can see that Buck is over 1,000 miles from home when he reaches Dyea and that he makes five trips of 603 miles, the distance from Dyea and Skagway to Dawson, in his first months in the Yukon.

FROM JOSEPH LADUE, *KLONDYKE FACTS. BEING A COMPLETE GUIDE TO THE GOLD REGIONS OF THE GREAT CANADIAN NORTHWEST TERRITORIES AND ALASKA*
(New York: American Technical Book Co., 1897, 203)

	Miles
Seattle to Juneau	899
Juneau to Dyea	96
Dyea to Lake Lindeman	28
Across Lake Lindeman	6
Portage, Lindeman to Lake Bennett	1 ¼
Across Lake Bennett to Caribou Crossing	30
Across Tagish Lake	19
Six-Mile River to Mud Lake	6
Across Mud Lake	20
Fifty-Mile River from Mud Lake to Lake LeBarge	50
Across Lake LeBarge	31
Thirty-Mile River to Hootalinqua River	30

Down Hootalinqua and Lewes Rivers to Fort Selkirk	187
Fort Selkirk down the Yukon to Dawson City	195
Total Distance from Dyea to Dawson City	603 ¼
Total Distance from Seattle to Dawson City	1598 ¼

THE CHILKOOT PASS

The first great obstacles to reaching gold country from the Alaskan Panhandle were the immense glaciated mountains that one had to cross to reach the interior of the Yukon. Two routes were available: the longer but less steep White Pass from Skagway, over which one could, reputedly, take pack animals, and the steep, ice-covered Chilkoot Pass from Dyea.

One of those who described their experiences on both passes was the highly respected author of a Yukon book, William B. Haskell, who characterized himself as "a returned gold miner and prospector." In 1898, Haskell published a handbook for travelers. It is to Haskell that we turn for a description of the second, more famous pass, the Chilkoot Pass from Dyea, Alaska. This is the pass over which Buck and Jack London traveled to reach Dawson and the gold fields. Though not as long as White Pass, Chilkoot was extremely difficult. The lower part was narrow and strewn with immense boulders. The upper was almost straight up to the summit. The entire pass was ice and snow filled, and those who went over it were in constant danger of being crushed by falling rocks or buried by avalanches of snow. Furthermore, men had to climb it time after time, packing from fifty to one hundred pounds up the steep incline as many as six times. The Chilkoot was too steep for pack animals. We see from *The Call of the Wild* that even the dogs had to be hauled over the summit with ropes.

FROM WILLIAM B. HASKELL, *TWO YEARS IN THE KLONDIKE AND ALASKAN GOLD-FIELDS*
(Hartford, CT: Hartford Publishing Co., 1898)

This does not look great on paper, and it is not; for mountain climbers are every day ascending steeps as great and twice as high. But they are not compelled to take along all they are to have to eat, to wear, and to use for a year or more. Therein lies one of the main difficulties in proceeding to the interior of Alaska. If one could depend upon warehouses within easy reach, could buy what he wanted as he journeyed from place to place, traveling in Alaska would have a few pleasures in it. At least it would not be difficult.

Joe and I were compelled to make forty trips over these steep places to get our outfit to the summit, and climbing a mountain forty times with a heavy pack on the back is different from climbing it once almost empty-handed and for fun. Many took all their goods to the Stone House at first, and then by another stage carried them to the "Scales"; then by another to the summit. We adopted different tactics. Having strapped our packs on, we continued to the foot of the last ascent, and there if the weather was bad we would leave them, otherwise we continued on to the summit. As the wind was blowing most of the time, this resulted in our having most of our outfit at the foot of the final ascent before we had many opportunities to view the summit, or any at all to indulge in a view from it.

The trail up to the "Scales" looks smooth when the snow lies deep over it, but it is, nevertheless, difficult, and by a single misstep the traveler may find himself buried to the armpits. Underneath are great masses of rocks, and part of the way fallen trees, but the timber belt ends completely at Stone House. One of the difficulties in the ascent lay in successfully passing those who were descending for another load, for the way is exceedingly narrow, and one must not step out of the trail except with the greatest caution. Occasionally a man would find himself at the bottom of a crevice forty feet or so below the trail, and he could make his way back only with the greatest difficulty.

The last climb of nearly seven hundred feet up a mountain peak that seemed to rise almost straight before us was the hardest of all. The trail winds in zigzag fashion in and around the boulders and over the glacial streaks, but at this time it was covered with snow, in some places fifty feet deep. In the steeper places steps were cut in the ice and snow, and in taking a pack up one was compelled to lean forward and use his hands on the icy steps. Occasionally a tired man would make a misstep, or his foothold caved off, and down the precipice he rolled, landing in the soft snow, from which he had to extricate himself and again attempt the tiresome climb. Its [*sic*] was drudgery in its simplest and purest form. One hundred pounds was the most that either of us could take, and then it required an hour to cover that seven hundred feet to the summit, which we generally found covered with a blinding snow storm or bathed in an ice-fog.

Fortunately, in returning we could make up for lost time. So steep and so treacherous was the trail, and so many were working up it, that the descent by the steps for another load was as trying work as the ascent. The grim mother of invention again came to the rescue. Nearly everybody fortified the seat of his trousers by sewing on a piece of canvas, and as there was a short cut back to the bottom of the trail, straight and smooth but too steep to climb, it was brought into use for the purposes of returning, a trench being formed thereby. One would sit down in this trench at the top, and just hold his breath till he struck the bottom. He need not hold it long. It took less time to slide down than it takes to tell of it. Once started there was no opportunity to stop, and no time to consider such a question. I remember that at the first trial I picked myself out of the snow and thought I would give up that sport. It seemed a little too much like riding an avalanche bareback. I was so much larger and heavier than the rest that gravity gave me a greater speed. In places the ditch was as much as four feet deep, but in other places it was shallow, and there was danger of jumping the track. Once I ran into a little man and was thrown completely out of the groove. Down the mountain side I plowed, plunging entirely out of sight in the soft snow at the bottom. I picked myself out and was not in the least hurt. The little man righted himself somehow, and came down the groove in good order. After awhile the experience began to have the flavor of true sport, and the more we tried it the better we liked it. (86–88)

IGNORANCE OF WOULD-BE MINERS

A. C. Harris, who billed himself as "a well-known author and traveler," illustrates the ignorance of many would-be gold miners with the following anecdote. A "sleeper" refers to a first-class railroad car where berths (beds) are provided for passengers who can pay the high price of the ticket.

A. C. HARRIS, *ALASKA AND THE KLONDIKE GOLD FIELDS*
(n.p.: W. Berton, 1897)

How little many would-be argonauts knew of the Klondike, or anything connected with it, was illustrated in a New York railroad ticket office. A well-dressed man pushed his way through the crowd, and throwing a big roll of bills on the counter, cried out:

"Give me a first-class, and a lower berth."

"Where to?"

"Klondike."

He was indignant when the ticket seller tried to explain that sleepers were not run regularly over Chilkoot Pass. (447)

Boat-building at Abbot Cove, Lake Bennett. Special Collections, University of Washington Libraries. Neg. # Hegg 266.

THE RAPIDS

After the would-be miner crossed the White Pass or the Chilkoot Pass, the next obstacle he had to face on his way to the gold fields was a series of treacherous rapids and gusty lakes. Our best descriptions of these water passageways in *The Call of the Wild* is in Chapter Three when Buck and the team have "a bleak and miserable camp" on Lake Laberge, where the wind "cut like a white-hot knife." On one side of the lake was "a perpendicular wall of rock" (15). Here it is that the sled dogs are attacked by the ravenous huskies.

In Chapter Five, Hal and Charles drive the starving dogs into the Five Fingers area. Despite the advice they have received to "lay over" until they can more easily see what they are doing in the spring thaw, they drive across the rotten ice covering the lake and fall in. Finally, in Chapter Six, Thornton and Buck get swept into the bad stretch of rapids on the Forty Mile Creek.

Josiah Spurr was a geologist who in 1896, before the gold rush, had been in charge of an expedition sponsored by the U.S. Geological Survey. In the following excerpt from his book, he recounts travel on the five lakes that must be crossed on the way to Dawson. The rapids in this area were so treacherous that the only way Spurr's party could navigate them was by leaving their boat and "lining" it down, that is, steering it through with a rope as they walked along the shore. Getting boats down was made more difficult by the large boulders, some entirely hidden under the water, on which boats could get caught or splintered. If the travelers chose to leave their supplies in their boats, both boats and supplies were sometimes lost. The number of boats the Spurr party found splintered on the rocks or washed up on shore below the rapids was multiplied a hundredfold after 1897. Of special interest here is Spurr's description of how to stand up from a sitting position with a heavy pack on one's back.

FROM JOSIAH EDWARD SPURR, *THROUGH THE YUKON GOLD DIGGINGS*
(Boston: Eastern Publishing Co., 1900)

We sailed down Lake Lindeman with a fair brisk wind, using our tent-fly braced against a pole, for a sail. The distance is only four or five miles, so that the lower end of the lake was reached in an hour. A mountain sheep was sighted on the hillside above us, soon after starting, and a long-range shot with the rifle was tried at it, but the animal bounded away.

At the lower end of this first of the Yukon navigable lakes there is a stream, full of little falls and rapids, which connects with Lake Bennett, a much larger body of water. According to Pete, the boat could not run these rapids, so we began the task of "lining" her down. With a long pole shod with iron, especially brought along for such work, Pete stood in the bow or stern, as the emergency called for, planting the pole on the rocks which stuck out of the water and so shoving and steering the boat through an open narrow channel, while we three held a long line and scrambled along the bank or waded in the shallow water. We had put on long rubber boots reaching to the hip and strapped to our belts, so at first our wading was not uncomfortable. On account of the roar of the water we could not hear Pete's orders, but could see his signals to "haul in," or "let her go ahead." On one difficult little place he manoeuvered quite a while, getting stuck on a rock, signalling us to pull back, and then

trying again. Finally he struck the right channel, and motioned energet-
ically to us to go ahead. We spurted forward, waddling clumsily, and the
foremost man stepped suddenly into a groove where the water was above
his waist. Ugh! It was icy, but he floundered through, half swimming, half
wading, dragging his great water-filled boots behind him like iron
weights; and the rest followed. We felt quite triumphant and heroic when
we emerged, deeming this something of a trial: we did not know that
the time would come when it would be the ordinary thing all day long,
and would become so monotonous that all feelings of novelty would be
lost in a general neutral tint of bad temper and rheumatism.

On reaching shallow water the weight of the water-filled rubber boots
was so great that we could no longer navigate among the slippery rocks,
so we took turns going ashore and emptying them. There was a smooth
round rock with steep sides, glaring in the sun, on this we stretched
ourselves head down, so that the water ran out of our boots and trickled
in cold little streams down our backs; then we returned to our work.

Before undertaking to line the Skookum through the rapids we had
taken out a large part of the load and put it on shore, in order to lighten
the boat, and also to save our "grub" in case our boat was capsized. The
next task was to carry this over the half-mile portage. Packing is about
the hardest and most disliked work that a pioneer has to do, and yet
every one that travels hard and well in Alaska and similar rough countries
must do it *ad nauseam*. In such remote and unfinished parts of the world
transportation comes back to the original and simple phase,—carrying
on one's back. The railroad and the steamboat are for civilization, the
wheeled vehicle for the inhabited land where there are roads, the camel
for the desert, the horse for the plains and where trails have been cut,
but for a large part of Alaska Nature's only highways are the rivers, and
when the water will not carry the burdens the explorer must.

In a properly-constructed pack-sack, the weight is carried partly by the
shoulders but mainly by the neck, the back being bent and the neck
stretched forward till the load rests upon the back and is kept from slipping by the head strap, which is nearly in line with the rigid neck. An
astonishing amount can be carried in this way with practice,—for half a
mile or so, very nearly one's own weight. Getting up and down with such
a load is a work of art, which spoils the temper and wrenches the muscles
of the beginner. Having got into the strap he finds himself pinned to the
ground in spite of his backbone-breaking efforts to rise, so he must learn
to so sit down in the beginning that he can tilt the load forward on his
back, get on his hands and knees and then elevate himself to the necessary standing-stooping posture; or he must lie down flat and roll over
on his face, getting his load fairly between his shoulders, and then work
himself up to his hands and knees as before. Sometimes, if the load is

heavy, the help of another must be had to get an upright position, and then the packer goes trudging off, red and sweating and with bulging veins. (69–73)

• • •

As we trembled on the brink, I looked up and saw our friends standing close by, looking much concerned. A moment later there was a dizzying plunge, a blinding shower of water, a sudden dashing, too swift for observation, past rock walls, and then Wiborg let out an exultant yell—we were safe. At that instant one of the oarsmen snapped his oar, an accident which would have been serious a moment before. On the shore below the rapids we found flour-sacks, valises, boxes and splintered boards, mementoes of poor fellows less lucky than ourselves. (94)

ANOTHER ACCOUNT OF THE RAPIDS

The English entrepreneur A. E. Ironmonger Sola provides another account of navigation on the rivers and lakes of the central Yukon Territory. The excerpt here, written on Sola's 1894 journey, begins at Lake Lindeman. Note that icy inlets and warm temperatures exist simultaneously on these summer Yukon days. The "portage" mentioned here means getting out of the boat and packing supplies on one's back over land, on the banks of the waterway. This had to be done where the rapids were too turbulent. Note that backpacking necessitates making numerous trips over the same trail, in this case, ten trips. The travelers must cut trees to build boats for this part of the trip, and when the boats wreck, they have to build new ones.

A. E. IRONMONGER SOLA, *KLONDYKE: TRUTH AND FACTS OF THE NEW EL DORADO*
(London: Mining and Geographical Institute, 1897)

June 11th [1894]. Thermometer 80°; south-west wind. Early in the morning we went up a small creek and chopped logs or small trees, and floated them down to the lake, being in the water up to our waists nearly all day.

Early that afternoon we rolled up in our blankets and slept until the morning of the 12th.

June 12th. That day we built our raft and loaded eight hundred pounds, our whole outfit, and started at 4 p.m. with a favourable south-west wind; the result being that we shipped a great deal of water and got all our provisions wet. Thermometer about 58°. At 11 p.m. we arrived at the end of Lake Lindeman, and had to camp, owing to the thick ice in the inlet, which prevented us from going through.

June 13th. Thermometer 66°. Laid in camp and watched for the ice to go out. Took our gold-pans, picks and shovels and prospected the small creeks for gold but failed to find any, neither did we see any game.

June 14th. Thermometer 68°; strong south-west wind. Left early in the morning and worked our way through the ice until 6.30 p.m., we then unloaded our raft and packed over the portage until 9.30 p.m., when we pitched our camp at the mouth of Lake Bennett. The portage is a distance of about one mile. During the time we packed from Lake Lindeman to

Lake Bennett a number of Stick Indians would peep at us from behind the trees in the woods. They looked very wild and curious, but did not attempt to molest us in any way.

The rapids between Lake Lindeman and Lake Bennett are about one mile long, and not much over seventy-five feet wide. The water is very quick, and it is impossible to navigate either a boat or raft with safety.

June 15th. Thermometer 62°; south-west wind. We started our raft from foot of Lake Lindeman through the rapids of Lake Bennett, intending to catch it at the head of Lake Bennett. In the centre of the rapids the raft stuck on the rocks, and we tried all day to get her off, but without success. In the attempt we lost all our rope, and had to abandon the raft.

June 16th. Thermometer 64°; south-west wind. Raft still on rocks. We went up another river at the mouth of Lake Bennett, which came in at the head of the left-hand side and pitched our camp. We got logs, and tried to float them down to the head of the lake, but they stuck in the rocks, and we wasted the whole day.

June 17th. Thermometer 60°; south-west wind. We decided to cross the Small River, and pitch our camp near a patch of timber about half a mile up the river, on a small knoll or hill. Finally we succeeded in crossing on three logs, and after having made at least ten trips managed to get our outfit across, which was all more or less wet. Early that night we turned in for a well-earned sleep.

June 18th. In the morning we cut down small suitable pines, built a saw-pit, and squared one tree for six inch lumber with a whip-saw. (57)

• • •

June 30th. Up to now we had made a distance of 215 miles, counting Juneau Juncan as the starting point.

At 8 o'clock that morning we left the camp and headed for the Miles Cañon. We drifted with the current at a speed of about two miles an hour, and arrived at the mouth of the cañon at 2 p.m.

Most people are very much afraid of the cañon, and they go to the enormous trouble of skidding their boat over the portage, which is a long and tedious operation.

We took out the most valuable of our cargo and examined the cañon before going through. We then took our boots and over-shirts off, and started through the rapids. The water was very rough and the channel narrow. It looks very dangerous, but really before we knew it we were through, and in an eddy at the other end. I think we travelled that mile in less than five minutes.

The cañon is a wonderfully beautiful bit of scenery. It is cut through a horizontal basalt bed, and the walls range in height from fifty to one hundred and twenty feet, being worn in all sorts of fantastic shapes. The average width of the cañon is about one hundred feet, and as the average width of the river above is about seven hundred feet, the force with which the great volume of water cuts through the steep ledges of rocks may be imagined.

A few remarks about the cañon, for the guidance of intending prospectors, would not be out of place.

Arriving in sight of the cañon, it is necessary to pull into an eddy on the right-hand side of the river. After shooting through the cañon pull hard to the right just at the foot, you can then land without difficulty, and load up your boat and proceed through the rocky channel to the head of the White Horse Rapids. This is not a dangerous thing to do, providing the men in the boat do not get in any way excited, and are competent to handle a boat properly.

July 1st. We had made a distance of 226 miles from Juneau. Thermometer varying from 60° to 95°. We resumed our journey at 9 a.m. Packed everything securely in boat, covered them over with tarpaulin and shot the rocky rapids between the cañon and the White Horse, a distance of about one and three-quarter miles.

We again unloaded our boat and packed everything over the trail to the foot of the Rapids; and owing to our having lost our rope, we also had to pack our boat, which was a very long and tedious operation.

On the rocks of the White Horse Rapids, we saw at least three boats stuck on the rocks and perfectly useless.

We met one man at the Rapids who had started into the Yukon alone, and had lost his boat and everything he possessed in it. He told us he had then been over two days without anything to eat. We, of course, fed him, and took him with us about two miles down the river, where we encountered another party who had more room in their boats than we had, and they very kindly took him with them down to Yukon.

July 2nd. Thermometer 65° to 85°. That morning we finished packing over the trail, and again loaded boat and resumed our journey at 2.30 p.m.

Below the White Horse Rapids, the river is very crooked, the scenery grand and beautiful, with ducks and geese in flocks. (61)

SCARCITY OF FOOD

The theme of starvation appears in *The Call of the Wild* when the incompetent newcomers end up taking along too many dogs and not enough food to feed them. Most of the dogs starve before the three-member family disappears beneath the ice. In reality, starvation in the Yukon led many men to eat their dogs or any available leather goods, including their shoes and the "traces" for the dog-sled.

In his 1897 guidebook, L. A. Coolidge mentions one of many dark aspects of Yukon gold hunting: the scarcity of food in the 1897–98 winter for the unexpected thousands who flocked to the Yukon. Everything from candles to vegetables had to be imported to the remote region. Moreover, it was impossible to import any supplies at all after the rivers froze. With so many unexpected people, many of whom had not packed adequate food or had lost it along the way, all food became very scarce.

FROM L. A. COOLIDGE, *KLONDIKE AND THE YUKON COUNTRY*
(Philadelphia: Henry Altemus, 1897)

There is one side of the Klondike picture which has been kept in the background, but about which whispers are beginning to be heard. It is a picture of suffering and starvation. One of the returned fortune makers is quoted as saying:

"You would find it easier to believe the most wonderful yarns I could tell you of the wealth of the country than some of the hardships I have known many men to undergo. Men can suffer a great deal and almost forget it if they eventually become rich, but for every man who has returned with a sack of dust there are now one hundred poor devils stranded and starving in that country.

"When I say starving I mean it literally. It seems incredible that a man would see another—his neighbor, at that—slowly dying by inches for want of food and deliberately refuse him a pound of bacon or pint of beans, yet that thing is happening every day, and God only knows how many frozen corpses will make food for wolves on Klondike this winter. When I left there was not enough food in the country to supply those already there, and as boats cannot take in much more before the river freezes, how are hundreds now on their way there to exist? It is not that men are selfish or avaricious, but few of the old miners have more than enough to keep them through the winter, and it is only a question of preserving their own lives or those of others." (73–74)

FOOD PRICES

When food was available, prices were astronomical by 1896 standards in the United States, as Josiah Spurr illustrates with the price of potatoes.

FROM JOSIAH EDWARD SPURR, *THROUGH THE YUKON GOLD DIGGINGS*
(Boston: Eastern Publishing Co., 1900)

In summer all prices were those of Circle City, plus forty cents freighting, plus ten cents handling. So a sack of potatoes, which I was told would cost twenty-five cents in the state of Washington, cost here eighty-five dollars.

MINING TERMINOLOGY

Joseph Ladue provides the neophyte miner with a list of terms that need to be mastered before claims can be staked or filed. Most mining done here involved panning for gold, as he later explains.

FROM JOSEPH LADUE, *KLONDYKE FACTS. BEING A COMPLETE GUIDE TO THE GOLD REGIONS OF THE GREAT CANADIAN NORTHWEST TERRITORIES AND ALASKA*
(New York: American Technical Book Co., 1897)

DEFINITION OF TERMS USED IN MINING.

"Mine," "placer mine," and "digging" shall be synonymous terms and shall mean any natural stratum or bed of earth, gravel or cement mined for gold or other precious minerals:

"Placer claim" shall mean the personal right of property or interest in any placer mine; and in the term "mining property" shall be included every placer claim, ditch, or water right used for placer mining purposes, and all other things belonging thereto or used in the working thereof. Placer claims shall be divided into creek diggings, bar diggings, dry diggings, bench diggings, and hill diggings:

"Creek diggings" shall mean any mine in the bed of any river, stream or ravine, excepting bar diggings:

"Bar diggings" shall mean any mine over which a river extends when in its flooded state:

"Dry diggings" shall mean any mine over which a river never extends:

"Bench diggings" shall mean any mine on a bench, and shall, for the purpose of defining the size of a claim in bench diggings, be excepted from "dry diggings:"

"Hill diggings" shall mean any mine on the surface of a hill, and fronting on any natural stream or ravine:

"Streams and ravines" shall include all natural watercourses, whether usually containing water or not, and all rivers, creeks and gulches:

"Ditch" shall include a flame, pipe, race, or other artificial means for conducting water by its own weight, to be used for mining purposes:

"Ditch head" shall mean the point in a natural watercourse or lake where water is first taken into a ditch:

"Free miner" shall mean a person, or joint stock company, or foreign company named in, and lawfully possessed of, a valid existing free miner's certificate, and no other:

"Legal post" shall mean a stake standing not less than four feet above the ground, and squared or faced on four sides for at least one foot from the top, and each side so squared or faced shall measure at least four inches on its face so far as squared or faced, or any stump or tree cut off and squared or faced to the above height and size:

"Record," "register," and "registration," shall have the same meaning, and shall mean an entry in some official book kept for that purpose:

"Record," when used without qualifying words showing that a different matter is referred to, shall be taken to refer to the record of the location of a placer claim:

"Full interest" shall mean any placer claim of the full size, or one of several shares into which a mine may be equally divided:

"Close season" shall mean the period of the year during which placer claims in any district are laid over by the Gold Commissioner of that district:

"Cause" shall include any suit or action:

"Judgment" shall include "order" or "decree":

"Real estate" shall mean any placer mineral land held in fee simple. (191–93)

CLAIM FORM

A. E. Ironmonger Sola includes practical help for miners in his book *Klondyke: Truth and Facts of the New El Dorado*. The following excerpt from that book is a form required to secure a claim and to begin mining a piece of land. Notice that the document gives the claimant the right to mine for gold on the land and to use the water that flows into it in the mining process, but ownership does not extend to surface rights or even to the soil between the surface and the gold deposit. Similar cases of dual ownership of the same piece of oil- or mineral-rich land have prevailed in other situations. In the depression of the 1930s, for example, landowners in need of money could sell the oil, coal, or gas resources in their land, beneath their houses, separating ownership of surface rights and mineral rights.

FROM A. E. IRONMONGER SOLA, *KLONDYKE: TRUTH AND FACTS OF THE NEW EL DORADO*
(London: Mining and Geographical Institute, 1897, 37)

FORM I.—GRANT FOR PLACER MINING.—DEPARTMENT OF THE INTERIOR.

No.   Agency,   18

In consideration of the payment of five dollars, being the fee required by the provisions of the Dominion Mining Regulations, clauses four and twenty, by (A. B.) of   accompanying his (or their) application No.   , dated   ,18 , for a mining claim in   (here insert description of locality)   .

The Minister of the Interior hereby grants to the said   (A. B.)   for the term of one year from the date hereof, the exclusive right of entry upon the claim   (here describe in detail the claim granted)   for the miner-like working thereof and the construction of a residence thereon, and the exclusive right to all the proceeds realized therefrom.

The said   (A. B.)   shall be entitled to the use of so much of the water naturally flowing through or past his (or their) claim, and not already lawfully appropriated, as shall be necessary for the due working thereof, and to drain his (or their) claim, free of charge.

This grant does not convey to the said   (A. B.)   any surface rights in the said claim, or any right of ownership in the soil covered by the said claim; and the said grant shall lapse and be forfeited unless the claim is continuously and in good faith worked by the said   (A. B.)   or his (or their) associates.

The rights hereby granted are those laid down in the aforesaid mining regulations and no more, and are subject to all the provisions of the said regulations, whether the same are expressed or not.

GOLD COMMISSIONER.

MINING OPERATIONS

In *The Call of the Wild*, reference is made to mining operations used in the Yukon when John Thornton tests areas in the far eastern Yukon for gold. He reaches "a shallow placer in a broad valley where the gold showed like yellow butter across the bottom of the washing-pan" (52).

Joseph Ladue, again in clearly understandable language, describes a variety of mining operations used in the Yukon, carrying the process from the digging up of gold-rich dirt to washing it out. Unlike gold fields in other areas of the world, California and Australia, for instance, miners in the Yukon had to melt the permanently frozen layers of earth to get to the gravel that held gold.

FROM JOSEPH LADUE, *KLONDYKE FACTS. BEING A COMPLETE GUIDE TO THE GOLD REGIONS OF THE GREAT CANADIAN NORTHWEST TERRITORIES AND ALASKA*
(New York: American Technical Book Co., 1897)

PLACER MINING.

Mining operations are thus far altogether placer mining, for the reason that the first discovery was of that nature and because no machinery was required. In fact, no machinery was immediately accessible, there being none in the territory. Placer mining is the crudest and most primitive kind of mining and the cheapest to operate. As conducted at Dawson City it consists simply in sinking a shaft to bed rock and then tunnelling in various directions. The ground is always frozen solid in winter, and in summer below a depth of two feet, and there is no need of shoring as there is no danger of its caving. These conditions are peculiar, to this interesting region, and in no other part of the world can shafts be sunk and tunnels made without great expense and loss of time in timbering and shoring, besides the loss of pay dirt in leaving columns standing, as is necessary anywhere else.

The pay dirt is taken out by a small windlass worked by hand and is simply thrown into a heap where it remains until spring, when it is washed out.

The depth necessary to go to reach bed rock—and it is always profitable to go to bed rock—varies from four to twenty feet.

The gold is found in nuggets, grains and dust. The largest nugget found

Miners in brutally cold weather, 1897. Photo
Collections, The Bancroft Library.

in the mines first discovered weighed forty ounces and was worth perhaps five hundred dollars, and from that size they run down to small
grains of pure gold. Nuggets weighing several ounces are quite common.
(93–94)

• • •

In placer mining the bed rock is often seamy and the gold is lodged
in the seams and crevices. When these conditions exist the miners dig
up the bed rock often to the depth of four feet and the richest finds have
been taken in that way. In fact the methods of placer mining are peculiar
to this strange and marvellously rich mineral country. The same methods
and conditions do not exist anywhere else in the known world.

As I have said above, the pay dirt, when hoisted to the surface, is
thrown into a pile and allowed to remain until spring, when it is washed.
The cost of lumber for sluice boxes, etc., is at this writing $130, and for
planed lumber $150 per thousand feet.

As very few outside of mining communities understand anything of the
nomenclature of the craft, or of the methods employed to separate the
very small quantities of the precious metal from the baser material with
which it is associated, a short description will not be out of place.

When a miner "strikes" a bar he "prospects" it by washing a few panfuls of the gravel or sand of which it is composed. According to the number of specks of "colors" he finds to the pan, that is, the number of specks of gold he can see in his pan after all the dirt has been washed out, he judges of its richness. Many of them have had so much experience that they can tell in a few minutes, very nearly, how much a bar will yield per day to the man.

The process of "placer" mining is about as follows: After clearing all the coarse gravel and stone off a patch of ground, the miner lifts a little of the finer gravel or sand in his pan, which is a broad, shallow dish, made of strong sheet iron; he then puts in water enough to fill the pan, and gives it a few rapid whirls and shakes; this tends to bring the gold to the bottom on account of its greater specific gravity. The dish is then shaken and held in such a way that the gravel and sand are gradually washed out, care being taken as the process nears completion to avoid letting out the finer and heavier parts that have settled to the bottom. Finally all that is left in the pan is whatever gold may have been in the dish and some black sand which almost invariably accompanies it.

This black sand is nothing but pulverized magnetic iron ore. Should the gold thus found be fine, the contents of the pan are thrown into a barrel containing water and a pound or two of mercury. As soon as the gold comes in contact with the mercury it combines with it and forms an amalgam. The process is continued until enough amalgam has been formed to pay for "roasting" or "firing."

It is then squeezed through a buckskin bag, all the mercury that comes through the bag being put back into the barrel to serve again, and what remains in the bag is placed in a retort, if the miner has one, or, if not, on a shovel, and heated until nearly all the mercury is vaporized. The gold then remains in a lump with some mercury still held in combination with it.

This is called the "pan" or "hand" method, and is never, on account of its slowness and laboriousness, continued for any length of time when it is possible to procure a "rocker" or to make and work sluices.

A "rocker" is simply a box about three feet long and two wide, made in two parts, the top part being shallow, with a heavy sheet iron bottom, which is punched full of quarter-inch holes. The other part of the box is fitted with an inclined shelf about midway in its depth, which is six or eight inches lower at its lower end than at its upper. Over this is placed a piece of heavy woollen blanket. The whole is then mounted on two rockers, much resembling those of an ordinary cradle, and when in use they are placed on two blocks of wood so that the whole may be readily rocked. After the miner has selected his claim, he looks for the most convenient place to set up his "rocker," which must be near a good supply of water. Then he proceeds to clear away all the stones and coarse gravel, gathering the finer gravel and sand in a heap near the "rocker." The shallow box on top is filled with this, and with one hand the miner rocks it, while with the other he ladles in water. The finer matter with the gold falls through the holes on to the blanket, which checks its progress, and holds the fine particles of gold, while the sand and other matter pass over it to the bottom of the box, which is sloped so that what comes through is washed downwards and finally out of the box. Across the bottom of the box are fixed thin slats, behind which some mercury is placed to catch any particles of gold which may escape the blanket. If the gold is nuggety, the large nuggets are found in the upper box, their weight detaining them until all the lighter stuff has passed through, and the smaller ones are held by a deeper slat at the outward end of the bottom of the box. The piece of blanket is, at intervals, taken out and rinsed into a barrel, as already mentioned.

Sluicing is always employed when possible. It requires a good supply of water with sufficient head or falls. The process is as follows: Planks are procured and formed into a box of suitable width and depth. Slats are fixed across the bottom of the box at suitable intervals, or shallow holes bored in the bottom in such order that no particle could run along the bottom in a straight line and escape without running over a hole. Several of these boxes are then set up with a considerable slope and are fitted into one another as the ends like a stove-pipe. A stream of water is now directed into the upper end of the highest box. The gravel having been collected, as in the case of the rocker, it is shovelled into the upper box and is washed downwards by the strong current of water. The gold is detained by its weight, and is held by the slats or in the holes mentioned; if it is fine, mercury is placed behind the slats or in these holes to catch it. In this way about three times as much dirt can be washed as by the rocker, and consequently three times as much gold is secured in a given time. After the boxes are done with they are burned, and the ashes washed for the gold held in the wood.*

*A great many of the miners spend their time in the summer prospecting and in the winter resort to a method lately adopted and which is called "burning." They make fires on the surface thus thawing the gound [*sic*] until the bed rock is reached, then drift and tunnel; the pay dirt is brought to the surface and heaped in a pile until spring when water can be obtained. The sluice boxes are then set up and the dirt is washed out, thus enabling the miner to work advantageously and profitably the year round. This method has been found very satisfactory in places where the pay streak is at any great depth from the surface. In this way the complaint is overcome which has been so commonly advanced by miners and others that in the Yukon several months of the year are lost in idleness. Winter usually sets in very soon after the middle of September and continues until the beginning of June and is decidedly cold. The mercury frequently falls to 60 degrees below zero, but in the interior there is so little humidity in the atmosphere

that the cold is more easily endured then on the coast. In the absence of thermometers, miners, it is said, leave their mercury out all night: when they find it
frozen solid in the morning they conclude that it is too cold to work and stay at
home. The temperature runs to great extremes in summer as well as in the winter;
it is quite a common thing for the thermometers to register 100 degrees in the
shade. (96–100)

TOO MUCH GOLD?

The drama of the Yukon experience inspired a fair amount of poetry and fiction. The following poem by W. D. Lighthall, originally published in *Songs of the Great Dominion* (London: W. Scott, 1889), speaks of a Yukon river rumored by the Indians to be running with gold. Although there actually *was* a tributary of the Klondike called Too Much Gold, the river in this poem seems more mythical than real.

The poet raises the question: just how much money is "enough"? Is there a point when an individual who has the prospect of endlessly making money decides to give up the struggle for more? Can money, if one gets enough of it, free a person from care? The reader is left wondering if the gold in this poem is more than just a yellow metal.

W. D. LIGHTHALL, "THE TOO-MUCH-GOLD RIVER," IN JOSEPH LADUE, *KLONDYKE FACTS. BEING A COMPLETE GUIDE TO THE GOLD REGIONS OF THE GREAT CANADIAN NORTHWEST TERRITORIES AND ALASKA*
(New York: American Technical Book Co., 1897)

THE TOO-MUCH-GOLD RIVER.

Which the Indians report to be situated beyond, and to be far richer than the Klondyke.

Far up the stern-precipiced Klondyke,
    In the Arctic drear, we are told,
There speeds a mysterious river,
    "The River of Too Much Gold."

O say, ye powers of darkness!
    Did the Yukon Indians dream
The longing they roused in our heart-chords
    When they named us that hidden stream?

There once was an El Dorado
    Men crazed their lives to behold;
But what was the merely Golden
    To the River of Too Much Gold?

O, if we could stand on its border,
    And after our sacks were distent,

Kick round us still beaches of nuggets,
    Would we feel we could then be content?

Would we feel, as we shouldered our million,—
    Pledge of pleasures ten thousand fold,
That even then this river
    Was a River of Too Much Gold?

Or when will the heart of mortal
    Be ready to cry "Enough!"
And what is the use of the struggle
    For the "stuff" if it does not stuff?

But however it be, I am longing
    As though it would free me from care,
For the banks of that Arctic river,
    And a little of what is there. (188–89)

THE SPELL OF THE YUKON

"The Spell of the Yukon" by Robert W. Service, the famous poet of the Yukon, asks some of the same questions raised in Lighthall's poem. Service, writing from the perspective of an unnamed miner who has made a fortune and left the Yukon, seems to be saying that what was really important was not gold, but the land itself and the adventure. In "The Heart of the Sourdough," Service's own "Call of the Wild," what the speaker longs for is, again, not gold and wealth, but a place untouched by society. Although Service, a Canadian, did eventually spend time in the Yukon around Lake Laberge, these poems were written before he had ever seen the Yukon and lend a mythical quality to his view of the land.

ROBERT W. SERVICE, "THE SPELL OF THE YUKON," AND "THE HEART OF THE SOURDOUGH," IN *THE SPELL OF THE YUKON AND OTHER VERSES*
(New York: Barse & Hopkins Publishers, 1907)

THE SPELL OF THE YUKON

I wanted the gold, and I sought it;
  I scrabbled and mucked like a slave.
Was it famine or scurvy—I fought it;
  I hurled my youth into a grave.
I wanted the gold, and I got it—
  Came out with a fortune last fall,—
Yet somehow life's not what I thought it,
  And somehow the gold isn't all.

No! There's the land. (Have you seen it?)
  It's the cussedest land that I know,
From the big, dizzy mountains that screen it
  To the deep, deathlike valleys below.
Some say God was tired when He made it;
  Some say it's a fine land to shun;
Maybe; but there's some as would trade it
  For no land on earth—and I'm one.

You come to get rich (damned good reason);
  You feel like an exile at first;

You hate it like hell for a season,
    And then you are worse than the worst.
It grips you like some kinds of sinning;
    It twists you from foe to a friend;
It seems it's been since the beginning;
    It seems it will be to the end.

I've stood in some mighty-mouthed hollow
    That's a plumb-full of hush to the brim;
I've watched the big, husky sun wallow
    In crimson and gold, and grow dim,
Till the moon set the pearly peaks gleaming,
    And the stars tumbled out, neck and crop;
And I've thought that I surely was dreaming,
    With the peace o' the world piled on top.

The summer—no sweeter was ever;
    The sunshiny woods all athrill;
The grayling aleap in the river,
    The bighorn asleep on the hill.
The strong life that never knows harness;
    The wilds where the caribou call;
The freshness, the freedom, the farness—
    O God! how I'm stuck on it all

The winter! the brightness that blinds you,
    The white land locked tight as a drum,
The cold fear that follows and finds you,
    The silence that bludgeons you dumb.
The snows that are older than history,
    The woods where the weird shadows slant;
The stillness, the moonlight, the mystery,
    I've bade 'em good-by—but I can't.

There's a land where the mountains are nameless,
    And the rivers all run God knows where;
There are lives that are erring and aimless,
    And deaths that just hang by a hair;
There are hardships that nobody reckons;
    There are valleys unpeopled and still;
There's a land—oh, it beckons and beckons,
    And I want to go back—and I will.

They're making my money diminish;
    I'm sick of the taste of champagne
Thank God! when I'm skinned to a finish
    I'll pike to the Yukon again.

I'll fight—and you bet it's no sham-fight;
    It's hell!—but I've been there before;
And it's better than this by a damsite—
    So me for the Yukon once more.

There's gold, and it's haunting and haunting;
    It's luring me on as of old;
Yet it isn't the gold that I'm wanting
    So much as just finding the gold.
It's the great, big, broad land 'way up yonder,
    It's the forests where silence has lease;
It's the beauty that thrills me with wonder,
    It's the stillness that fills me with peace. (11–14)

THE HEART OF THE SOURDOUGH

There where the mighty mountains bare their fangs unto the
    moon,
There where the sullen sun-dogs glare in the snow-bright, bitter
    noon,
And the glacier-glutted streams sweep down at the clarion call of
    June.

There where the livid tundras keep their tryst with the tranquil
    snows;
There where the silences are spawned, and the light of hell-fire
    flows
Into the bowl of the midnight sky, violet, amber and rose.

There where the rapids churn and roar, and the ice-floes
    bellowing run;
Where the tortured, twisted rivers of blood rush to the setting sun—
I've packed my kit and I'm going, boys, ere another day is done

                    * * * * * *

I knew it would call, or soon or late, as it calls the whirring
    wings;
It's the olden lure, it's the golden lure, it's the lure of the timeless
    things,
And to-night, oh, God of the trails untrod, how it whines in my
    heart-strings!

I'm sick to death of your well-groomed gods, your make-believe
    and your show;
I long for a whiff of bacon and beans, a snug shake-down in the
    snow;
A trail to break, and a life at stake, and another bout with the foe.

With the raw-ribbed Wild that abhors all life, the Wild that would
   crush and rend,
I have clinched and closed with the naked North, I have learned
   to defy and defend;
Shoulder to shoulder we have fought it out—yet the Wild must
   win in the end.

I have flouted the Wild. I have followed its lure, fearless familiar,
   alone;
By all that the battle means and makes I claim that land for mine
   own;
Yet the Wild must win, and a day will come when I shall be
   overthrown.

Then when as wolf-dogs fight we've fought, the lean wolf-land
   and I;
Fought and bled till the snows are red under the reeling sky;
Even as lean wolf-dog goes down will I go down and die. (15–17)

LESS OPTIMISTIC VIEWS ON THE YUKON

Views of the Yukon less romantic than those of Lighthall and Service are expressed by two men who carved their verses into trees while struggling to the Yukon through the Canadian trails. Miners-to-be discovered that the route through the Stikine Mountains was impassable, though the Canadian government and newspapers urged its citizens to take that Canadian route to the Yukon.

HUGH WELLS, "THERE IS A LAND," AND ANONYMOUS, "THIS IS THE GRAVE," CARVED INTO TREES ON THE WAY TO THE YUKON
(Pierre Berton, *The Klondike Fever* [New York: Alfred A. Knopf, 1897], 226)

There Is a Land

There is a land of pure delight
Where grass grows belly-high;
Where horses don't sink out of sight;
We'll reach it by and by.

This Is the Grave

This is the grave the poor man fills,
After he died from fever and chills,
Caught while tramping the Stikene Hills,
Leaving his wife to pay the bills.

PROJECTS FOR ORAL OR WRITTEN EXPLORATION

1. To the people of the Renaissance, "gold" signified heaven, Eden, and ideal perfection. To modern generations, it usually means worldly greed. Write an essay on these two divergent concepts. Are either or both meanings embraced in *The Call of the Wild*?

2. Make a list of expressions, songs, and titles that use the word "gold" and conduct a discussion of gold's multiple meanings. Which of these has significance for a study of this novel?

3. Discuss why an economic depression would intensify a gold rush or gold fever.

4. Imagine that you are absolutely penniless in 1896. Make a list of the ways you might raise enough money to try your luck in the gold fields of the Yukon.

5. Write an essay on other ways in which people have sought their fortunes through adventure.

6. Some political theorists may argue that people and things are always hurt in the unbridled search for wealth. Conduct a formal debate on this question.

7. Consult some maps of the Yukon and trace the three major routes taken to the gold fields. From your research, calculate the mileage of each and the pluses and minuses of each.

8. Suppose that you are living in late-nineteenth-century America and have read the news article from the *San Francisco Call* on the gold rush. Make a list of questions to which you would want to find the answers before you left. From the material presented here, do you think that there are some things for which you would simply not be prepared? If so, what are they?

9. After reading the excerpts from the *Call* article and the Coolidge handbook, stage a dramatic scene in which one person encourages a young man to go to the Yukon and another advises him to stay away.

10. Considering that Canadian officials insisted that anyone entering the Yukon have a year's supply of food and that Coolidge's list is for a month only, make an estimate of what food or supplies one would need for a year. Does it appear to you that Coolidge lists some things that you could live without? If in the Yukon you found, as did Hal and company, that you had to leave things behind, what things on Coolidge's list could you do without?

11. From maps and other data, try to figure exactly how many miles Buck travels before he joins the wild.

12. Compare the treatment of horses on the White Pass, as described by Jack London and William B. Haskell, with the treatment of dogs in the novel.

13. Many of the Yukon's dangers can be classified as hidden beneath the surface. Write an essay on this concept, considering both the literal and metaphoric dimensions of hidden danger in the Yukon.

14. Consider the questions raised by Lighthall's poem. Does he imply that for people with gold fever there is never enough? Consider whether money always frees people from cares. Conversely, is money always a curse? Construct a question on the value of gold or money and debate it.

15. How are the two poems carved in the trees different in tone from the three more conventional poems?

16. In light of the documents presented in this chapter, do you think, that *The Call of the Wild* is romantic or realistic in its depiction of the Yukon? Be prepared to back up your conclusions with specific evidence from the novel.

SUGGESTIONS FOR FURTHER READING

Adney, Tappan. *The Klondike Stampede*. New York: Harper & Brothers, 1900.

Berton, Pierre. *The Klondike Fever*. New York: Alfred A. Knopf, 1958.

———. *The Klondike Quest: A Photographic Essay, 1897–1899*. Toronto: McClelland & Stewart, 1983.

Friesen, Richard J. *The Chilkoot Pass and the Great Gold Rush of 1898*. Ottawa: National Historic Parks and Sites Branch, Parks Canada, 1981.

MacDonald, Ian, and Betty O'Keefe. *The Klondike's "Dear Little Nugget."* Victoria, B.C.: Horsdal & Schubart, 1996.

Mayer, Melanie J. *Klondike Women: True Tales of the 1897–98 Gold Rush*. Athens, OH: Swallow Press, 1989.

Mcdill, Robert Bell. *Klondike Diary: True Account of the Klondike Rush of 1897–1898*. Portland, OR: 1949.

Wells, E. Hazard. *Magnificence and Misery: A Firsthand Account of the 1897 Klondike Gold Rush*. Garden City, NY: Doubleday, 1984.

Wharton, David. *The Alaska Gold Rush*. Bloomington: Indiana University Press, 1972.

4 ————————————

The Sled Dog

The Call of the Wild, the best-known of Jack London's dog stories, reflects the dog-centered world of the Yukon during the gold rush. Travel by dogsled was the only viable means of navigating the vast subarctic plains. Dogs were the only means of carrying hundreds of pounds of supplies across this frozen land. As a consequence, dogs were the most valuable commodities in the Yukon, and their value prompted an unscrupulous business in the buying and stealing of dogs stateside to be shipped to the Yukon. At least 1,500 dogs worked at the mine sites, and Dawson, the village center of the Yukon, was inhabited by some 1,500 dogs. One reporter claimed that no community on earth of the size of Dawson could boast so many dogs.

From all reports, Jack London had an intimate knowledge of dogs stemming from a lifetime of dog ownership and study. At the age of ten, London had a dog named Rollo. Later, while living in Oakland, he owned for a time a collie that he had rescued from the Oakland marshes. As a young man, he had a husky named Brown Wolf. Toward the end of his life, well after he had written *The Call of the Wild*, he owned another dog named Possum. His abiding interest in dogs is certainly apparent in his fiction, in which they sometimes play a major role and often are integral or incidental to the story. More than knowledge, London had great sym-

Dogsled in the Yukon, 1897. Photo Collections, The Bancroft Library.

pathy with and understanding of dogs. In 1916, after London's death, Marshall Bond, the California Princeton graduate who, with his brother Louis, met London in the Yukon, where they were prospecting, wrote of London's high regard for the Bonds' dog Jack, on whom Buck is based. Bond stated that he was struck even at the time with London's unique way of dealing with dogs. While others patted and caressed dogs, London "always spoke and acted toward a dog as if he recognized his noble qualities, respected them" (Marshall Bond, Jr., *Gold Hunter* [Albuquerque: University of New Mexico Press, 1969], 39). Bond suggested that while others acted toward dogs as if they were children, London respected them as equals. In his story of this dog-centered world, London incorporates the information about dogs that he had observed and that was then known to be true of the species—the origin of dogs, dog breeds, and the life of dogs in the Yukon gold rush.

The origin of dogs is fundamental to the story of Buck and his sled mates in the Yukon, for their ancient history reverberates in

Buck's dreams throughout the narrative—the hairy caveman in the life of his dog ancestors who was short of leg and long of arm and did not walk erect, and Buck's wild ancestors who ranged through the forest and killed their own meat. Also, specific references to dog breeds—the St. Bernard, the Scotch shepherd, the fox terriers, the Indian huskies, the spitz, and others—are essential to characterization in *The Call of the Wild*. Moreover, details of dog behavior, in relation to other dogs and men, and the peculiar culture of the working sled dog, shaped by men and the environment, inform the action of the narrative.

THE HISTORY OF DOGS

> "In vague ways he remembered back to the youth of the breed." (14)

Jack London, a reader of the work of Charles Darwin and other scientific writers, was privy to the debates in the late nineteenth and early twentieth centuries about the history of the dog. At this time, some naturalists were still arguing that certain breeds (for example, the spitz, the breed of Buck's rival of the same name) derived from the fox. In fact, the spitz was classified by some naturalists in the late nineteenth century as a "fox-dog," in large measure because of its foxlike head. There were also scientists who believed that some dogs derived from early mixed breeding with bears and tigers. But by the turn of the twentieth century, this theory had largely been discredited, behaviorists pointing out that there were no known cases of wild dogs breeding with foxes, bears, or tigers. Some scientists even rejected the theory that any present dog breeds derived from any species other than wild dogs, like the Australian dingo, the African and Asian jackal, the dhole of India, or the wild "Indian" dogs of North and South America. Those who held that the wild dog was the only progenitor of the present-day dog argued against the wolf (the most likely other candidate for the dog's ancestor) on the grounds that the most wolf-like dogs, those of the arctic and subarctic regions, had tails that curled upwards, unlike the straight, drooping tail of the wolf.

> "His muzzle was the long wolf muzzle. . . . His cunning was wolf cunning." (56)

But the prevailing theory of Jack London's day, and one that present DNA evidence corroborates, is that the domestic dogs descend from either the wild dog or the wolf or mixtures of the two. What scientists suspected in Jack London's day has been confirmed by DNA testing that shows that the DNA of the dog is identical to that of the wolf. According to Marion Schwartz, writing in *A History of Dogs in the Early Americas* (New Haven, CT: Yale University Press, 1997), the dog has one direct ancestor, and that is the wolf. Schwartz suggests the relations of the dog in this way: the father of the dog is the wolf; the siblings are wolves and coyotes; and the cousins are foxes.

> "The vision of the short-legged hairy man came to him more frequently." (53)

The scenario developed to speculate on how the dog developed a relationship with man is consistent with London's assumptions about Buck's ancestry in *The Call of the Wild*. The story suggested by archeological evidence is that there was a relationship between cavemen and dogs over 20,000 years ago. One scenario is that wild dogs distantly followed wandering groups of humans to glean any leavings from their hunts. At first, humans were suspicious of any wild animal and reluctant to share any portion of their food with the wild dogs. However, over time, humans sensed that the noisy dogs warned them of the approach of animals that were really dangerous to humans. Perhaps the dogs even frightened away bears and tigers. Without the wild dogs around, primitive man felt more uneasy. Very gradually, perhaps over hundreds of years, primitive hunters began encouraging jackals or other wild dogs to follow their camps by deliberately leaving food for them. Eventually, dogs joined men in the hunt.

The theory is that some wolves living near human communities or different wild dogs from other areas bred with the hunting dogs to produce new characteristics. Sometimes, for no apparent reason, a very different dog would be produced and then bred, its difference continuing in its progeny. Especially in arctic and subarctic regions, the wolflike dog flourished. These dogs were lanky and gray, with small, recessed eyes and pointed faces. Early explorers in the region declared that it was impossible to distinguish between the working dogs used there and the wolves in the wild. Scientists have long concluded that northern breeds, especially Eskimo dogs, Samoyeds, and Russian laikas are descended from wolves.

When dogs first joined men in the hunt, the two species struck a bargain. In exchange for protecting humans, helping them in the hunt, and carrying their kill back to camp, dogs were allowed to share in the kill. The supposition is that as long as man was primarily a hunter, he regarded other animals as his equals. This is one of the stages in the developing relationship between humans and dogs that Buck frequently dreams about.

At some point, however, the relationship between man and dog changed. Humans became agricultural. The need for dogs in the hunt diminished. Perhaps, it is thought, a litter of orphaned pups was introduced into the human circle as playmates for the children and companions for the women in camp.

It has been established that the animals most likely to be domesticated are those with hierarchies and sociability within their own numbers. We know that wolves, particularly, are highly sociable; they work together; and they run in packs, unlike deer, for example. There is also a strict line of authority within the pack, with the pups bound to a mother and all adult members following or being subjected to the leader. These two behaviors were easily continued with humans as wolves became part of the human "pack" and followed a master.

At the same time that dogs became domesticated, the old equality between dogs and humans changed. The dog gradually lost its freedom and independence. Instead of being the human's cohunter, the dog became his property, dependent on him for food and shelter and often for affection. The domestication, which is to say the subjugation, of the dog became complete when dogs lost their freedom and self-determination. The dog was often chained outside the human's shelter. Like slaves in one respect, domesticated dogs lost the fruits of their labor. Humans even took control of the dog's breeding by neutering it or selecting its mates. Thus the dog began to change biologically in form and behavior as a result of its relationship with humans.

We know that dogs played an important role in ancient societies. Both dog and human remains have been found together in the excavations of cave dwellers from Denmark to Switzerland. European cave drawings suggest that even primitive man was selectively breeding dogs.

Through archeology, art, and literature, we know that several kinds of dogs were kept three to five thousand years ago in Egypt, where they were regarded affectionately and with veneration. Many Egyptian families went through formal periods of mourning when their dogs died. Among the many other societies in which dogs were also cherished companions were ancient Assyria, Persia, Greece, Rome, and Britain. Positive references to dogs abound in early literature. One of the most famous illustrations of this can be found in Homer's *Odyssey*. After many years away fighting in the Trojan War, the hero finally comes home, to be recognized and greeted by his faithful dog. Another example is in the ancient religious testament of Persia, the Book of Zend-Ayesta, in which we find rules for the good treatment of dogs.

> "From Spitzbergen through the Arctic, and across Canada and the Barrens, [Spitz] had held his own." (23)

Of special interest to readers of *The Call of the Wild* is the history of the dog in North America. Dogs were brought to the Western Hemisphere by migrants from northern Asia who first made their appearance in the arctic and subarctic areas of the continent where Buck's story takes place. Consequently, it is appropriate that as Buck is moved closer to those places where his species initially appeared in North America, he begins dreaming of the caveman and the dog around the campfire.

> "The camp was suddenly discovered to be alive with . . . starving huskies . . . who had scented the camp from some Indian village." (16)

From the Arctic, men with their dogs moved into the western coastal areas and the Great Plains. Among arctic peoples, dogs were generally used as hunters of seals and moose and as haulers. Dogs were regarded in other ways in other settlements. Often they were watchdogs. In other North American societies, dogs were regarded as pets and companions and were not used to work at all. At the other end of the spectrum, some Native American societies sacrificed dogs in religious rituals, others ill-treated them, and still others bred dogs only to eat them.

As a result of the interbreeding of many different kinds of wild dogs and different kinds of wolves, a number of distinct breeds had developed by the time Europeans arrived in the New World. In 1920, naturalist Glover Allen listed some seventeen types of dog in the New World even before Europeans introduced their dogs to the mix. Among these types are what are undoubtedly the progenitors of many of the dogs in *The Call of the Wild*, including the Eskimo dog, the Hare Indian dog (both located in the Great Northwest), the Plains Indian dog, the Sioux dog, and the larger or common Indian dog. Even one of the small house dogs on Judge Miller's ranch, the Mexican hairless, already existed as an American breed before Europeans arrived in the New World.

> "His cunning was wolf cunning, and wild cunning; his intelligence, shepherd intelligence and St. Bernard intelligence."
> (56)

With European settlement came European dogs, and the breeds of the Old World were now mixed with those of the New. Spanish dogs that had been brought to settlements in what are now Florida and Louisiana traveled into the interior of the continent and bred with the wolf-dog mix on the plains. In some instances, much larger dogs were developed, which in the Arctic, for example, increased the use of dogs for hauling.

CHARACTERIZATION BY BREED IN *THE CALL OF THE WILD*

Jack London mentions at least eleven breeds of dogs in *The Call of the Wild* to help establish the animal characters he develops. The most numerous breed in the novel by far is what is referred to generically as "the husky." The "wolfish" dogs Buck sees when he gets off the boat in Dyea are described as huskies. They impress Buck with their uncivilized, uncontrollable violence. It is this group of dogs that kills Curly. Billee and Joe, the siblings who join the dogsled team when it starts out for Dawson, are also "true huskies," though they are of opposite temperaments: Billee is good natured and grovels, while Joe is a bad-natured snarler. Soon an old, experienced husky, Sol-leks, moves into one of the leadership positions on the team. He is also sour natured and a loner, like Dave. Finally, there are the semiwild, starving huskies, attached to an Indian village, who viciously attack the team. Except for Billee, who seems to illustrate that not all dogs in a breed are exactly alike, the huskies in the novel are wild, unpredictable, solitary, bad tempered, and even vicious.

For the 1897 gold miners and other earlier adventurers in the Northwest, the word "husky" was used to describe a number of different types of dogs, including the Siberian husky and the Alaskan husky, some of which are not recognized as official breeds, but are only loosely called types, and some of which were only introduced into the Yukon during the gold-rush days. Today the term "husky" is still used to describe several kinds of sled dogs. The one statement that can be made about the origin of huskies is that they are all complicated mixes of several breeds of dog with the wolf. Some huskies are described as crosses between wolves and Eskimo dogs, Eskimo dogs, in turn, being regarded as a type of spitz mix. The Alaskan husky may include many mixtures, such as Irish setter, bloodhound, and wolf. Most of the huskies in *The Call of the Wild* are likely descendants of American Indian wild dogs, wolves, and the wild dogs domesticated by Eskimo tribes. Such huskies may have worked with native peoples in the arctic regions 10,000 to 15,000 years ago.

In appearance they are much like wolves, as early travelers to the region noted, in that they typically have small, erect ears, small, recessed eyes, and sharp muzzles. These dogs weigh about sixty to eighty pounds and have long, heavily boned, muscular legs and slim chests. Most are what is called "double coated," with a very dense furlike undercoat and an equally dense outercoat, usually of a gray, black, or white hue. The one feature that distinguishes the husky from the wolf is its bushy, upwardly curling tail. These physical traits make huskies extremely well suited for life as sled dogs in bitterly cold climates. They are not as heavy and strong as many northern breeds, but few dogs can match their speed and endurance.

Like wolves, the husky typically does not bark like a dog, but howls like a wild animal. Temperamentally, huskies are, as a type, still not recommended as pets for children because they tend to be independent, bad tempered, suspicious, and, on occasion, vi-

cious. Like the wolf, as opposed to the usual family dog, they typically do not retain in maturity an adolescent playfulness. Some
have speculated that a long history of brutal treatment, as well as
its closeness to the wild, has shaped the temperament of the husky.
The husky was also well known for fighting, and London's observation of these dogfights, like one he saw on his way back from
Skagway, helped shape his account of the attack of the starving
huskies on Buck's team.

In addition to the husky, the spitz breed is important in char-
acterizing a dog in the novel. Buck's rival Spitz is named for his
breed, whose origin is associated with islands north of Norway.
There are written reports of the breed going back to the fifteenth
century. This dog's usefulness caused the breed to spread throughout the arctic and subarctic world. The spitz is not only one of the
oldest known domesticated breeds, but it has changed least over
the years from crossing with other breeds. Many of today's distinct
breeds, including the Samoyed, the St. Bernard, and the Eskimo
dog, can be traced in part to the spitz. In the fifteenth and sixteenth centuries, the spitz was a relatively small dog, weighing
about twelve pounds, but by Jack London's day, it weighed about
fifty pounds. Its heavy dense coat was sometimes compared to that
of a sheep or Angora rabbit. The dogs that live in the coldest mountain climates are usually white, and those that live in the warmer
valleys are somewhat darker. The tail of the spitz, like that of the
husky, curls upward. The most distinctive feature of the breed,
however, is its foxlike head with its "laughing" mouth and sharp
nose. The spitz's head is so similar to that of the fox that it has
long been classified as a "fox-dog" along with the Pomeranian. Authorities on the dog long ago mistakenly thought that the spitz was
descended from foxes.

Spitz dogs were so well suited for hauling in bitterly cold climates that they were a familiar breed in Canada's Northwest Territories by the time of the Yukon gold rush. Even though the dog
named Spitz in the novel has recently arrived in the area on a
whaling boat, unlike Buck, he seems to be immediately at home
in the cold weather among the wild huskies, and he already knows
the work of a sled dog well.

More than anything else, it is the foxlike nature of the breed that
characterizes Spitz. Spitz has the unpleasant slyness of the fox
about him in his attacks on Buck until Buck beats him at his own

game by undermining him in the pack. Spitz is described as "smiling into one's face the while he meditated some underhand trick" (7). His tendency to "laugh" like a fox, especially after Curly dies, earns him Buck's undying hatred.

Curly is the only Newfoundland in *The Call of the Wild*, but the breed was important in dogsled travel in the Yukon and other parts of the Canadian Great Northwest. The Newfoundland also figures in the history of the St. Bernard, the breed of Buck's father. The Newfoundland dog was originally from Norway, not Newfoundland, to where it was brought from Norway only later. In the first mention of the Newfoundland in 1732, it is called a "bear dog." This is still one of the most apt descriptions of this densely furred, massive, and powerful dog, usually black, with the enormous square head and flat face of the mastiff. Indeed, the Newfoundland likely has its origins in the breeding of the extremely large, short-haired mastiff with the spitz fox-dogs. It is variously classified as a water dog, a working dog, and one of the "hero" dogs, for it was not only used for guarding and hauling in arctic weather, but was also known for rescuing drowning humans. Many of these dogs, described as having webbed feet, proved something of a nuisance when brought to England, where, under the impression that they were observing a drowning, they insisted on pulling swimmers out of the water.

The "good nature" and friendliness of Curly are consistent with the even temper of the Newfoundland breed. Unfortunately, it is Curly's friendliness that spells her doom, for when she makes overtures toward a wolflike husky, he rips her face open, pushes her down, and makes her vulnerable to the killing attack by the whole pack.

Other breeds are mentioned in passing: the Japanese pug and Mexican hairless, who live in Judge Miller's house; his fox terriers, used for hunting; and Thornton's two dogs, an Irish setter and a bloodhound-deerhound mix. But the dogs whose blood runs in Buck's veins are the St. Bernard (his father) and the Scotch shepherd (his mother). The narrator says that Buck got size, weight, and intelligence from his St. Bernard side. While the St. Bernard was often thought to be one of the oldest and most original breeds, nineteenth-century naturalists found that it was actually one of the newer and most mixed of the recognized breeds. Legend had it that St. Bernards came from a Swiss monastery around 962 A.D., having been bred and trained to rescue travelers in distress in the snow and ice. There were fantastic stories of a legendary St. Bernard named Barry that had rescued up to seventy people after a devastating avalanche in the Swiss Alps.

Later naturalists, however, came to doubt the stories of the breed's great age and Barry's heroic feats. They argued that the breed made its first appearance around 1815 and that, in developing the dog, breeders had used the mastiff, the Newfoundland, the spitz, the bloodhound, the Great Dane, and the Great Pyrenees. They also argued that these monastery dogs were never used to rescue travelers in the snow, but rather to carry food and drink for the monks when they traveled from home. Whatever their origins, the St. Bernard was soon recognized in England and America as an impressive and valuable dog. The St. Bernard has the Newfoundland's massive size, averaging two hundred pounds as an adult. Its body is also thick and extremely muscular. Its chest is broad and its coat is dense. Its face is distinctive in that it has a massive, broad head, a prominent brow, a short muzzle and square nose, and deep-set eyes. Its drooping lower eyelid and heavy jowls are one of the most prominent features of the breed. In Jack London's day, it was known as a dog with a gentle personality and well suited as a pet for small children. We see that Buck, on the Miller ranch, can be trusted to play with the judge's grandchildren, carrying them on his back and rolling them in the grass.

The shepherd or collie (like the one London had as a boy) is also pertinent to the novel. Buck's mother was such a breed—the Scotch shepherd. From her he inherits intelligence and shape. This breed, originating from the wild dog, was often called the "old Scotch Colley." Today, the breed is called "collie." The Scotch shepherd was a work dog used to herd sheep, originally in Scotland alone. Legend has it that the first collie, who worked for a sheep stealer, would divert sheep from one man's herd into his master's herd as they were driven to market. For many years the breed was never allowed outside Scotland. The collie has the slim, pointed face of the wild dog and heavy, long, sable and white hair. The collie's chief asset was known to be its quick intelligence, and stories of its intellectual feats are legend. Dogs of this breed were rumored to understand an impressive range of human language. Some claim that a famous collie in the nineteenth century could play cards and usually win at his game. Unlike the husky, the shepherd grew to be an ideal family dog, protective and patient with children.

Buck seems to have the best of the domestic canine world in his blood. He is courageous and strong, good natured, and intelligent.

SLED DOGS OF THE FAR NORTH

For centuries before the Yukon gold rush in 1897, dogs had been used in far northern climates to carry heavy loads. From their first domestication, dogs had been put to use in carrying game home from the hunter's kill. In Alaska, the Great Northwest Territories, the Yukon, and Canada, wild dogs and wolves, newly domesticated, were widely used by the Eskimos and American Indians to carry provisions across the ice.

At the same time that tribal men took dogs with them on the hunt, women in some areas, who had once shouldered the entire burden of carrying supplies, now enlisted dogs to help them with their work. In some tribes, the breed of dog used by the women was markedly different from that of the men's hunting dogs. Sacks, similar to saddlebags, were placed over the dog's back in much the same manner as horses were loaded. Entire tents, lumber, and cooking pots would be lashed to the backs of dogs in parts of the Yukon among the predominant Athapaskan Indians.

Eventually, it became obvious that dogs could drag more weight than they could carry on their backs, and both dogs and humans began pulling loaded sleds or sledges, as they were often called. From using single dogs to drag one sled each, it was natural to move to a team of dogs carrying heavier loads. Different native peoples had different ways of harnessing and arranging the dogs, but a standard arrangement used by many Indians and Eskimos was passed along to the explorers and in 1897 to the gold prospectors. Teams were comprised of from four to six dogs, the usual number for the Hudson's Bay Company's teams. On some teams, the dogs were arranged in order of skill and strength, with the first, lead dog being the most intelligent and experienced, and the last dog being the least dependable. On other teams, the last dog, closest to the sled, was the strongest and one of the most important. This is the case in *The Call of the Wild*, where the position is held by Dave. The man who drove the team usually followed, whip in hand.

Natives made harnesses of reindeer, moose, or seal skin. Some of the nonnative gold hunters were known to use strips of heavy canvas. One strap of the harness formed a collar around the dog's neck. Other straps were fitted to each of the dog's front legs. The three straps were attached to a single thick strap that went down the dog's back and was connected to the sled. This connecting strip was known as the trace. Thus a dog who was injured or intractable could be eliminated by "cutting it from the traces"— merely cutting the trace that connected it with the sled. Some teams were not only linked to the sled, but to each other by the traces. In either case, getting these traces entangled when, for example, two dogs got into a fight or one dog did not know what it was doing (as is the case with Buck when he is first harnessed) could cause the driver untold trouble and delay. Some sled drivers contended that dogs were capable of untangling the traces by themselves; others confessed that the only way of dealing with tangled traces was to cut them. A few tribes fed the traces between the front and back legs of the dogs, necessitating the castration of male sled dogs.

The dogs were fanned out so that all the weight would not be along one single strip, especially in traveling over unpredictable ice that could give way at any moment. Many dogs wore bells around their necks, to keep them awake and lively, and leather shoes on their feet, to prevent sores that would render them unable to do their jobs.

The lead dog, sometimes called the foregoer, ran about twenty feet ahead of the sled, setting the pace and directing the rest of the dogs on the driver's vocal orders, given in the language of the far north, at least before gold-rush days. The last dog ran about ten feet ahead of the native driver, who usually sat on the sled. With his whip, an experienced native driver could tap any individual dog who was out of line without touching any other dog. Such a team could travel fifty or sixty miles a day, or about three hundred to four hundred miles a week.

Eskimo and Indian dogs were fed a diet of dried and fresh fish, meat, and birds. In the coldest winter, many of them slept in the tents or igloos of their masters. Others burrowed under the snow to sleep in winter and under mud to protect themselves from mosquitoes in summer. Natives freed their dogs in summer to fend for themselves. In winter the dogs returned for food and were put to work again.

When Europeans began to explore the great unknown Northwest and the Yukon, they also used sled dogs to carry necessary provisions as they forged their way into the country. The surveyors and independent trappers who followed them also used dogsleds. These were the outsiders who brought news of the rich resources to be found in the Yukon, and the way was prepared for business companies, eager for profits from Yukon furs. In the eighteenth century the Russian-America Company in Alaska and in the nineteenth the Hudson's Bay and the Great Northwest companies in the Yukon used as their chief means of transportation a complex system of dog teams—the only viable means of crossing the ice and snow to travel from Canadian settlements to company outposts.

In the Yukon in the mid-nineteenth century, after the activities of the Hudson's Bay Company had greatly diminished in the Yukon, scattered independent miners had less use for as many large teams of dogs in that area. But with the discovery of the rich gold fields and the stampede to the Dawson area in the Yukon, the need for dogs to pull sleds exploded. Some young hopefuls (like Jack London) served as their own pack animals, but getting all the way from Dyea or Skagway without dogs to haul one's gear was extremely difficult for most outsiders. For one thing, it was a very long way from these seaports to the rich gold fields—some six hundred miles. There were no roads, no railroads, and no clearly defined trails. The second consideration was that there were no stores along the way where one could replenish food or provisions. Everything needed for an entire year had to be carried for six hundred miles. (Remember that the Canadian border guards began turning back newcomers who did not have a year's worth of supplies.) Consequently, most people needed some form of pack animal to get them and their supplies to the Dawson area.

But traditional pack animals in the lower United States—horses, donkeys, and mules—were quickly found to be totally unsuitable. The trails from Canada or from the Alaskan Panhandle were narrow, constantly changing, and ill defined, with insufficient room for such animals to pass. Some routes were too steep for traditional pack animals, who were also too heavy to be hauled over such passes. Prospectors might be able to bring in mules and horses by boat from St. Michael, down the Yukon River, but the winter climate was too cold for them to survive outside, and they were too heavy and physically ill suited to travel on snow or ice.

Furthermore, there was no fodder to be found in the Yukon for such animals, and it was impossible to bring in enough fodder to keep them alive.

The answer for those who needed transportation to Dawson and in the gold fields (and for later arctic and antarctic exploration) was the dog. Unlike horses and mules, it could be hauled over steep passes like the Chilkoot. Dogs could eat what was native to the Yukon—fish and wild game—and could survive on a much lesser volume of food. In a pinch, as one old-timer mentioned cheerfully, dogs could be fed on each other.

As a consequence of the dog's suitability for Yukon travel and the crisis created by thousands of people pushing into the area at once, the demand for and price of dogs skyrocketed. Unpedigreed dogs that might before have been given away or sold for under $10 apiece were suddenly being sold for hundreds of dollars, some for as much as $350, at a time when such an amount of money was a small fortune. Dog stealing and the illicit trade in dogs were epidemic, especially throughout the western United States and Canada. Northwest mounties warned people to keep their dogs locked up in their basements. Ironically, Jack London's friends' dog Jack, on whom Buck was modeled, was stolen on his return trip home from the Yukon.

THE 1925 DOGSLED RESCUE

The use of dogs for hauling in the Northwest continued on a less colossal scale after the gold rush cooled off. With the arrival of railroads and highways, including the great Alcan Highway, the total dependence on sled dogs was bound to diminish some. But sled dogs continued to be used for hauling in many quarters of the Northwest—by Eskimos near the Arctic Circle, to the remote areas unserviced by rail, and in the mines that were still in operation. Moreover, sled dogs had another function: they began to be used frequently for sport. Dogsled racing became one of the most popular forms of entertainment in many localities, and numerous teams competed for championships. We see an early version of the use of dogs for sport in the scene in *The Call of the Wild* where a group gathers outside the saloon to watch and place bets on Buck's being able to break a heavy sled out of the ice.

Despite the lessening use of sled-dog teams for necessary hauling, sled dogs earned their place in history by responding to a medical emergency. This dramatic story began in late January 1925 in Nome, a small village of 1,400 people located in northern Alaska, only 140 miles from the Arctic Circle. Nome had been a gold-rush town in the years following the Yukon gold rush, when gold was discovered in Alaska. During the gold rush, it had once been a large, thriving town, but afterward had dwindled again to a village. Because no railroad serviced the town, the easiest way to get supplies in and out of Nome was over the Bering Sea, but in winter the sea was usually frozen over, leaving Nome isolated except for the information that could be conveyed by its telegraph office and the supplies and mail that could be brought in by dogsled, somewhat in the manner of Perrault and François in *The Call of the Wild*.

It was in such a season of isolation that Dr. Curtis Welch, the only local doctor in Nome, made a horrifying discovery during his rounds of patients. Three children he saw in one day were dying with what he diagnosed as diphtheria. In 1925, diphtheria was an especially virulent and horrible disease—horrible in that it attacked the throats of its victims, usually children, swelling and paralyzing their throats, tongues, tonsils, and larynxes until they literally strangled to death. In two of the cases Welch saw that day, the disease had advanced so far that he was unable to pry their mouths open to examine them. The disease was virulent because it was highly contagious. Medical advances in the treatment and prevention of the disease were just then getting under way. Some 210,000 cases of diphtheria, resulting in 20,000 deaths, were recorded in the United States in 1925.

Welch realized instantly that he had a crisis on his hands, that the disease could become epidemic at any time and wipe out the children of Nome, Alaska. He had only a small supply of out-of-date toxoid on hand, the U.S. Public Health Service having ignored his pleas for more. In the middle of a brutally cold winter, even for Alaska, the Bering Sea was too frozen to allow boats to bring in more medicine by that route. Nor in those days was airplane carriage to Nome an answer, for it was assumed that fuel, oil, and pilot would freeze solid given the rudimentary designs and the primitive, open cockpits.

There was only one possibility: dogsled teams. An appeal was made to dogsledders or mushers,[1] as they were called, to get the diphtheria serum from Anchorage to Nome. From the first, this presented an almost impossible challenge for several reasons. First, the serum had to be rushed to Nome in a few days if the inoculations were to stem the epidemic and save lives. Second, the weather was even more bitterly cold than usual, temperatures dropping below fifty degrees below zero. In such temperatures, men's lungs froze if they even breathed improperly, through their mouths. The membranes inside their noses and the ends of their noses could freeze if they were not extremely careful. Also, the loins of even the most densely furred dog began to freeze at fifty below zero. When this began to happen, everything came to a standstill.

Despite the perils, authorities sought the help of the most famous dog-team driver in Alaska, Leonard Seppala, and his partner, Gunnar Kaasen, both of whom drove dogs around the camps of mining companies. Seppala, commandeered the two best dogs in the mining companies' kennels for the trek. These two dogs, now among the most famous in the world because of this feat, were Togo and Balto.

From Anchorage, the 300,000 units of serum were carried by rail to Nenana. From there, teams of dogs, involving twenty drivers, were to carry the precious cargo to Nome in relays. For example, one team of seven dogs picked up the serum from the train in Nenana and took it to Whiskey Creek. Another picked it up there immediately and took it to Galena, and another team took it from Galena to Nome.

There were several spectacular legs in this journey. One was the 91-mile stretch from Shaktoolik to Golovin along the Norton Sound shoreline, driven by Seppala on January 31. An obvious shortcut was to drive across the sound rather than around the shore, but high winds had made the ice extremely unstable, leading Eskimos in the area to advise him strongly against it. Conditions were so unpredictable that huge blocks of ice had been known to break away and carry Eskimos out to sea or to dump entire dog teams into the icy water below. Nevertheless, Seppala was determined to take the shortcut because time was of the essence and he was confident that Togo could spot and evade bad ice and get them to Golovin. Against all odds and under the most perilous conditions, Togo was able to do this, and they arrived safely on the other side of the sound.

Another spectacular run was made by Charlie Olson, who picked up the serum from Seppala in Golovin on February 1. In Olson's 25-mile run to Bluff, high winds blew the dogs off the trail into dangerous, smothering snowdrifts. Olson had no sooner gotten back on the trail than the dogs immediately began to slow down. Olson recognized this as a deadly sign: it meant that the dogs' loins were freezing. The only way he could save the team was to wrap each dog in blankets. In performing this difficult feat, Olson froze his fingers.

At Bluff, Gunnar Kaasen took over from Olson, depending on the rugged and heroic dog Balto. The team drove into a dreadful blizzard that blew them into paralyzing snowdrifts. They had to struggle out of the drifts and then laboriously make their way back to the trail. Nor were the team's troubles over when they regained the trail. Balto suddenly stopped dead still as they were crossing the Topkok River, his feet in water in a crack in the ice. Kaasen had to take him out of the traces to get his feet dry before they could proceed.

After passing a spot named Solomon, Kaasen's team ran headfirst into another raging blizzard that flipped the sled over, throwing the package of serum into a deep snowbank where the driver had to hunt for it with his bare hands. Because of confusion in communication, Kaasen's relief driver at Point Safety was not expecting the team for several hours after it actually arrived. Kaasen, finding no lights on and the relief team unhitched, decided not to take the time to wake his relief driver. Instead, he went on with Balto and his team. At 5:30 A.M. on February 2, having driven 53 miles, Kaasen arrived at the Nome hospital door with the serum. Both he and his dogs were so weak with exhaustion that they were crawling the last few feet.

The 674 miles covered by the drivers and their dogs in five and one-half days remains a world record to this day. Five days later, more serum arrived in the Alaskan Panhandle and was also taken to Nome by dogsleds in record time. At great risk to their own lives, the drivers and their dogs had averted the diphtheria epidemic.

THE IDITAROD: DOGSLEDDING IN THE NORTHWEST CONTINUES

In 1967, the one hundredth anniversary of the purchase of Alaska, a dogsled race was held in commemoration of the 1925 dogsled run from Nenana to Nome. Called the Iditarod, the race followed some of the same trails used by the 1925 teams. Some sections of that trail had been blazed by mail and freight carriers during the Alaskan gold days in 1910 and 1911 between the village called Iditarod (for which the trail and the race are named) and an area just south of Anchorage. From 1973 to the present, the race has been run from Anchorage to Nome, a total distance of 1,137 miles.

The dogs involved in the race are descendants of those who were already in North America when Europeans first set foot in the New World, native dogs that bred with dogs brought in by gold prospectors. The main breeds in the area, now recognized by the American Kennel Club, are malamutes and the smaller Siberian huskies. The huskies were found to be more suitable for racing. Still, most of the dogs who race are of mixed rather than pure blood. They not only must have the speed of the Siberian husky but the ability to drag heavy weights. The dogs must carry from three hundred to five hundred pounds, including the driver. (Drivers must start with 7 to 18 dogs and end up with no less than five dogs.)

In this continuation of the tradition of dogsledding, about which Jack London wrote in *The Call of the Wild*, the great care with which the dogs are treated is in marked contrast to their treatment in the Yukon gold-rush days of 1897. Veterinarians must examine all the dogs shortly before the race to approve that each is fit to participate. Moreover, veterinarians examine every dog at each checkpoint and have the authority to pull out any dog in substandard condition.

The requirements include rests for the dogs every twenty-four hours, protective booties, nonchafing harnesses, two pounds of food per day for each dog, and adequate supplies of dog medicine. As Tim Jones writes in his history of the Iditarod, *The Last Great Race: The Iditarod*, "As far as food and health care go, the dogs fare much better than the mushers" (Harrisburg, PA: Stackpole Books, 1988: 19).

The following documents include excerpts from examinations of (1) the history of the dog; (2) some breeds pertinent to the novel; and (3) the manner of traveling by dogsled. A newspaper account of the 1925 race to Nome concludes this chapter.

THE ORIGIN OF THE DOG

Robert Leighton, writing in 1910 about the origin of the dog, contends that the present domestic dog likely descended from the breeding of wild dogs and wolves. This is very much in line with the sentiment in London's novel, in which Buck seems to recognize the wild wolves of the Yukon as his forefathers. As his evidence, Leighton presents the dog's and the wolf's similar skeletons, the pack habits of both, their gestation periods, and their closeness in size and color within a particular area. Leighton answers the question of how so many different types of dogs could have come from the wolf: his comment is that there are as many different types of wolves as there are of dogs.

FROM ROBERT LEIGHTON, *DOGS AND ALL ABOUT THEM*
(London: Cassell & Co., 1910)

This last habit of the domestic dog is one of the surviving traits of his wild ancestry, which, like his habits of burying bones or superfluous food, and of turning round and round on a carpet as if to make a nest for himself before lying down, go far towards connecting him in direct relationship with the wolf and the jackal.

The great multitude of different breeds of the dog and the vast differences in their size, points, and general appearance are facts which make it difficult to believe that they could have had a common ancestry. One thinks of the difference between the Mastiff and the Japanese Spaniel, the Deerhound and the fashionable Pomeranian, the St. Bernard and the Miniature Black and Tan Terrier, and is perplexed in contemplating the possibility of their having descended from a common progenitor. Yet the disparity is no greater than that between the Shire horse and the Shetland pony, the Shorthorn and the Kerry cattle, or the Patagonian and the Pygmy; and all dog breeders know how easy it is to produce a variety in type and size by studied selection.

In order properly to understand this question it is necessary first to consider the identity of structure in the wolf and the dog. This identity of structure may best be studied in a comparison of the osseous system, or skeletons, of the two animals, which so closely resemble each other that their transposition would not easily be detected.

The spine of the dog consists of seven vertebræ in the neck, thirteen in the back, seven in the loins, three sacral vertebræ, and twenty to twenty-two in the tail. In both the dog and the wolf there are thirteen pairs of ribs, nine true and four false. Each has forty-two teeth. They both have five front and four hind toes, while outwardly the common wolf has so much the appearance of a large, bare-boned dog, that a popular description of the one would serve for the other.

Nor are their habits different. The wolf's natural voice is a loud howl, but when confined with dogs he will learn to bark. Although he is carnivorous, he will also eat vegetables, and when sickly he will nibble grass. In the chase, a pack of wolves will divide into parties, one following the trail of the quarry, the other endeavouring to intercept its retreat, exercising a considerable amount of strategy, a trait which is exhibited by many of our sporting dogs and terriers when hunting in teams.

A further important point of resemblance between the *Canis lupus* and the *Canis familiaris* lies in the fact that the period of gestation in both species is sixty-three days. There are from three to nine cubs in a wolf's litter, and these are blind for twenty-one days. They are suckled for two months, but at the end of that time they are able to eat half-digested flesh disgorged for them by their dam—or even their sire.

We have seen that there is no authenticated instance of a hybrid between the dog and the fox. This is not the case with the dog and the wolf, or the dog and the jackal, all of which can interbreed. Moreover, their offspring are fertile. Pliny is the authority for the statement that the Gauls tied their female dogs in the wood that they might cross with wolves. The Eskimo dogs are not infrequently crossed with the grey Artic wolf, which they so much resemble, and the Indians of America were accustomed to cross their half-wild dogs with the coyote to impart greater boldness to the breed. Tame dogs living in countries inhabited by the jackal often betray the jackal strain in their litters, and there are instances of men dwelling in lonely outposts of civilisation being molested by wolves or jackals following upon the trail of a bitch in season.

These facts lead one to refer to the familiar circumstance that the native dogs of all regions approximate closely in size, coloration, form, and habit to the native wolf of those regions. Of this most important circumstance there are far too many instances to allow of its being looked upon as a mere coincidence. Sir John Richardson, writing in 1829, observed that "the resemblance between the the North American wolves and the domestic dog of the Indians is so great that the size and strength of the wolf seems to be the only difference. I have more than once mistaken a band of wolves for the dogs of a party of Indians; and the howl of the animals of both species is prolonged so exactly in the same key that even the practised ear of the Indian fails at times to discriminate between them."

As the Eskimo and Indian dogs resemble the North American wolf, so the dog of the Hare Indians, a very different breed, resembles the prairie wolf. Except in the matter of barking, there is no difference whatever between the black wolf-dog of the Indians of Florida and the wolves of the same country. The same phenomenon is seen in many kinds of European dogs. The Shepherd Dog of the plains of Hungary is white or reddish-brown, has a sharp nose, short erect ears, shaggy coat, and bushy tail, and so much resembles a wolf that Mr. Paget, who gives the description, says he has known a Hungarian mistake a wolf for one of his own dogs. Many of the dogs of Russia, Lapland, and Finland are comparable with the wolves of those countries. Some of the domestic dogs of Egypt, both at the present day and in the condition of mummies, are wolf-like in type, and the dogs of Nubia have the closest relation to a wild species of the same region, which is only a form of the common jackal. Dogs, it may again be noted, cross with the jackal as well as with wolves, and this is frequently the case in Africa, as, for example, in Bosjesmans, where the dogs have a marked resemblance to the black-backed jackal, which is a South African variety.

It has been suggested that the one incontrovertible argument against the lupine relationship of the dog is the fact that all domestic dogs bark, while all wild *Canidæ* express their feelings only by howls. But the difficulty here is not so great as it seems, since we know that jackals, wild dogs, and wolf pups reared by bitches readily acquire the habit. On the other hand, domestic dogs allowed to run wild forget how to bark, while there are some which have not yet learned so to express themselves.

The presence or absence of the habit of barking cannot, then, be regarded as an argument in deciding the question concerning the origin of the dog. This stumbling block consequently disappears, leaving us in the position of agreeing with Darwin, whose final hypothesis was that "it is highly probable that the domestic dogs of the world have descended from two good species of wolf (*C lupus* and *C latrans*), and from two or three other doubtful species of wolves—namely, the European, Indian, and North African forms; from at least one or two South American canine species, from several races or species of jackal; and perhaps from one or more extinct species"; and that the blood of these, in some cases mingled together, flows in the veins of our domestic breeds. (6–9)

THE ST. BERNARD

Jack London acknowledged using dog expert Edward Jesse's 1878 *Anecdotes of Dogs* in writing *The Call of the Wild*. Here Jesse describes the St. Bernard, the breed of Buck's father. We note in his description the very characteristics that belong to Buck in *The Call of the Wild*. In the first place, members of this breed are intelligent. In the second place, they have early on had the uncanny ability to communicate with humans like the Swiss monks who seemingly developed the breed. They are dogs who thrive in intense cold; they have been able to endure great physical trials; and they are strong. Buck's ability to save John Thornton seems appropriate to his heritage from dogs who traditionally were thought to be rescuers.

FROM EDWARD JESSE, *ANECDOTES OF DOGS*
(London: George Bell & Sons, 1878)

Sir Walter Scott said that he would believe anything of a St. Bernard dog. Their natural sagacity is, indeed, so sharpened by long practice and careful training, that a sort of language is established between them and the good monks of St. Bernard, by which mutual communications are made, such as few persons living in situations of less constant and severe trials can have any just conceptions of. When we look at the extraordinary sagacity of the animal, his great strength, and his instinctive faculties, we shall feel convinced how admirably he is adapted to fulfil the purpose for which he is chiefly employed,—that of saving lives in snow-storms.

The peculiar faculty of the St. Bernard dogs is shown by the curious fact, that if a whelp of this breed is placed upon snow for the first time, it will begin to scratch it, and sniff about as if in search of something. When they have been regularly trained, they are generally sent out in pairs during heavy snow-storms in search of travellers, who may have been overwhelmed by the snow. In this way they pass over a great extent of country, and by the acuteness of their scent discover if any one is buried in the snowdrift. (241)

• • •

These dogs, however, do not always escape being overwhelmed by a sudden avalanche, which falls, as is most usual, in the spring of the year.

Two of the domestics of the convent, with two or three dogs, were escorting some travellers, and were lost in an avalanche. One of the predecessors of these dogs, an intelligent animal, which had served the hospital for the space of twelve years, had, during that time, saved the lives of many individuals. Whenever the mountain was enveloped in fogs and snow, he set out in search of lost travellers. He was accustomed to run barking until he lost his breath, and would frequently venture on the most perilous places. When he found his strength was insufficient to draw from the snow a traveller benumbed with cold, he would run back to the hospital in search of the monks.

One day this interesting animal found a child in a frozen state between the Bridge of Drouaz and the Icehouse of Balsora. He immediately began to lick him, and having succeeded in restoring animation, and the perfect recovery of the boy, by means of his caresses, he induced the child to tie himself round his body. In this way he carried the poor little creature, as if in triumph, to the hospital. When old age deprived him of strength, the prior of the convent pensioned him at Berne by way of reward. He is now dead, and his body stuffed and deposited in the museum of that town. The little phial, in which he carried a reviving liquor for the distressed travellers whom he found among the mountains, is still suspended from his neck. (244–45)

A DOG OWNER'S DESCRIPTION OF HIS ST. BERNARD

Egerton Young, a missionary to the Northwest Territories, regarded himself as a dog lover and an expert on dogs. Jack London had read his book before he wrote *The Call of the Wild* and was often accused, unjustly, of plagiarizing Young's book. Several of the dogs and incidents regarding dogs that appear in Young's book are similar to those in London's novel, but similar instances of dog behavior are reported in almost every account of Northwest dog-sledding.

One of the more interesting portraits in Young's book is his description of his St. Bernard, Jack, who is typical of the breed, and who reminds us of Buck in *The Call of the Wild*. Note the height and weight of Young's dog and his great intelligence, courage, and regard for his master—all somewhat parallel to Buck. Note also Jack's ability to "break in" a new dog on the dogsled, much as Spitz did in the novel. In an earlier passage, Young writes about how Jack constantly whirls back in leading the dogsled to make sure that his master is safe from danger. In a passage included here, the author gives an account of Jack's intelligence and heroism in saving men and dogs from what seemed like a sure death in a blizzard, a feat that reminds one of Buck's saving of Thornton in the rapids.

FROM EGERTON YOUNG, *MY DOGS IN THE NORTHLAND*
(New York: Fleming H. Revell Co., 1902)

Jack, when he reached his prime, was thirty-three inches high at the fore-shoulder. (68)

• • •

His weight averaged from one hundred and eighty to two hundred pounds. Like all my dogs, his weight was at the lowest point when we returned from our long toilsome trips, often of weeks' duration. (69)

• • •

In the work of breaking in obstinate young dogs, I found that Jack was my best assistant. He delighted in the work, and it was simply marvellous at times to see the cleverness and thoroughness with which he seconded my efforts. The plan I generally adopted in breaking in a big, stubborn young dog, was to harness him up in a train with three strong, well trained ones in front of him and Jack in harness behind him. When "Marche!", the word for "Go!", was shouted, the old dogs would, of course, at once spring to advance. This the new dog would generally attempt to prevent, by stubbornly balking. Most desperately would he exert all of his strength to hold his ground against the efforts of the dogs in front. This was Jack's opportunity to show what he could do in speedily bringing the young dog to his senses.

"Go for him, Jack," was all I had to say. With a rush and a roar Jack would spring at the stubborn dog, and with more noise and furor than actual biting, he would so frighten the now terrified young animal, that he was glad to spring to his feet and make the most desperate effort to get beyond the reach of the enormous dog that was making it so lively in his rear. As long as the youngster kept going on straight in the trail, Jack did not molest him, but it often happened that a stubborn dog hated to yield quickly, and so tried various other tricks. One was to try to run ahead of the steady dogs in front. This Jack easily prevented. Sometimes he would rush forward, and suddenly seizing the transgressor by a hind leg or his tail, would speedily drag him back into his place. At other times he would throw himself back with such force that the delinquent was speedily jerked back into line. Thus every trick or artifice of the young dog would be so promptly met and defeated that it was not long ere the training lessons were completely learned, and the young dog was thoroughly fitted for his work. (72–73)

• • •

JACK TRIUMPHANT IN THE BLIZZARD

"I'll never see my mother again and you will never see your wife and little ones!"

Such was the pathetic cry of a fine young Indian lad when he and I found ourselves lost in a blizzard storm out on Lake Winnipeg, one wild fierce wintry day. We had started away from our home several days before this, on a winter trip of several hundreds of miles. We were each driving a splendid train of dogs. We had no guide or experienced Indian attendant. It was a risky experiment we were making but I did not see my way clear to do otherwise. (96)

• • •

As long as the wind had, as we thought, remained steadily blowing from the one quarter, we had kept up our courage. We knew that we were going in the right direction when we had our last glimpses of the distant point, and since that time we had been trusting the wind. Now, as in the eddying gusts the wind began whirling around us, coming apparently from every quarter, we were most emphatically brought to realize that in all probability we had been running in a very erratic course, for the last two or three hours at least.

Utterly bewildered, I stopped my dogs, and as Alec's train came up near I shouted to the lad:

"Alec, I am afraid we are lost."

"Yes, we are surely lost," was his not very comforting reply.

"It is a blizzard, and that is where we have blundered," I said, "in allowing ourselves to be caught in it and we so far from shore."

At the mention of blizzard, so dreaded by those who know them best, Alec at once lost heart, and by the utterance of the words I have already quoted, and others in a similar strain, showed that he was well aware of our great danger. (100–101)

• • •

I was now so completely bewildered by the fierce whirling blizzard that I had not the slightest idea of any of the points of the compass. The cold was terrible and of course we could not stay there. On we must go somewhere, and so in sheer desperation I shouted out to Jack, as he was the second dog in the train. Eager and alert to start he had been, from the first word shouted to Koona, but like a well trained dog he knew his place, and that he was expected to follow his leader. He had, however, been showing a good deal of impatience at the hesitancy of Koona, and so now I saw that he was ready for any call that might be made upon him. So I shouted, "Go on, Jack, whichever way you like, and do the best you can, for I do not know anything about it!"

Nothing more was necessary. The noble dog at once seemed to realize that on him rested the responsibility of rescuing us from our perilous position. And grandly did he perform the tremendous task, as with one of his cheery barks he sprang forward in the tempest, Koona, with slackened traces, gladly dropped back, and was quite content to resign the leadership to the more powerful dog. During the long run that followed, never once did the bewildered dog seem to wish, as many a dog does, to again take his position as leader. Koona seemed to have had enough dog sense to know that Jack, in this trying ordeal, could do better work than he, and so he ran beside the larger dog and at times cleverly availed himself of the protection thus afforded to shield himself from some of the fiercest blasts of the storm.

So thoroughly was the blizzard lifting the snow from the ice, that we were able to travel with a good degree of speed. Hours succeeded hours, and still the storm shrieked and howled around us. With undiminished vigour Jack kept to his work. Occasionally I would shout out to him some cheery word, and back through the gale would come his well-known bark. It had in it the ring of victory, and strangely kept up our spirits and hopefulness, and the assurance that we were yet going to escape this peril, although we could but be conscious of the fact that we were indeed in very great danger of perishing. The cold was now so gripping us that it seemed as though we must freeze to death. The very necessary precaution of tying ourselves on our sleds made it impossible for us to spring off and run, as we frequently did under ordinary circumstances. (105–7)

· · ·

Our dogs under the marvellous leadership of Jack, seemed to have caught his enthusiastic, indomitable spirit, and so, hour after hour, were gallantly pressing on through the storm as though they saw in the distance the welcome camp fire, and scented their supper of white fish thawed out for them before the blazing flame.

So there was no need of losing heart while the dogs were setting us such an example of confidence and courage. Then we were both young and strong, and had with us our camp outfit of robes and blankets, and if our dogs became rattled or discouraged we might spread out these robes and blankets, and getting under them, with our dogs huddled around and partly on us, we could at least try to keep alive during the night. So trusting in a loving Providence, who had more than once before marvellously opened up our way, we resolved in quiet restfulness of spirit to make no change as long as Jack, the glorious fellow, kept pushing on with such confidence and courage. From my knowledge of dogs, I decided that he was confident of his course, or he never would have continued on at such a rate, and so inspiring all the other dogs with confidence and assurance—save Koona. So with the exception of the occasional cheery calls to Jack, to which he always responded, and the warning cries to my young Indian comrade not to go to sleep in spite of the bitter cold, I managed to keep, or was kept, in a comfortable state of mind without anxiety or fear.

Thus on we were whirled over the great frozen lake, where, we knew not. But it was evident that if the dogs could keep up such a rapid gait they would certainly in time, bring us out somewhere, and so we resolved that we would try and keep from freezing, or even going to sleep, for under such conditions sleep might mean death without waking.

It was perhaps three hours after dark, when I was agreeably startled by the fact that the dogs had detected something and were much excited by the discovery. It was a long time since I had been able to see them, owing to the darkness of the night and the density of the storm, but it did not require a view of them to tell one accustomed to dogs that they had suddenly become possessed of some knowledge that their drivers knew not of. At first I was inclined to think that perhaps some roaming wild beast had become bewildered in the blizzard, and was near us, far out on the great lake, and that the scent of it had only excited the hunting instincts of my dogs. However, there was but little time or chance for theorizing, or any thing else, except to hang on to the sleds and exercise all the skill possible to keep them from capsizing, as the now thoroughly excited dogs madly dashed along. Such a burst of speed could not last very long, nor was it necessary, for in a short time they gave us a very tangible evidence of the correctness of their keenness of scent, and noble Jack won all honours possible, as the peerless leader.

The fellow had, after a run of sixty or seventy miles in the teeth of a first-class blizzard, with the temperature anywhere from thirty to fifty below zero, gallantly led the way to the icy accumulations cut out, and piled up day by day, by a number of Indian families who, living on the shore, come out here for their daily supply of water. As for months these Indians had been here cutting out the ice that froze each night, there was quite a large pile of it. Squarely did Jack strike that pile, and gallantly aided by the dogs behind he sealed its jagged sides and, before I fully realized what it was, we were in a pellmell sort of a style tumbling down on the other side. Fortunately we did not fall in the open water-hole, but struck finely the beaten trail that led up in the forest to the wigwams of the Indians. Over it the dogs fairly flew. Soon we knew we were being pulled up the steep side of a bluff and in a few minutes more as we were being hurled along the smooth but crooked trail, we saw the welcome sparks flying out of the top of the birch-bark wigwams. A blessed sight indeed was this, for we were safe at last; and can any one blame me if, after our notes of thanksgiving to a kind Providence, we shouted out:

"Well done, Jack!" (106–12)

THE NEWFOUNDLAND

Edward Jesse describes another important dog in *The Call of the Wild*, the Newfoundland. This is Curly's breed in London's novel. Note the mention of traits displayed by Curly—docility, affection, serenity, and nobility. In fact, it is Curly's trusting friendliness that causes the vicious husky to attack her. Jesse also repeats the stories of the Newfoundland's record of saving drowning humans.

FROM EDWARD JESSE, *ANECDOTES OF DOGS*
(London: George Bell & Sons, 1878)

I have seen such courage, perseverance, and fidelity in the Newfoundland dog, and am acquainted with so many well-authenticated facts of his more than ordinary sense and utility, that I think him entitled to be considered as little inferior to the Irish wolf-dog.

When we reflect on the docility of the Newfoundland dog, his affectionate disposition, his aptitude in receiving instruction, and his instantaneous sense of impending danger, we shall no longer wonder at his being called the friend of his master, whom he is at all times ready to defend at the risk of his own life. How noble is his appearance, and at the same time how serene is his countenance! (134)

• • •

No animal, perhaps, can show more real courage than this dog. His perseverance in what he undertakes is so great, that he never relinquishes an attempt which has been enjoined him as long as there is a chance of success. I allude more particularly to storms at sea and consequent shipwreck, when his services, his courage, and indefatigable exertions, have been truly wonderful. Numerous persons have been saved from a watery grave by these dogs, and ropes have been conveyed by them from a sinking ship to the shore amidst foaming billows, by which means whole crews have been saved from destruction. Their feet are particularly well adapted to enable them to swim, being webbed very much like those of a duck, and they are at all times ready to plunge into the water to save a human being from drowning. Some dogs delight in following a fox, others in hunting the hare, or killing vermin. The delight of the Newfoundland dog appears to be in the preservation of the lives of the human race. (135)

CUFFY, THE NEWFOUNDLAND

Egerton Young also owned a Newfoundland named Cuffy that many readers believed was the model for London's Curly. Cuffy, like Curly, is typical of the breed, quickly adjusting to Young's household, eager and capable of serving her master and of charming both man and beast. It is useful to keep these two portraits in mind in evaluating the excerpt from Egerton Young's work in Chapter Five, which discusses attitudes toward and treatment of dogs in Jack London's day.

FROM EGERTON YOUNG, *MY DOGS IN THE NORTHLAND*
(New York: Fleming H. Revell Co., 1902)

Cuffy was the most beautiful dog I ever owned. She was a thoroughbred Newfoundland of the short curly-haired variety. Every curl upon her seemed absolutely perfect, and they were apparently all of the same size. She was always an object of admiration to every lover of these noble animals. Even persons who had but little love for dogs would stop and admire beautiful Cuffy. (125)

• • •

She was very easily taught to fetch and carry, and nothing gave her greater pleasure than to be sent into other rooms for well-known articles. She became quite an adept at this work, but never equalled Jack, as some of his triumphs were simply marvellous. Cuffy acquired the art of opening every door in the house, when she was on the side where it opened from her, but she was completely foiled when the door opened towards her. With but a few lessons I taught Jack how to accomplish the feat, and he never had any difficulty afterwards, but poor Cuffy never could get possession of the knack of pulling the door towards her and thus opening it. However, this did not much bother her, if Jack happened to be about, and they were generally together; for after making an attempt on the door and as usual failing, she would march over to the spot where Jack was comfortably sleeping upon his fur rug, and unceremoniously seizing him by the ear, would lead him to the closed door and in expressive dog language would order him to immediately open it.

With this demand he always quickly complied, for Cuffy was a bit of a tyrant and, presuming on her sex, lorded it over him most thoroughly.

In fact she had him in the most thorough subjection, and it often gave us lots of amusement to watch her coquettish and tantalizing ways, and Jack's patience and quiet dignity. Yet, like many a hen-pecked spouse, it seemed that the more she imposed upon him, the greater his love and jealous care. (125, 128–29)

THE COLLIE

Robert Leighton offers a portrait of one of the most intelligent breeds of dog, the Scotch shepherd or collie. This is the breed of Buck's mother. From her he gets his superior intelligence, the quickness with which he learns his work as a sled dog, and the cunning with which he defeats his enemy Spitz and takes over the dog team. Note that the collie is a work dog that is capable of learning many jobs: it can be a sheep dog, a sporting dog, a guard dog, a companion, or a killer of vermin. This breed has even been trained to work with ambulances on the battlefield.

FROM ROBERT LEIGHTON, *DOGS AND ALL ABOUT THEM*
(London: Cassell & Co., 1910)

THE COLLIE

The townsman who knows the shepherd's dog only as he is to be seen, out of his true element, threading his confined way through crowded streets where sheep are not, can have small appreciation of his wisdom and his sterling worth. To know him properly, one needs to see him at work in a country where sheep abound, to watch him adroitly rounding up his scattered charges on a wide-stretching moorland, gathering the wandering wethers into close order and driving them before him in unbroken company to the fold; handling the stubborn pack in a narrow lane, or holding them in a corner of a field, immobile under the spell of his vigilant eye. He is at his best as a worker, conscious of the responsibility reposed in him; a marvel of generalship, gentle, judicious, slow to anger, quick to action; the priceless helpmeet of his master—the most useful member of all the tribe of dogs.

Few dogs possess the fertile, resourceful brain of the Collie. He can be trained to perform the duties of other breeds. He makes an excellent sporting dog, and can be taught to do the work of the Pointer and the Setter, as well as that of the Water Spaniel and the Retriever. He is clever at hunting, having an excellent nose, is a good vermin-killer, and a most faithful watch, guard, and companion. Major Richardson, who for some years has been successful in training dogs to ambulance work on the field of battle, has carefully tested the abilities of various breeds in discovering wounded soldiers, and he gives to the Collie the decided preference.

It is, however, as an assistant to the flock-master, the farmer, the butcher, and the drover that the Collie takes his most appropriate place in every-day life. The shepherd on his daily rounds, travelling over miles of moorland, could not well accomplish his task without his Collie's skilful aid. One such dog, knowing what is expected of him, can do work which would otherwise require the combined efforts of a score of men.

Little is known with certainty of the origin of the Collie, but his cunning and his outward appearance would seem to indicate a relationship with the wild dog. Buffon was of opinion that he was the true dog of nature, the stock and model of the whole canine species. He considered the Sheepdog superior in instinct and intelligence to all other breeds, and that, with a character in which education has comparatively little share, he is the only animal born perfectly trained for the service of man. (53–54)

SLED DOGS IN THE YUKON

As we see in the account of H. M. Robinson, dogs were being used by Europeans new to the Yukon in the nineteenth century. Robinson, who worked for the Hudson's Bay Company, traveled from post to post via dogsled. At this time, as early as the 1870s, long before the gold rush, dogs brought a good price.

In the following passages, Robinson describes the appearance of the dogs used to draw sleds in the Yukon. To his knowledge, these Eskimo dogs are part wild dog, part Indian dog, and part wolf— sometimes, he writes, they are entirely wolf. Robinson describes a variety of ways of harnessing the dogs used by the Hudson's Bay Company travelers and natives. He also believes that it is necessary to brutalize many of these wilder dogs in order to use them for drawing sleds. As we will see in subsequent accounts, these dogs— mixtures of wild dogs and wolves—were frequently called huskies.

FROM H. M. ROBINSON, *THE GREAT FUR LAND; OR, SKETCHES OF LIFE IN THE HUDSON'S BAY TERRITORY*
(New York: G. P. Putman's Sons, 1879)

But here comes the winter vehicle of the Fur Land! The traveler who lingers long at any season of the year about a Hudson Bay Company's fort will be stuck with the unusual number of dogs lying about the square court during the day, or howling and fighting underneath his windows at night. To leave his door open at any time is only to invite an invasion of the wolfish brutes, who come crowding up, and seem inclined to take possession of the apartment. During the summer season they do nothing for man, but pass their time in war, love, robbery, and music, if their mournful howls can be dignified by that name. And yet, neglected as are these noisy, dirty animals in their months of idleness, unfed, kept in bare life by plunder, the mark for every passer's stick or stone, they are highly prized by their owners, and a team of fine, good, well-trained dogs will bring a handsome price when the winter season approaches. Then two well-broken dogs become as valuable as a horse; then it is the dogs that haul the sledges and that perform, in fact, nearly all the work of the country.

These animals are mostly of the ordinary Indian kind, large, long-legged, and wolfish, with sharp muzzles, pricked ears, and thick, straight, wiry hair. White is one of the most usual colors, but brown, blue-grey, red, yellow, and white marked with spots of black, or of the other various hues, are also common. Some of them are black with white paws, others are covered with long rough hair, like Russian setters. There are others of a light bluish-grey, with dark, almost black spots spread over the whole body. Almost all of them have black noses, but with some of the lighter-colored ones this part is red, brown, or pink, which has a very ugly effect. Most of them are very wolfish in appearance, many being half or partly, or all but entirely, wolves in blood. One frequently sees dark-grey dogs which are said to be almost pure wolves. Seen upon the prairie, it is almost impossible to distinguish them from the ordinary wolf of the middle-sized variety; and their tempers are spoken of as a match for their looks. Indeed it often happens that the drivers of such dogs are obliged, before harnessing or unharnessing them, to stun them momentarily by a blow on the nose, on account of their savage natures. Many of the others, moreover, are nearly as bad, and need a touch of the same rough treatment. In some instances the worse animals are emasculated, with a view of improving their tempers without rendering them unfit for work.

It sometimes happens, however, that among this howling pack of mongrels there may be picked out a genuine train of dogs. There is no mistake about them in size or form, from foregoer to hindmost hauler. They are of pure Esquimaux breed, the bush-tailed, fox-headed, long-furred, clean legged animals, whose ears, sharp-pointed and erect, spring from a head embedded in thick tufts of wooly hair. Or there may be a cross of Esquimaux and Athabascan, with hair so long that the eyes are scarcely visible. These animals have come from the far-northern districts, and have brought a round sum to their owners. They are of much more equable temper than their wolfish brethren, and frequently have a keen appreciation of kindness. To haul is as natural to them as to point is natural to a pointer. Longer than any other dogs will their clean feet hold tough over the rough ice. But it is with dog-driving as with everything else; there are dogs and dogs, and the difference between their mental and physical characteristics are as great as between those of average men. (222–25)

• • •

Dogs in the Fur Land are harnessed in a number of ways. The Esquimaux run their dogs abreast. On the coast of Hudson's Bay they are harnessed by many separate lines into a kind of band or pack; while in Manitoba and the Saskatchewan they are driven tandem. Four dogs to each sledge form a complete train, though three and even two are used, and are harnessed to the cariole by means of two long traces. Between these traces the dogs stand one after the other, with a space intervening between them of perhaps a foot. A round collar, passing over the head and ears and fitting closely to the shoulder, buckles on each side to the traces, which are supported by a back-band of leather. This back-band is generally covered with tiny bells, the collar being hung with those of larger size, and decorated with party-colored ribbons or fox-tails. In no single article of property, perhaps, is greater pride taken than in a train of dogs turned out in good style; and the undue amount of beads, bells, and ribbons, frequently employed to bedizen the poor brutes, produces the most comical effect when placed upon some terror-stricken dog, who, when first put into harness, usually looks the picture of fear, resembling a chief mourner clad in the garb of *Pantaloon*. The ludicrous effect is intensified when the victim happens to be young in years, and still retains the peculiar expression of puppyhood.

The rate of speed usually attained in sledge-travel is about forty miles per day of ten hours, although this rate is often nearly doubled. Four miles an hour is a common dog-trot when the animals are well loaded; but this can be greatly exceeded when hauling a cariole containing a single passenger upon smooth snow-crust or a beaten track. Very frequently extraordinary distances are compassed by a well-broken train of dogs. An instance is recorded where a young Scotch half-breed, driving the mail-sledge between Fort Garry and Pembina, was desirous of attending the wedding of his sister, which was to occur at seven o'clock of the morning following the evening of his regular departure for the latter place. To do this he would have to make the journey in a single night. Leaving Fort Garry at five o'clock in the evening, he reported again with his return mail at a quarter to seven o'clock the following morning, having compassed a distance of one hundred and thirty-five miles in a single night with the same train of dogs. This remarkable speed is capable of ample verification. Sixty to eighty miles per day is not infrequently made in the way of passenger travel. (226–28)

A husky. Courtesy of W. Ostell Johnson.

THE HUSKY

Robert Leighton writes of the "husky" or "Eskimo" dog with which miners in the 1897 gold rush were well familiar. In addition to relating the history of the arctic dog, he describes the physical appearance of the dog, noting that it inherits its appearance, temperament, and habits from the wolf.

Leighton raises a point that we find repeatedly in accounts of dogs in the Northwest: the determination to keep them hungry. Some writers have said that it made the dogs more eager to perform their work if they were fed only infrequently, after long trips. Leighton, otherwise sympathetic, makes the callous statement that these dogs do not need to eat often. Having concluded this, Leighton and other writers then ironically accuse these half-starved dogs of being incurable thieves or even make fun of them for eating anything in sight, including dishrags, soap, and candles.

Leighton also brings up the subject of madness in arctic dogs. While some students of *The Call of the Wild* argue that the madness of Dolly is actually rabies, writers of the time when the novel was written, including Leighton, contend that the not-infrequent madness of these arctic dogs is not to be confused with rabies, but is due to severe environmental conditions. Finally, Leighton supposes that the viciousness of these semiwild dogs may well be due to constant "ill-treatment, hunger and the lash."

FROM ROBERT LEIGHON, *THE NEW BOOK OF THE DOG*
(London: Cassell & Co., 1907)

The uncivilised Polar tribes, both those who inhabited the Siberian tundras, and the Eskimos of America and Greenland, had discovered long before Arctic expeditions had begun, a safe and easy means of traversing the barren, trackless regions of the frozen North: namely the sledge drawn by dogs. They were a semi-nomadic people, moving their habitations at certain seasons of the year in accordance with the varying facilities for procuring food, and the need for a convenient method of locomotion by land and the absence of any other animal fitted for the work of hauling heavy burdens very naturally caused them to enlist the services of the dog. Nor could a more adaptable animal have been chosen for travelling over frozen ground and icebound seas, had these inhabitants of the frigid zone been at liberty to select from the fauna of the whole earth. Had the horse been possible, or the reindeer easily available, the necessity of adding fodder to the loaded sleds was an insuperable difficulty; but the dog was carnivorous, and could feed on blubber, walrus skin, fish, bear, or musk ox, obtained in the course of the journey, or even on the carcases of his own kind; and his tractable character, the combined strength of an obedient pack, and the perfect fitness of the animal for the work required, rendered the choice so obvious that there can hardly have been a time when the Arctic peoples were ignorant of the dog's value.

The Eskimos are not an artistic race; but the few ancient records rudely inscribed on rock or bone give proof that in the very earliest times their sledges were drawn by dogs. In the sixteenth century Martin Frobisher, who voyaged to Greenland in search of gold, and the early navigators who penetrated far into the Arctic seas to seek a north-west passage, observed with interest the practical uses to which the wolf-like dog of the north was put. In later times the European explorers recognised the advantage of imitating the Eskimo method of locomotion in circumstances which made the use of the sailing boat impossible, and the modern explorer into Arctic regions regards his teams of sledge dogs as being as much a necessary part of his equipment as fuel and provisions. (526–27)

. . .

They are irregular in their feeding, and are content if they get a good meal thrice a week and for lack of better food they will devour almost anything from a chunk of wood to a coil of tar rope, their own leather harness, or a pair of greasy trousers. In the severest Arctic weather they do not suffer from the cold, but they are subject to diseases uncommon in civilised kennels. Paralysis of the legs, and convulsions, are deplorably frequent, but the worst complaint is the epidemic madness which seems to attend them during the season of protracted darkness. True rabies are unknown among the Eskimo and Indian dogs, and no one bitten by an afflicted dog has even contracted the disease.

The Eskimo . . . is a sturdy, well-boned animal, with excellent body qualities, and admirable limbs. His resemblance to his wild relative is accentuated by his long, snipy muzzle, and his erect triangular ears, although it may be noted that his Eskimo owner has a fancy for the ear carried low. The eyes are set obliquely, like those of the wolf, and the jaw is formidable, with excellent dentition. With a strong, arched neck, a broad chest, and muscular quarters, he is apparently made for work, and for accomplishing long journeys, with tireless endurance. His tail is long and bushy, and in the adult is usually carried over the back. His coat is dense, hard and deep, especially on the back, where it may be from two to four inches in length, with a woolly undercoat to resist the penetrating snow and cold. It is longer about the neck and the thighs, but shorter on the legs and head. In colour it is the same as that of the wolf, black or rusty black with lighter greyish markings on the chest, belly and tail. Often a pure white dog may be seen, as Peary's Lion, who was very little different from the Siberian breed, and in all there is the characteristic light spots above the eyes. The height of the Eskimo dog may average 22 inches at the shoulder.

Many lupine traits are observable in the Eskimo dog. He does not habitually bark but has a weird wolfish howl; and he is remarkable for his thievishness and his destructiveness towards smaller animals. . . .

The "Huskies" so frequently referred to in Jack London's "Call of the Wild," are of the Eskimo and wolf cross, and the "Giddies" are of similar parentage, bred specially by the Indians for hauling purposes. These last are willing workers, but vicious brutes, who fight their way through summers of semi-starvation and winters of too much ill-treatment, hunger and the lash. (529–30)

A DOG OWNER'S DESCRIPTION OF THE HUSKY

Egerton Young also lived with and here describes the arctic husky, a dog identical in his mind with the Eskimo dog. Young's account is valuable for its specific description of the dog's physical appearance—size, color, and shape. Like other writers, Young reveals that he rid himself of his huskies because they were incurable thieves.

FROM EGERTON YOUNG, *MY DOGS IN THE NORTHLAND*
(New York: Fleming H. Revell Co., 1902)

Still these Eskimo, or Huskie dogs—for they are sometimes called by one name and sometimes by the other, have justly won for themselves a name and a record that will cause them to hold a high place among animals that have been of real service to the human race. But few of them are ever kept for mere pleasure or pastime. It is because they are so serviceable to man, and at times absolutely invaluable to him, that they deservedly stand in such esteem with the admirers of the canine race.

The pure Eskimo dog is not devoid of beauty. His compact body, well furred; his sharp-pointed, alert-looking ears; his fox-like muzzle; his good legs and firm, hard feet; his bushy tail, of which he often seems so proud; and his bright, roguish eyes, place him in no mean position among the other dogs of the world. His colour varies from the purest white to jet black. I owned two so absolutely white that not a coloured hair could be found on either of them. They were named Koona and Pa-qua-sha-kun, Snow and Flour, by the Indians, on account of their spotless whiteness.

A favourite colour is a kind of light mouse-grey. Dogs of this kind are, however, rare, but when obtained from the natives are considered of greater intelligence than others and are valued accordingly. Still the colour, as a general thing, is not often taken into consideration, or considered as evidence against the purity of their blood.

The working weight of my Eskimo dogs ranged from sixty to a hundred and thirty pounds. It seemed rather remarkable that some of the lighter dogs were quite equal in drawing power to others that were very much larger and heavier. In my first winter's experience with dogs in the Hudson's Bay Territories, I was the fortunate or unfortunate owner of twelve of them. It was evident from their appearance that, in the eyes of an expert, they would not all have been classed as pure bred Eskimo. Still there was enough of that breed in them to dominate everything else and to cause them to act in the most thoroughbred fashion.

They had, in common with all other dogs—and there were hundreds of them in the Indian village where we resided—the habit of setting up the most discordant howlings three or four times during the night, especially in the winter months. (18–20)

DOGSLEDS

Egerton Young graphically shows why dogs were at a premium in the Great Northwest and provides us with one of the most thorough descriptions of the dogsleds in this area. Not only does he describe sleds similar to the ones drawn by Buck and his mates, but he details what supplies were ordinarily pulled on the sleds.

FROM EGERTON YOUNG, *MY DOGS IN THE NORTHLAND*
(New York: Fleming H. Revell Co., 1902)

With the dogs of the Northland, and "journeyings oft" with them we are now concerned. Travellers in the burning deserts can write whereof they know about the patient camel, but this chapter is to be devoted to a description of a trip with dogs and Indians through the wilds of the Great Northland. Why with dogs? Simply because there is positively no other way possible.

The whistle of no railroad engine or steamer has ever aroused the echoes of these northern interior solitudes, neither is it likely to do so for long years to come.

There are absolutely no roads, or paths, or trails, for hundreds, nor even thousands, of miles. The result is that there is absolutely no other way of winter travelling than with dogs, except going on foot, and even that becomes impossible when distances are greater than those where men can carry their own supplies. For their supplies mean much more than merely the food a man would consume. It means his bedding, weapons of defence, axe, snow-shoes and various other things, in addition to kettles in which to cook his food. Hence to those who would there travel, the dog is simply invaluable, in spite of his many defects.

As so much is said in other parts of this book about dogs in general, as well as about some individual ones, I need not in this chapter give any further description of them. My readers must imagine that we are travelling with the splendid dogs elsewhere described or with others like them.

The dog-sleds are not always of the same form or construction. In those regions where there is but little dense forest country, the sleds are made much wider than are those which are used where the trails run through the densely wooded regions. Then in many places experience has shown that the sleds constructed with strong runners, which keep the body of the sled well up from the ground, are the best for travelling through certain sections of broken country, and especially over the great rough ice fields of the Northern seas.

The perfect sled, however, for use in the forest and lake regions, where we spent our years when in that Northland, was made exactly on the same plan as are the toboggans of Quebec. From the Red River Settlement we had sent out to us by boats in the summer time, some good oak boards. They were twelve feet long, eight or nine inches wide, and an inch thick. Two of these were matched and then firmly fastened edge to edge to each other with strong cross-bars. Then one end was planed down, until it was not more than half of the thickness of the rest of the boards. The thin end was then thoroughly steamed for at least a day, and then, in a place prepared, was bent in the shape required for the head of the sled. Strong deer-skin thongs, well tied, held every part in its right position, and so, as soon as the parts softened by the steam had become hard and rigid, the sled was about finished. Two strong deer-skin loops were fastened at the front, to which the traces of the dogs were attached when desired. Then much larger loops were firmly secured on each side of the sled for the purpose of fastening on the loads, and now the sled is considered completed, and ready for use. A cariole was one of these sleds fixed up with a comfortable back and parchment sides. Often it was gaily painted and with fur robes and a good trail was a cosy vehicle in which to ride.

For a long trip of, say, several hundreds of miles, during which I would be absent from home for perhaps six weeks, I would take with me three of these oak sleds and a cariole.

Four dogs constituted a train sufficiently strong to draw a loaded sled. The dogs with us were harnessed up in tandem style. Any other method would not have been suitable in such a densely wooded country.

The taking of so many dogs and sleds may appear at first extravagant. But the explanation is simple. It must be borne in mind that these long journeys were made in a country so wild that there were not only no hotels or lodging places of any kind from the beginning to the end of the route, but also there were no shops, or places of any description, where supplies could be secured for love or money. The only possible exception to this rule was when we were so fortunate as to cross the trail of a hunter who might have been lucky enough to have just shot a moose or a reindeer. Then we might be able to purchase some venison. But even that meant giving in exchange supplies from our sleds, as all bargains were by barter; so we really were not much better off.

Our loads were of a most miscellaneous character. The supplies of food for ourselves and the fish for our dogs generally constituted the heaviest part. For cooking our food and making tea for all, we had a supply of kettles as well as a quantity of unbreakable dishes. Then there were our axes, of which we had to take a liberal supply, as we were continually breaking them on account of the intense frost, making the steel almost as brittle as glass. Some guns and ammunition were also in our loads although not nearly as much as on a summer trip. Then we would expect to find sufficient game to keep our pot boiling, but now in this bitter winter weather there was but little game. So our guns were more carried now, as a precautionary measure against prowling grey wolves that could make themselves troublesome at times and give us an exciting hour or two, or even a whole sleepless night. Our bedding constituted no inconsiderable part of our loads. To sleep out in the open air in a hole scooped out in a snow drift, and the cold so intense that the mercury is frozen in our thermometers, requires for comfort a considerable amount of bedding. These blankets and fur robes add considerably to the bulk and weight of our loads. Then add to what has already been enumerated, medicines in case of sickness or accidents, articles to mend breakages to dog harness or sleds, a liberal supply of presents for the different bands of Indians we hope to visit, and our necessary changes of clothing, and it will be easily seen that a long trip by dog trains, is not a light or trifling undertaking. (244–49)

TRAVELING BY DOGSLED

William Haskell writes of dogsledding during the gold rush in the Yukon. He describes the manner of traveling by dogsled and gives some indication of the perils to both man and dog. He repeats the oft-stated claim that these dogs need be fed only once a day, despite the backbreaking labor required of them. Some writers claimed that dogs needed to be fed only three times a week. Haskell also recounts their thieving tendencies, seemingly, like his comrades, drawing no connection between sparse feedings and thievery as well as their eagerness to eat anything made out of leather.

FROM WILLIAM B. HASKELL, *TWO YEARS IN THE KLONDIKE AND ALASKAN GOLD-FIELDS*

(Hartford, CT: Hartford Publishing Co., 1898)

After observing something of the town, and making some arrangements for a temporary abode, Joe and I went back to our boat, where we learned other facts concerning the ways and possibilities of the country. While we were away the dogs had swam out to our boat, chewed off the rope by which it was held, and dragged it ashore. There they tore open every sack of provisions we had, and, when we approached, were having a regular feast. They had even chewed up some of the flour sacks and the dishrag, the flavor of which was undoubtedly agreeable to them. Everything in the boat was wet, and the damage we figured up to amount to forty dollars. Everyone who gets along well in Alaska must have a proper understanding of dogs, and a few facts concerning them may be established at this point, though the pioneer may not acquire a complete knowledge of them until he has been some time in the country.

Dogs are fed here but once a day, unless they find an opportunity to feed themselves, and they rarely let an available opportunity slip, even if they have to bite through a tin can or climb a pole. They are fed dried fish, whenever it can be obtained; if unobtainable, bacon and flour. All provisions must be set up on a cache, and that should be as high as possible, or they will climb up to it when there is no one at hand to disturb them. They will lie down innocently enough near a tent, watching and waiting for hours for the owner to leave and give them a chance to ransack it. I have known them to come into my tent, go up to a boiling pot of beans on the stove, push off the cover, take out the piece of bacon, and walk off with their tails curled up over their backs in the most nonchalant manner.

But they are too precious to shoot. They are a prime necessity in Alaska, and are sometimes worth almost their weight in gold. They do nearly all the packing in the summer, and they will carry from forty to fifty pounds, keeping up with a man. In the winter they do all the freighting, haul all the wood, and carry the mails. Harnessed tandem to sleds—and I have seen twenty in a single string—they will go anywhere, ninety miles from Circle City to the mines, or a thousand to Juneau, and if a man wishes to take out for a drive one of the few young ladies of the city who conforms to his ideas of respectability, and whose acquaintance is, therefore, of considerable value, he rigs up a couple of dog teams, for Yukon sleds hold but one, and off they go. But there is very little driving for pleasure over the Arctic snows, though the experience is not without its delights, so unique are all the conditions. (165–67)

· · ·

Two good dogs will haul from five to six hundred pounds on a good trail, and run twenty-five miles in six hours, and they will haul a man from forty to fifty miles a day and show little sign of weariness. A native Yukon dog is much more valuable than any importation because they endure the climate so much better. The natives are of all colors, and most of them have very long hair, as fine as wool. They look like wolves, but they rarely bite or bark at persons. They simply howl. They are faithful to the last degree in their work, and have that single failing—they are born thieves.

Buckskin moccasins are provided by many owners to keep the feet of the faithful little animals from becoming raw and sore on the ice and snow. They are made like a child's stocking, about nine inches long. Sometimes pack-saddles are used, whereby a dog can carry from ten to twenty pounds, besides drawing a sled. A dog harness commonly weighs a little over two pounds. The collar, which is usually made of leather, faced with sheepskin, and stuffed with deer hair, slips over the dog's head—fumbling with buckles would be severe on the fingers in Arctic weather—and on each collar are rings, to which the traces are attached. These traces are usually made of heavy web material, otherwise the dogs would eat them up. They have an insatiable appetite for leather, and will devour their collars if they are allowed a chance. They have to be kept separate when harnessed, or they will eat each other's collars, and when the web traces become oily they will eat them. They are so adroit that, sooner or later, even with the most careful master, they will devour their trappings. An Arctic appetite is something enormous in a man, but it is completely distanced by that of a dog.

An old prospector in Alaska told me that once when he was driving a pair of native dogs one of them slipped his collar while he was camping for the night near Fort Yukon, and ate up a pair of large gauntlet gloves, all the leather off a snow-shoe, a whip, and a part of the handle, a long leather strap on a gun case, and the leather binding on the canvas case, and badly chewed a part of the harness. When the man got up in the morning the dog was asleep, and never showed any signs of the night's dissipation. But these dogs will do a good day's work on four pounds of dried fish. (167–68)

• • •

A good leader is generally placed ahead, but dogs will often lie down in the trail unless kept going. They are driven with a dogwhip, a device which is a miracle in the hands of an expert, but a dangerous thing in the hands of a novice. It has a handle about nine inches long, and a lash about thirty feet long, and weighs four pounds. The lash is made of folded and plaited seal-hide, and for five feet from the handle averages about one and a half inches in diameter; then, for fourteen feet, it gradually tapers off, ending in a single thong half an inch thick and eleven feet long. When traveling the lash drags along at full length behind, and, when the driver wishes to make use of it, he gives a skillful jerk and twist of the wrist which cause the lash to fly forward, the thick part first, the tapering end continuing the motion till it snaps at full length ahead. Sometimes it is merely snapped over the heads of the dogs as a reminder or warning, but a skillful driver can pick out any dog in a team and touch almost any spot on a dog's back, and, if hit just right, the fur will fly. But till the driver is used to the management of this weapon, he is liable to receive most of the injury himself, for when awkwardly thrown the lash may wind about him like a snake and inflict painful injuries on his own face.

The standard sled for an Arctic traveler consists of a narrow box four feet long, the front half being covered or boxed in, mounted on a board eight feet long, resting on runners. In this box the passenger sits, wrapped in skins so that he can hardly move, with only his head and shoulders projecting. In front and behind and on top of the box is placed all the luggage, covered with canvas, and securely lashed, to withstand all the jolting and possible upsets, and the snow-shoes are kept within easy reach. (171)

• • •

The dogs are harnessed to the front of the sled, sometimes each by a separate trace. The nearest dog is about fifteen feet from the sled and the leader with bells on his neck, as far off as the number of dogs in the team. They are guided by the voice, using husky Esquimaux words, "owk"—go to the right; "arrah"—to the left; and "holt"—straight on. If the driver runs ahead on snow-shoes, as is frequently required, the dogs will follow him. (172)

• • •

It was a great day in Circle City, so they said, when the news of the Klondike richness came with such force and authenticity that even the skeptical old miners began to believe it and quietly made their plans to go up the river. It was carried down by J. M. Wilson, of the Alaska Commercial Company, and Thomas O'Brian, a trader, and they also had with them some of the Klondike gold. When it was seen that a few were starting, of course, nothing more was needed. It at once grew into a stampede. The price of dogs jumped almost out of sight. In a few days they were so valuable that they began to be sold by the pound, first at one dollar and fifty cents a pound, and then as high as two dollars and fifty cents. One man told me that he saw one dog sold for twenty ounces of gold dust, and, as in trade an ounce is worth seventeen dollars, the dog sold for three hundred and forty dollars. The purchaser was determined to go, and he had the money. He was bound to have dogs no matter what they cost. It was a melancholy time for the Circle City saloon-keepers, who saw the signs of prosperity vanish, but many of them joined in the rush for the new diggings. It was a melancholy time, also, for those who had failed to go up when the river was open, and now had not the means to buy the fancy-priced dogs, for they were too wise to think of setting out without at least four months' provisions, and it required dogs to drag that quantity over the rough ice of the Yukon in the face of the biting blasts of the dead of winter. Yet it was the greatest exodus that was ever known on the Yukon. As many as four hundred men and women worked their way up, and none of them lost their lives, though several had their faces and toes frozen. (285–86)

• • •

So many small parties had been going out that dogs were extremely scarce. The price had started at one hundred and fifty dollars, but had soon risen to two hundred dollars, and when we began to think about them they were worth about two hundred and fifty dollars. We smoked and thought again.

With good dogs we figured that we could reach the coast in about thirty days; without them it would take about forty under good conditions. But Alaskan travel is uncertain, with or without dogs. One thing, however, was certain; the dogs would eat up a good part of what they would draw before they reached the coast unless we made remarkably good time, so we concluded to save our money, even if we lost some time, and draw the sleds ourselves.

So one morning late in November we blade good-bye for a time to Dawson and the Klondike, and started for the coast in a blinding snow storm. The mercury bottles were frozen solid. The river was rougher than the rocky road to Dublin. It had frozen once, then broken up and frozen again so that it was all humps and bumps, and the only way to maintain a tolerably smooth course was to cross back and forth where the way seemed to open out best. In spite of every precaution the sleds were continually overturning while we were slipping and sprawling. Parties with dogs fared even worse. The dogs could go anywhere, but the sleds followed them sometimes right side up, but more often on one side. Many sleds were broken. Soon many of the dogs had badly lacerated feet, and in some cases they were frozen, so that we were rather glad we had concluded to depend upon ourselves, though the dog teams quickly got ahead of us and others overtook us.

All the way from Dawson to the mouth of the Pelly River the river was so rough that dogs were hardly able to haul more than enough to last them to the coast, and it was hard, cold drudgery for Joe and me. (507–8)

THE 1925 DIPHTHERIA RESCUE BY SLED DOGS

Twenty-seven years after sled dogs were used to support the gold mining of individuals that Jack London observed in the great Yukon gold rush of 1897, they were still being used by mining companies in Alaska. But in 1925, these sled dogs were called upon for a higher purpose: to bring diphtheria serum to isolated Nome, Alaska. At the time of this front-page, one-and-a-half-inch-headlined article in the *San Francisco Chronicle*, the fate of the diphtheria serum on its way to Nome was still gravely in question. The cause for alarm was a blizzard that hit Alaska as the team was traveling north, placing in danger the men and their dogs, severing communication, and threatening to freeze the serum or burst the containers.

As the article indicates, people were hoping for news of the team when it reached Solomon, but Gunnar Kaasen, the driver, never saw the sign posted for him at Solomon and thus never communicated with Ed Rohn, his contact at Safety. The desperation with which Dr. Welch and his fellow citizens waited for the serum in Nome intensified as the three initial cases of diphtheria grew to twenty-seven.

FROM "NOME DOGS BATTLE BLIZZARD"
(*San Francisco Chronicle*, Monday, February 2, 1925)

WIND CHECKS TEAMS WITH SERUM UNITS

Storm Makes Time of Arripal [*sic*] With Antitoxin Very Uncertain

New Cases Registered

Two Additional Victims of Diphtheria Await Arrival of Racers

NOME Alaska, Feb. 1 (by the Associated Press).—A blizzard is raging along the Bering sea coast today, the temperature hovering around 10 below zero and the wind blowing eighteen miles an hour and increasing rapidly. Communication lines are down and there was no means of ascertaining the whereabouts of the dog team with the antitoxin serum. The time of its arrival here has been rendered very uncertain.

At 5 o'clock this afternoon no word had been received here from the dog team. The storm will probably make it dangerous to travel at night, due to the chances of getting lost, in which event the anti-toxin serum might freeze, if it has not already frozen, and break the containers.

NOME, Feb. 1 (by the Associated Press).—Ed Rohn, with a fast race team, is waiting at Safety for the arrival of the relay team speeding toward Nome with 300,000 units of anti-toxin. Rohn will take the precious cargo from Safety to Nome, a distance of twenty-one miles, in record-breaking time.

No word has been received from the relay team since it left Unalakik, distant from Nome 200 miles by land, or 100 miles across Norton sound, yesterday.

Communication Between Alaska Towns Difficult

Communication between Unalakik and Solomon, 30 miles from Nome, is difficult and the relay team will probably not be heard from until it reaches Solomon.

If plans work perfectly, the anti-toxin will reach here late today.

Two new cases of diphtheria developed here yesterday afternoon, both children. This brings the total number of cases up to 27, a recheck by the board of health yesterday morning having shown 25 cases. Instead of 23 as previously reported.

Number of Contacts Is Not Officially Reported

The number of contacts has not been officially determined, but must be nearly 100. No more deaths are reported.

Special by Leased Wire to The Chronicle

NOME, Feb. 1.—Bearing life in their fleeting feet, the pick of the dog teams of the North are racing into Nome tonight with their load of anti-toxin.

As the speeding dogs near their goal the lives of twenty-five people, stricken with diphtheria in the epidemic that is sweeping Nome, swing in the balance. Three more victims were reported today.

Leonard Seppella, undefeated musher of the north, gave over his precious cargo to fresh relay teams this morning. Perhaps he has broken his record. He left Kaltag, 320 miles from Nome, Friday afternoon.

Nome is hanging on to the passing moments as the fresh dogs pick up the race. No one has learned at what point Seppella met the first of the fresh teams, but they have been placed in relays, several miles apart, along the last lap of the journey.

No such excitement has prevailed since the gold rush.

Veteran mushers were almost breathless in their anxiety when they learned that Seppella was going to make the dash across the frozen ice of Norton sound. This morning when word traveled along the relay line that he had made it, and that his cargo had been transferred to the first of the fresh teams, the sigh of relief was audible.

The champion's team of great huskies, the prize-winning dogs of the North, cut off twenty-five miles by the desperate race over the ice instead of running along the coast from the Norton bay station.

The temperature ran from 25 to 50 degrees below zero during Seppella's great run. (1–2)

NOTE

1. A musher is a sled driver. The story about the origin of the term is that the French drivers' yells of "Marche!" (or "Run!") was heard and repeated as "musher."

PROJECTS FOR ORAL OR WRITTEN EXPLORATION

1. Write a history of the life of Buck's ancestors from the scattered account in the novel. Use other accounts of the history of dogs found in the introduction and documents of this chapter to flesh out your history.

2. Prepare a class report on any one breed of dog. By consulting library resources as well as the Internet, make it as thorough as possible, including the history of the breed, its place of origin, physical and temperamental characteristics, the work it may have been used for, and its suitability as a pet.

3. Certain "wildlike" behavior manifests itself in some of the domestic dogs in *The Call of the Wild*. Discuss all the instances of this that you can find.

4. Compare and contrast sled-dog behavior in *The Call of the Wild* with similar examples in the documents of this chapter, for example, lead dogs breaking in newcomers.

5. Read London's earlier short story entitled "Bâtard," which he claimed was very different from the story of Buck. Compare and contrast this story with the novel, noting any concepts that are common to both works.

6. London has been said to "anthropomorphize" the dogs in *The Call of the Wild*; that is, he gives them human characteristics. Investigate the extent to which this is true, using two dogs in the novel. Mention other examples in present culture of anthropomorphizing animals.

7. London has sometimes been accused of plagiarizing the nonfictional work of Egerton Young, who is liberally quoted in this chapter. From reading the Young excerpts, how would you respond to the idea that London borrowed too heavily from Young? Consider tone and ideas as well as similar incidents.

8. Research the Iditarod using the Internet, archives of your own local paper, or the *New York Times* on microfilm. Has modern technology taken all the risk from dogsledding, or do the Iditarod drivers and their teams face many of the perils experienced by similar teams in the Yukon in 1897?

SUGGESTIONS FOR FURTHER READING

Allen, Glover. *Dogs of the American Aborigines*. Cambridge: Harvard University Museum, 1920.

Caldwell, Elsie Noble. *Alaska Trail Dogs*. New York: Richard R. Smith, 1945.

Clutton-Brock, J. *Domesticated Animals from Early Times*. London: Heinemann, 1981.

Coppinger, Lorna. *The World of Sled Dogs*. New York: Howell Book House, 1977.

Denlinger, Milo, Albert Heim, Mrs. Henry H. Hubble, Gerda Umlauff, and Joe Stetson. *The New Complete Saint Bernard*. 4th ed. New York: Howell Book House, 1973.

Drury, Mrs. Maynard K., ed. *This Is the Newfoundland*. 2nd ed. Jersey City, NJ: T.F.H. Publications, 1978.

Freedman, Lew. *Iditarod Classics*. Sausalito, CA: Epicenter Press, 1992.

Hart, Ernest H. *Encyclopedia of Dog Breeds*. Jersey City, NJ: T.F.H. Publications, 1968.

Jones, Tim. *The Last Great Race: The Iditarod*. Harrisburg, PA: Stackpole Books, 1988.

Lawrence, R. D. *The North Runner*. New York: Ballantine Books, 1980.

Serpell, James. *In the Company of Animals*. Oxford: Basil Blackwell, 1986.

Undermann, Kenneth A. *The Race to Nome*. New York: Harper and Row, 1963.

Vesey-Fitzgerald, Brian. *The Domestic Dog*. London: Routledge and Kegan Paul, 1957.

Zeuner, F. E. *A History of Domesticated Animals*. London: Hutchinson, 1963.

Web Sites

"The Road Ahead Project" Lathers Elementary School, 1999. http://www.nfie.org/ra/low/mi-gc/iditarod/html.

"Iditarod SuperSite" at Dogsled.com.2000. http://www.dogsled.com.

"Updates, History, Photos, Musher Bios" *Anchorage Daily News*, 1999. http://www.adn.con/pf/mushing/links.html.

5

Humans' Relationship with Animals: The Issue of Cruelty

Jack London explores the relationship between man and beast in many of his stories. In *The Call of the Wild*, he inquires into the specific theme of man's treatment of wolves and dogs. The suffering inflicted by man on the dogs in the novel is an issue that London painted in even more graphic detail in his other stories of the Yukon. Man is not alone in inflicting cruelty in the novel. Nature itself, including the dogs, is also shown as intensely cruel. But man must assume the greater blame because of his power over other animals—a power that he abuses.

HUMAN MASTERY OVER BUCK

The reader becomes aware in the early pages of *The Call of the Wild* that the human's power leads inevitably to cruelty. In the beginning of Buck's story, the power that Judge Miller holds over Buck is benign. But despite Buck's physical prowess, he is completely subject to his human owner. As a result of that ancient bargain wherein dogs relinquished their freedom in exchange for the food and shelter that man could provide, Buck is, in a sense, a privileged slave, albeit highly regarded, with no alternative than to be subjected to Judge Miller.

This places the dog in a vulnerable position. As long as the protective circle placed around the pet by a caring owner remains perfect, the animal fares well. But when death or illness or economic distress or (as in this case) the briefest inattention creates even a temporary crack in this protective circle, the dog, no longer self-sufficient because of his ancestors' ancient bargain, is open to attack. While the judge is temporarily away, Buck's trust in man gives Manuel power over him, enabling Manuel to betray him by luring him away from the judge's house and attaching a rope to his collar.

Once the bargain has been made between man and dog, man is able to secure mastery over the dog. For man still has the cunning that is blunted in the trusting domesticated dog; thus the ease with which Manuel turns Buck over to his torturers. Man's special kind of intelligence and his physique allow him to use with greater facility than other animals certain tools—the chain, the whip, the gun, and especially in *The Call of the Wild*, the club—to secure his mastery over the dog. These tools become extensions of man and, like his control of the dog's food and shelter, opportunities for abuse. The story of Buck follows the pattern found in the history of mankind's power over the dog: Manuel's trickery and Buck's trust lead to the rope on the collar, the cage, and the club, first wielded by the man in red.

ANIMAL CRUELTY IN *THE CALL OF THE WILD*

Although Buck is a valuable commodity, he is subject to extreme cruelty and neglect after his kidnapping, in the course of his move to and through the Yukon. The first instance occurs when the man to whom Manuel sells him twists the rope attached to his collar:

> Then the rope tightened mercilessly, while Buck struggled in a fury, his tongue lolling out of his mouth and his great chest panting futilely. . . . But his strength ebbed, his eyes glazed, and he knew nothing when the train was flagged and the two men threw him into the baggage car. (3)

For several days he receives no food or water and is constantly tormented: "the ill treatment had flung him into a fever, which was fed by the inflammation of his parched and swollen throat and tongue" (4). Then he is attacked with a club by the man in red:

A dozen times he charged, and as often the club broke the charge
and smashed him down.

After a particularly fierce blow, he crawled to his feet, too dazed
to rush. He staggered limply about, the blood flowing from nose
and mouth and ears, his beautiful coat sprayed and flecked with
bloody slaver. Then the man advanced and deliberately dealt him a
frightful blow on the nose. All the pain he had endured was as
nothing compared with the exquisite agony of this. (5–6)

The dogs are consistently overworked and underfed and, after
falling into the hands of Charles and Hal, are treated brutally. The
loads they are required to pull are far in excess of their abilities.
Dub, one of the dogs, wrenches his shoulder blade and is shot.
Then the food runs out and the dogs begin starving one by one:

And through it all Buck staggered along at the head of the team as
in a nightmare. He pulled when he could; when he could no longer
pull, he fell down and remained down till blows from whip or club
drove him to his feet again. (38)

Finally, Hal's cruelty is on the brink of killing Buck:

So greatly had he suffered, and so far gone was he, that the blows
did not hurt much. And as they continued to fall upon him, the
spark of life within flickered and went down. It was nearly out. He
felt strangely numb. As though from a great distance, he was aware
that he was being beaten. The last sensations of pain left him. He
no longer felt anything, though very faintly he could hear the impact
of the club upon his body. (40)

CRUELTY FROM INCOMPETENCE

Dogs were abused by both the Yukon natives and the outsiders
flooding into the area looking for gold. The Indians reportedly
rarely fed their dogs adequately, and hunger led the dogs to try to
eat their own harnesses.

Prospecting miners also starved their dogs. Dogs were usually
the last to be fed. Routinely, even with the heavy work they per-
formed, dogs were fed at the most once a day. Drivers sometimes
claimed that dogs needed to be fed only three times a week. In
hard times when food was scarce, dogs would not be fed at all,

would be fed to each other, or would be eaten by their drivers. This last fact was listed as one of the great advantages of taking dogs to the Yukon: they could not only pull heavy loads, but could be the source of food for both men and dogs. In the summer of 1897, the crush of people in Dawson, coupled with inadequate supplies, created a severe famine in the entire area, and the thousands of dogs in the area suffered horribly. Chroniclers recalled seeing hundreds and hundreds of starving dogs roaming the streets of Dawson. It was said that one could travel from one end of Dawson to the other on the backs of dead animals.

Some of the cruelty to dogs and horses was a result of incompetence and ignorance. This partially accounts for the behavior of Hal and company in *The Call of the Wild*. Their attempt to get the dogs to break the sled out of the ice, their overloading of the sled, their taking more dogs than they could feed, and traveling over unstable ice are all examples.

Many other such examples can be found in the accounts of travelers to the Yukon. Old and sick horses, mules, and donkeys were driven over White Pass, often incorrectly reined, saddled, and shod, inadequately fed, and invariably thrown off balance by excessively heavy loads on the perilous and narrow trails. Such ignorance accounted for some three thousand deaths of pack animals on the pass. Often animals who broke their legs or fell down crevasses were not even mercifully shot, but were left to a slow, agonizing death.

Incompetence and ignorance also caused the suffering of dogs. With dogs at a premium, many prospectors just brought to the Yukon whatever dogs were at hand. Many of these were also too old or ill to pull heavy loads or to survive the cold. In far too many cases, those on a stampede to the gold mines in the Yukon would bring shorthaired dogs that were completely unsuited for survival in subarctic weather. It is no wonder that eyewitnesses reported seeing greyhounds, Chihuahuas, and other shorthaired dogs frozen to death before they even began their treks up the Chilkoot Pass to the gold fields. There were reports of death by freezing of many of even the most densely furred dogs. Even those dogs more suited for the climate died from being overworked, incorrectly harnessed, and unprotected by owners who were ignorant of the ways of the subarctic.

But incompetence and irresponsibility were not the only causes of violent cruelty in the Yukon. Dog drivers invariably took out their frustrations on their animals in gratuitous acts of cruelty. Repeatedly, eyewitnesses to life in the Yukon during the gold rush recalled incidents of extreme cruelty, especially when travel to the gold fields did not go as smoothly as planned. Dogs were beaten to death in their traces when they were physically unable to move, not only with whips, but with clubs. Dogs were kicked to death, knifed, and thrown against walls or the frozen ground. Jack London did not exaggerate the painful life led by this valuable animal.

CRUELTY AND GREED

What provokes man's cruelty to creatures over which he has power? The most obvious reason given in *The Call of the Wild* is greed. Manuel's greed for money to pay his gambling debts, the kidnappers' greed for profit from the sale of an exceptional dog, the dog breaker's greed for a fee for his services, Perrault and François's greed for the salary that they can take home by driving their dogs in record time, and the three incompetents' greed for gold all attest to the underlying avarice in man's behavior. Greed leads men to starve, overwork, choke, club, and whip the dogs under their control.

REJECTION OF THE TRADITIONAL RELATIONSHIP WITH MANKIND

In a sense, for a creature like Buck, domestication and loss of freedom have in themselves become a form of cruel oppression. At the conclusion of the novel, Buck returns to the wild, joining the wolves. When he approaches members of the pack, the dog alters his position in the world and rejects his dependence on and subservience to humans. He is no longer man's work dog, no longer man's slave, no longer man's pet, not even man's companion. In fact, he no longer lives in man's world at all.

A CULTURE OF CRUELTY TO ANIMALS

The cruelty to animals in the Yukon, while it occurred on a massive scale, was scarcely uncharacteristic of human behavior toward animals at the time. Animal literature in the nineteenth century and when London was writing his novel just after the turn of the twentieth century is filled with tales of the suffering routinely inflicted on animals by humans. Many of the accounts described unadulterated and routinely conducted sadism perpetrated out of rage or for amusement. Mark Twain's portrait of Arkansas in *Adventures of Huckleberry Finn* includes a scene of men encouraging dogs to attack a nursing sow and "putting turpentine on a stray dog and setting fire to him" (Chapter 21). Stephen Crane, in "The Dark-Brown Dog," writes of a tormented puppy in a poverty-stricken household of adult drunks, one of whom eventually slings the dog out of a fifth-story window. Even the one human who cared for the pup had taken delight in continually beating him. Other such accounts of typical behavior, at that time unpunishable by law, are too grim to linger over.

Some instances of cruelty to animals arose from neglect and irresponsibility—animals kept chained, unclean, and starved. Other instances of cruelty were less sadistic, if equally senseless in that they did and do feed the human mania for fashion. For instance, horses were placed in reins that painfully forced their heads up at an unnatural angle because it was the fashion. The tails and ears of dogs were docked without anesthesia to create a distinctive, fashionable look. Wild animals suffered excruciating pain in traps designed to secure fur for fashionable coats. Baby harp seals were clubbed to death to provide humans with their much-coveted white fur. Sports, only some of which are illegal, did and do often result in excruciating pain for animals, whether they be certain means of hunting, cockfighting, bullfighting, dogfighting, rodeos, dog-track racing, or circus acts.

In the process of providing society with the food of animals, many practices resulted in or result in pain for animals: the raising of chickens or young calves for veal in pens that restrict all movement, the castrating of cattle without anesthesia, the branding of cattle, or the painfully slow and haphazard killing in the slaughterhouse. Even now, much of this cruelty is condoned by law because it is conducted in the process of providing humans with a product, that is, food or clothing.

MAN AS THE CENTER OF THE UNIVERSE

The toleration of cruelty to animals in the United States in the nineteenth and early twentieth centuries has much to do with the character of Western culture itself and its view of nature, including animals. The Western world tended philosophically to separate man and nature, the natural and the spiritual, into separate entities. Therefore, rather than embracing the oneness of all things, humans tended to see themselves as set apart from other creatures. Animals, it was argued, had no souls and were of "lower" orders. To call a man an "animal" or a "brute" or a "beast" is an insult. To call him "humane" is praise. Spirit and soul were reserved for man, and in man's pursuit of spirit, it is his aim to rise above the natural world and animals. This separation of the world into lower and higher entities tended to give humans a callous and superior attitude toward animals, as if to say, "Animals are not in our camp and are less admirable than we are, so we can treat them as we like."

This dual view of the world has its roots in the Greeks, who argued that animals were created for man's pleasure and use. This theory of animals continued in the Judeo-Christian tradition. Man was viewed as the center of the universe, and a separation and moral/spiritual hierarchy emerged. The view clearly set forth in Genesis is that man was made in God's image and the animals were created for man to use in any way he wanted. God intended for nature to be exploited by humans. Since animals were thought to have no souls, feelings, or intellect, to ponder treating them in an ethical fashion was silly and pointless. In both the Old and New Testaments the most pejorative phrase that can be applied to a human is being "like a dog." The one conspicuous exception to this way of thinking in Christian history was St. Francis of Assisi.

Nor did animals fare much better with less religious thinkers. French philosophers in the eighteenth century buttressed the idea that animals were altogether separated from human beings. Animals other than man were little more than feelingless machines. The philosophers argued that while even the stupidest human communicated with a language, even the most intelligent animal had no language. Therefore, they argued, machines, that is, animals, were deficient in feelings, intelligence, and soul. The conclusion they reached was that such creatures could have no rights because machines could have no rights, and humans did not need to worry themselves about treating lower animals with compassion.

As a result of these views, Robert S. Brumbaugh writes, between 1637 and 1859, with the emergence of the machine and the Industrial Revolution, animals began to disappear. "Less efficient than tractors, more ornamental dead than alive (as hat plumes or shoe leather), and more useful as food sources, they became dispensable" ("Of Man, Animals, and Morals: A Brief History," in *On the Fifth Day*, edited by Richard Knowles Morris and Michael W. Fox [Washington, DC: Acropolis Books, 1978], 15).

The idea that began to challenge this view of the separation between animals and man was evolution, proposed by Charles Darwin primarily in *On the Origin of Species* in 1859 and in *The Descent of Man* in 1871 and summarized by Harvard professor Asa Gray in 1880 in *Natural Science and Religion*. In arguing that higher orders evolved from lower orders and in stressing the similarities and continuities between man and beast, science supported the belief that we are one and need to have consideration for one another. It is interesting to note that by the time Jack London was in the Yukon in 1897, he was already familiar with Darwin's theories, promulgated in America by Asa Gray less than twenty years earlier but rejected by Christianity. Much more slowly, science also came to endorse what many workers with animals had long observed: animals do have feelings—of grief and affection, for instance. Animals do exhibit considerable intelligence. Animals do have languages of their own.

Another view of animals that allowed humans to inflict pain on them with impunity was the concept of animals as property. Especially with the rise of capitalism, a person's rights in his property were sacred. A person's property could not be infringed upon by others, whether that property was a factory, a bank account, land, slaves, or animals. Slave owners were allowed, by and large, to beat and torture slaves because slaves were their property to do with as they pleased. For the same reason, there was and is a reluctance to interfere with the brutal treatment of animals by their owners. Note, for example, that in a moment of horrible brutality in *The Call of the Wild*, when John Thornton objects to Hal's clubbing of Buck into insensibility, Hal retorts, "It's my dog" (41).

CONFRONTING CRUELTY TO ANIMALS

There are hints in *The Call of the Wild* that humans were not insensitive to cruelty to animals. A group gathers to watch Hal and company attempt with a whip to get exhausted dogs to pull an overloaded sled that is frozen to the ground. One of that group tells Hal and Charles that the dogs need a rest. Another is obviously furious about the whipping of the dogs:

> One of the onlookers, who had been clenching his teeth to suppress hot speech, now spoke up.—
>
> "It's not that I care a whoop what becomes of you, but for the dogs' sakes, I just want to tell you, you can help them a mighty lot by breaking out that sled." (34)

The only protection of animals, so brutally misused in the Yukon, comes in the form of risky individual intervention. This we see when John Thornton intervenes on Buck's behalf by disarming Hal and cutting Buck from the traces. Indeed, in much of the United States, the only protection animals had came in the form of rare intervention on the part of private citizens who witnessed abuse.

PROTECTION SOCIETIES

Until 1960, when the Humane Slaughter Act was passed insisting on the humane slaughter of most animals, laws protecting animals were (and largely still are) local matters passed by counties or city governments at the urging of protection societies and were enforced only sporadically. At the time of the publication of *The Call of the Wild*, the "law" of property superseded most attempts to protect animals from cruel treatment.

No single individual is better known for altering the way in which Americans regarded animals and for pioneering the prevention of cruelty to animals than Henry Bergh. Born in 1813 to a wealthy and aristocratic family in New York, from his childhood Bergh was conscious of and objected to the pain inflicted on animals by people. As an adult, Bergh sought the advice of similar-minded Englishmen who were considerably ahead of Americans in organizing for the prevention of cruelty to animals. A British Society for the Prevention of Cruelty to Animals was formed in 1824 and received royal endorsement from Queen Victoria in 1840. In the spring of 1865, Bergh, who had decided to establish a similar organization in the United States, called on the earl of Harrowby, the president of the renamed society, the Royal Society for the Prevention of Cruelty to Animals. Bergh returned home determined to work on his project, and on April 10, 1866, he received a charter from New York State for the American Society for the Prevention of Cruelty to Animals (ASPCA), the first organization for the protection of animals in the United States. Nine days later, on April 19, the first law prohibiting cruelty to animals was passed in New York State. While jurisdiction of the law was limited to New York State, the ASPCA inspired similar societies throughout the country.

The second most active society was organized in Massachusetts two years later, in 1868, by George Thorndike Angell, a Boston attorney. With the help of Bergh, Angell was also able to get laws enacted forbidding cruelty to animals. Angell believed that the key to preventing cruelty to animals was education. To this end, he established a house newsletter entitled *Our Dumb Animals* and in 1881 organized a network of clubs designed to educate and involve children in anticruelty measures.

These two societies were important first steps for holding some people discovered to be cruel to animals accountable in court. Unfortunately, the courts resisted the enforcement of the law in far too many cases. Judges, reflecting the general attitudes of the community, decided that certain creatures (like turtles) were not technically animals. Sometimes they ruled that the animals in question did not feel pain, or it was decided that the animals enjoyed their abuse (as was argued in the case of roosters or dogs used in fights for human sport). Sometimes it was argued that a measure of cruelty to animals should be tolerated to provide for the wants or needs of humans—as, for example, in raising, bringing to market, and slaughtering animals for food.

Bergh was able to make much gratuitous cruelty to animals—that is, the infliction of cruelty on an animal for no reason, as when someone chained up a dog and left it to starve—illegal and punishable. However, cruelty to animals inflicted in the course of legally sanctioned activities (such as castrating or dehorning cattle without anesthesia in the course of preparing them for human consumption) was not considered legally cruel or prosecutable. But Bergh was a determined advocate for animals and remained a thorn in the side of those he viewed as causing animals unnecessary pain.

By 1873, over half the states in the United States had some kind of anticruelty society based on the ASPCA. In addition to the creation and enforcement of laws and educational programs, the activities of these societies included the maintaining of animal hospitals and shelters and the design of more humane equipment used in slaughterhouses and animal work situations.

PLEAS IN LITERATURE FOR PREVENTION OF CRUELTY TO ANIMALS

Prior to the publication of Jack London's *Call of the Wild*, two nineteenth-century animal novels stand out as pleas for the prevention of cruelty to animals. One is Anna Sewell's *Black Beauty*, a novel subtitled *The "Uncle Tom's Cabin" of the Horse* and described as arguably the most important and influential anti-cruelty novel ever written. In 1877, Sewell, who was dying at the time, dictated the novel to her mother. She never lived to know the phenomenal success of her work, which was sponsored by the Massachusetts SPCA and sold around 250,000 copies annually. *Black Beauty* has for well over a century continually been reprinted in numerous editions and made into films, one considered a film classic.

Black Beauty is the story of a horse told in the first person from the horse's point of view. It resulted in specific legislation concerning horses and was responsible for altering public attitudes toward the condition of all animals and arousing greater public sympathy for laws to lessen the pain suffered by animals.

Black Beauty heightened the public's sympathy for horses (like Ginger in the novel) who were beaten and overworked, forced to carry excessively heavy loads until they died. It opened the readers' eyes to the fact that the mean temper of animals was usually the result of cruel treatment. But the real eye-opener for readers of the novel was the pain caused to the horse by ordinary, accepted customs, justified only in the interest of tradition and fashion: tail bobbing, blinkers, double bits, check reins, risky jumps during hunting, and what Beauty calls his loss of liberty when he is shut up in a stall.

Sewell also mentioned the cruelty suffered by other animals. Her scene of the hunting of a rabbit, in which the dogs descend on the creature and Beauty says with horror, "We heard one shriek" (5), resonates in *The Call of the Wild.* Sewall also devotes a long paragraph to the inhumane docking of dogs' tails and ears.

The other nineteenth-century novel that is an argument for humane treatment of animals is *Beautiful Joe*, Margaret Marshall Saunders's 1893 novel about a dog that was published only four years before Jack London went to the Yukon. Like *Black Beauty*, *Beautiful Joe* is an unapologetic polemic for the prevention of cruelty to animals and support for humane societies. It is dedicated to George Thorndike Angell, the society he founded, and the American Band of Mercy, an educational society founded by Angell. Like *Black Beauty*, it is also told in the first person from an animal's point of view, in this case a dog's. Joe suggests that his inspiration for the story was a book admired by his mistress that is "the story of a horse's life," an obvious reference to *Black Beauty*. Like the horse, Joe decides that "it will help a little [to end cruelty to animals] if I tell a story" (2).

The early pages of Joe's story document the cruelty he suffered under the ownership of Jenkins, a wicked milkman. Cruelty to animals was often ignored because, it was argued, animals had no language, no feelings, no soul. But Saunders, in giving her animal narrator a voice, also gives him feelings. The first-person nature of the account elicits our sympathy for the puppy who is both physically and psychologically scarred. He is kicked repeatedly as a puppy, and his mother is whipped until she is covered with blood and scars. Even worse, Jenkins brutally kills all Joe's tiny siblings in front of their mother and, in a rage, chops off Joe's tail and ears with a hatchet.

Advocates of humane treatment of animals often argued that humans who mistreated animals also abused fellow humans. This argument is set forth in the character of Jenkins, who not only abuses his dogs, cows, and horses, but mistreats his wife and children and is later discovered to be a dangerous thief.

In the response of a young man, Harry, to Jenkins's attack on Joe, the reader sees that a single individual can make a difference by intervening on behalf of a defenseless animal. We also see that there are laws to protect Jenkins's animals and punish their torturer—laws put in place by societies to prevent cruelty to animals.

Several pertinent issues are taken up in the course of Joe's narrative. The description of the Morris household in which the relationship to animals is an ideal one is exceptional. The book addresses part of the philosophy behind toleration of cruelty to animals and answers to it as well: actions taken in response to the problem of cruelty to animals.

Many of the situations mentioned in the novel are ones that, the characters say, may never have been perceived as cruelty by most citizens. A few examples include the deliberate or accidental shootings of hunting dogs; the training of dogs to fight; the cramming of cattle into railway cars; the careless and painful killing of animals for food; the use of cruel traps for wild animals; the misfitting of reins and shoes on horses; the overdosing of horses and dogs; and the abandonment of animals.

Behind the toleration of this cruelty is the Christian notion that animals are creatures without souls who will not go to heaven. Therefore, somehow, how humans treat them is of no consequence. Another rationale for condoning cruel behavior is given voice by a young gentleman in the story who argues that they were put on earth to suffer and die in the course of being used by man. If animals are not killed, he says, they will overrun the earth.

The first argument is addressed by three of the more humane characters in the novel, Laura, Maxwell, and Harry, who agree that while there is no biblical proof that animals go to heaven, many of their owners could scarcely regard heaven as heavenly without the presence of their beloved animals. Further, they decide, the question of whether or not animals go to heaven should have nothing at all to do with how we treat them on earth. Indeed, it is after this conversation that these characters decide to devote their lives to preventing cruelty to animals.

The second argument, that animals must suffer and die in the service of man, is answered by an elderly gentleman who concedes that animals may have been put on earth for use by man and that animals may have to die to serve man. But, he retorts, there is no reason why they have to suffer in the course of working and dying: "The Lord made the sheep, and the cattle, and the pigs. They are His creatures just as much as we are. We can kill them, but we've no right to make them suffer" (105).

A number of characters in the novel, like Harry, who rescues Joe, make it a policy in their everyday lives to do what they can to stop cruelty to animals. In addition, the author makes reference to the group effort to eradicate cruelty to animals. She mentions whole communities who attempt to rid themselves of cruel behavior, and the Band of Mercy and the Boston American Humane Education Society, which encourage young people to work in the best interests of animals.

THE CURRENT ISSUE OF CRUELTY

While a few people like Saunders, Sewell, Angell, Bergh, and their followers were concerned about many kinds of cruelty to animals, throughout the nineteenth century and well into the twentieth century during Jack London's life, cruelty to animals, especially to those used for food, work, and sport, was widespread and largely ignored by the general population. Only in the most blatant cases—beatings, starving, or torturing, for instance—would an ordinary private citizen take note or, even more rarely, intervene to stop the abuse.

However, in 1954, the Humane Society of the United States was formed to represent the interests of animals. In 1960, one of the first pieces of national legislation was signed into law to prevent cruelty to animals. This was the Humane Slaughter Act, first introduced by Senator Hubert Humphrey. Other legislation in the last half of the twentieth century passed to prevent cruelty to animals includes laws concerning both wild and domesticated horses, laboratory animals, zoo and aquarium animals, marine mammals, dogs and cocks (often chosen for fighting), fur seals, farm animals, calves raised for veal, and wild birds.

ANIMAL WELFARE AND ANIMAL RIGHTS

Two approaches to human responsibility to animals are in evidence at the turn of the twenty-first century. The animal welfare movement, which was first formalized in the United States in the nineteenth century, accepts the use and even the slaying of animals, for example, as food, to perform work, in entertainment, in the sport of hunting, and in scientific experimentation, but insists that such use be accomplished without causing unnecessary pain to the animal. Thus a worker in the animal welfare camp would acknowledge that animals must be raised and slaughtered for food, but would insist that such animals not be jammed into pens and railway cars, that they not be raised in cruel conditions of confinement, and that they not be slaughtered irresponsibly and painfully.

A more radical view of animal protection arose in the last decades of the twentieth century. This position, the animal rights movement, differs from the long-standing animal welfare movement in its refusal to condone any exploitation of animals by humans for food or in scientific research, entertainment, and sport. This last school of thought has been marked in recent decades by more militant advocates of animal liberation who, in addition to accepted methods of boycotting, have at times used violent means to halt cruelty to animals. They have resorted on occasion to illegal entry into scientific laboratories to release animals used in scientific research, the sabotage of these laboratories, and the symbolic throwing of red paint on fur coats worn by men and women.

The issue of humankind's relation to animals, raised by Jack London's *Call of the Wild*, is explored in the following documents. Excerpts from the Book of Genesis illustrate the Judeo-Christian attitude that animals exist to serve mankind. Several selections show the hard lives of animals in the Yukon, especially during the gold rush when the fictional dog Buck worked there. Included as well are a paragraph on dogs in *Black Beauty* and a selection from the mission statement of People for the Ethical Treatment of Animals (PETA), which works to prevent cruelty to animals.

GENESIS: THE WESTERN-WORLD TRADITION

The following verses from Genesis, the first book of the Old Testament, present part of the story of God's creation of the earth in the Garden of Eden. Next, man is created. Man is different from the other creatures in that he is created in the image of God—to look like God—which from the first implies that man has a status and a consecration that the other creatures lack. Then, according to the biblical story, man is given unlimited power over all other creatures and is told to "subdue" the earth. These sentiments are repeated in the story of Noah when God reminds him again that he is a special creation of God who has been given all the rest of creation to do with as he will.

These verses and others like them reinforce the sentiment in Western thought that man is at the center of the universe and that all the rest of creation exists for his use. Within certain rules for cleanliness, then, man was given by his religion free reign to slaughter and eat animals, harness them and load them to help him in work, and use them to amuse him in any way he wanted. If in the course of using animals, it became inconvenient or tiresome to treat them humanely or if it amused him to give them pain, there was no religious prohibition directing him otherwise.

FROM THE FIRST BOOK OF MOSES CALLED GENESIS IN THE
KING JAMES VERSION OF THE BIBLE

CHAPTER ONE

20 And God said, Let the waters bring forth abundantly the moving creature that hath life, and fowl *that* may fly above the earth in the open firmament of heaven.

21 And God created great whales, and every living creature that moveth, which the waters brought forth abundantly, after their kind, and every winged fowl after his kind: and God saw that *it was* good.

22 And God blessed them, saying, Be fruitful, and multiply, and fill the waters in the seas, and let fowl multiply in the earth.

23 And the evening and the morning were the fifth day.

24 And God said, Let the earth bring forth the living creature after

his kind, cattle, and creeping thing, and beast of the earth after his kind: and *it was* so.

25   And God made the beast of the earth after his kind, and cattle after their kind, and every thing that creepeth upon the earth after his kind: and God saw that *it was* good.

26   And God said, Let us make man in our image, after our likeness: and let them have dominion over the fish of the sea, and over the fowl of the air, and over the cattle, and over all the earth, and over every creeping thing that creepeth upon the earth.

27   So God created man in his *own* image, in the image of God created he him; male and female created he them.

28   And God blessed them, and God said unto them, Be fruitful, and multiply, and replenish the earth, and subdue it: and have dominion over the fish of the sea, and over the fowl of the air, and over every living thing that moveth upon the earth.

29   And God said, Behold, I have given you every herb bearing seed, which *is* upon the face of all the earth, and every tree, in the which *is* the fruit of a tree yielding seed; to you it shall be for meat.

30   And to every beast of the earth, and to every fowl of the air, and to every thing that creepeth upon the earth, wherein *there is* life, *I have given* every green herb for meat: and it was so.

• • •

CHAPTER NINE

1   And God blessed Noah and his sons, and said unto them, Be fruitful, and multiply, and replenish the earth.

2   And the fear of you and the dread of you shall be upon every beast of the earth, and upon every fowl of the air, upon all that moveth *upon* the earth, and upon all the fishes of the sea; into your hand are they delivered.

3   Every moving thing that liveth shall be meat for you; even as the green herb have I given you all things.

• • •

6   Whoso sheddeth man's blood, by man shall his blood be shed: for in the image of God made he man.

TREATMENT OF SLED DOGS IN THE YUKON

With a much more sensitive eye than the writers in Chapter Four, H. M. Robinson, who traveled with dogs for the Hudson's Bay Company long before the gold rush, shows us in the following passages something of what this work was like for the dog—something of the sled dog's life in the Arctic. Notice the beatings he records (with sympathy for the dog) and the general brutality with which the drivers generally drove dogs beyond the limit of their endurance.

FROM H. M. ROBINSON, *THE GREAT FUR LAND; OR, SKETCHES OF LIFE IN THE HUDSON'S BAY TERRITORY*
(New York: G. P. Putnam's Sons, 1879)

To begin my journey, I purchased a board about nine feet long and sixteen inches wide, which was duly steamed and turned up at one end. To it wooden bows were fastened, while over it was stretched a stout covering of raw-hide. This accomplished, the board resembled the front of a slipper. To complete the likeness, a heel-top was made by attaching an upright back about two feet from the rear end, and extending the raw-hide covering to it. Then the shoe was submitted to an Indian friend, who decorated its outer surface with mystical emblems in red and yellow pigments, covering the whole with a coating of oil. When the motive power was furnished, the ship would be ready to sail.

The selection of the propelling force was more difficult of accomplishment. Dogs of high and low degree were brought for inspection; for dogs in the North have but one occupation—to haul. From the Esquimaux down through all the stages of canine life to the Indian mongrel, all are alike doomed to labor before a sledge of some kind during the winter months; all are destined to howl under the beatings of a brutal driver; to tug wildly at the moose-skin collar; to haul until they can haul no longer, and then to die. When I look back at the long line of seared and whip-marked heads, whose owners were put through their best paces in demonstration of their perfect fitness for the work, what a host of sadly-resigned faces rises up before me! There were heads lacking an ear, an eye; heads bearing the marks of blows with sticks, whips, the heels of boots; heads that had been held down and beaten out of all semblance of life; the heads yet all bleeding and torn with the brutal lashings thought necessary to impart an air of liveliness before a probable purchaser! The same retrospect brings up the hybrid drivers of those dogs, upon the majority of whose countenances a painful indifference to suffering and an inherent brutality were plainly visible—dusky, athletic fellows, whose only method of dealing with the poor dog, who gave up everything in life for them, was by blows and fierce invective. (3–4)

• • •

Suppose . . . that the gently-undulating motion of the sledge, in accommodating itself to the inequalities of the frozen surface, which seemed so suggestive of a canoe floating cork-like upon rippling water, felt, now that one is seated in the sledge, like being dragged over a gravel-walk upon a sheet; or that the track has been completely snowed up, and the wretched dogs are unequal to the emergency. Mistatim, the leader, is willing, but young, thin, and weak; the middle one, Shoathinga, is aged and asthmatic; and the shafter, Kuskitaostiquarn, lame and lethargic. From morning till night the air resounds with howling and the cries of their drivers anathematizing Shoathinga and Kuskitaostiquarn. The sledges constantly upset from running against a stump or slipping over a hillside; and, when one hauls and strains to right them, the dogs lie quietly down, looking round at him, and not offering to pull an ounce to help. When the driver, aggravated beyond endurance, rushes up, stick in hand, and bent on punishment, they make frantic exertions, which only render matters worse, resuming their quiescent attitude the moment he returns again to haul at the sleigh. (8)

• • •

The snow having been cleared away by the toe of a snow-shoe used as a shovel, and our own supper prepared and eaten, we turned our attention to the dogs who had borne the burden if not the heat of the day; for the sledge-dog's day is one long tissue of trial. Put to a task from which his whole nature revolts, he is driven to the violation of every instinct by the continual lashings of a driver's whip. Before Night has lifted her sable mantle to shroud the stars, the sledge-dog has his slumbers rudely broken by the summons of his master. Close by the camp, under the protecting lee of stump or fallen tree, he has lain coiled in the roundest of balls during the night. Perhaps, if his lines are cast in pleasant places, he has encroached upon his driver's blanket, and contributed his vital heat to the comfort of that merciless functionary. Perhaps, too, the fast-falling flakes of the snow-storm have covered him in their soft folds, adding to his sense of warmth, and revealing his presence only in the shape of a rounded hillock of snow. He may, perchance, dream the dreams of peace and comfort, or imagine that his soft covering will render

him undistinguishable from the surrounding mass of white; to be awakened from his delusion by blow of whip-stock, a kick of the driver's foot,
and the stern command to find his place in the gaudy gear of moose-
skin and bells awaiting him—an ornamented and bedizened harness that
mocks the pathos of his whip-marked face and trembling figure. (13)

• • •

As the education of the Cree, so far as regarded the French language,
had seemingly been conducted with an eye single to the acquirement of
anathemas, which long practice enabled him to use with such effect that
the dogs instinctively dodged them as if they had been the sweep of a
descending lash, our speed at first was not materially affected by the
attempted haltings of the weary animals. But, as the storm increased in
violence, and the swirl of powdery snow swept in their faces, the dogs
turned about more frequently, and seized every opportunity of shirking.
Then ensued that inhuman thrashing and varied cursing, that howling of
dogs and systematic brutality of drivers, which make up the romance of
winter-travel, and degrade the driver lower than the brutes. The perversion of the dog from his true use to that of a beast of burden is productive
of countless forms of deception and cunning; but a life of bondage every-
where produces in the slave vices with which it is unfair to blame him.
Dogs are often stubborn and provoking, and require flogging until
brought into subjection; but lashings upon the body while laboring in
the trains, systematic floggings upon the head till their ears drop blood,
beatings with whip-stocks until nose and jaws are one deep wound, and
poundings with clubs and stamping with boots till their howls merge into
low wails of agony, are the frequent penalties of a slight deviation from
duty.

Of the four dogs attached to the provision-sledge, three underwent
repeated beatings at the hands of the Cree. By mid-afternoon the head
of Whiskey was reduced to a bleeding, swollen mass from tremendous
thrashings. Chocolat had but one eye wherewith to watch the dreaded
driver, and Brandy had wasted so much strength in wild lurches and
sudden springs, in order to dodge the descending whip, that he had none
remaining for the legitimate task of hauling the sledge. But one train of
dogs out of the six sledges fared better, and that one was composed of
animals of the Esquimaux breed. Fox-headed, long-furred, clean-legged,
whose ears, sharp-pointed and erect, sprang from a head imbedded in
thick tufts of woolly hair, hauling to them was as natural as to watch is
natural to the watch-dog. And of the whole race of dogs, the Esquimaux
alone should be made a hauling-dog. He alone looks happy in his work,
and is a good hauler; and although other dogs will surpass him in speed

for a few days, only he can maintain a steady pace throughout a long journey, and come in fresh at its end. (22–24)

• • •

At an early hour a start was again made in the usual manner—the harsh command "Marche!" followed by deep-toned yells from the crouching dogs; then, a merciless beating and thumping, and the cowering animals at length set off with the heavy loads, howling as if their hearts would break. After the thrashing came the abuse and curses. Coffee would be appealed to "for the love of Heaven to straighten his traces." Chocolat would be solemnly informed that he was a migratory swindle, and possessed of no character whatever. Brandy would be entreated to "just see if he couldn't do a little better;" that he was the offspring of very disreputable parents, and would be thrashed presently. (25)

BRUTALITY TOWARD HORSES AND DOGS IN THE YUKON

While Robinson recorded the brutality of a sled dog's life at mid-century, largely at the hands of Indian drivers, Arthur Treadwell Walden shows the same pattern of brutality toward both horses and dogs on the part of the hopeful gold miners of the 1897 gold rush, of which he himself was a part. The first passages are about his observations in Skagway and the passes north of Skagway and Dyea. The final paragraph is about the situation in Dawson, where so many animals had been allowed to starve to death.

FROM ARTHUR TREADWELL WALDEN, *A DOG-PUNCHER ON THE YUKON*
(Boston: Houghton Mifflin Co., 1928)

Of course conditions are unusual when enormous crowds of men, coming from all parts of the world, stream through a country in which there is practically no law or organization of any kind. The place was supposed to be under civil law, but that, in the early history of our country, meant no law at all. Any crime could be committed with impunity, and might made right.

The cruelty to animals was something terrible, and strange to say it was not practiced on by the so-called rougher element who knew something about handling animals. The worst men were those who in former life were supposed to be of the better class. These men lost their heads completely. I have seen horses that had stuck in the mud abandoned and left to die. They were not even killed, in the rush to hurry on. . . .

Men left valuable stuff on the horses' backs, not even stopping to unpack it. I saw one man who, after having made his way over the pass and onto the lakes, where it was all smooth going, got mad at his dogs, and, after beating them with a club till they were unable to go, began with the leader and pushed them all down a water-hole under the ice. He cut the traces of the last dog, leaving himself absolutely stranded with no means of locomotion. Then he sat down and cried.

It is no use harrowing the reader with further details of these acts of brutality, and it would mean almost endless repetition. The whole trail was strewn with dead animals of all kinds, and there was no interference with this cruelty whatsoever. The unwritten law of the trail seemed to be, "Mind your own business." In any case it would have been of little use to interfere, as you would have to do it fifty times a day. Furthermore, when men are in this state of mind it would be necessary to kill them first in order to stop what they were doing. To show you how much we minded our own business, I remember seeing a dead man with the back of his head smashed in and every one passing him and paying no attention. This was probably the work of Soapy and his gang. (133–34)

• • •

I did not see a horse that was either hurt or frightened, but then they were Western ponies. The following year, when thousands of people tried to get into the country over the newly discovered White Pass, twenty-five hundred or three thousand horses were killed.

Besides the bad traveling and hard work getting over Chilkoot Pass, terrible storms often raged for days, making it impossible to move from camp. When men were caught halfway up, pack and load had to be abandoned and a stampede made for camp. Quantities of goods were lost during the winters, and the Indians made a business of picking them up when the snows went off.

A curious thing happened up here, which for some unknown reason affected us very queerly and was a good deal talked about. The weather had turned cold. A man was driving a team composed of the usual long-haired dogs of the country, together with one short-haired greyhound. One morning the short-haired dog was found frozen solid, standing up: there he stood with his tail between his legs, his back arched and his head down. The owner was very much criticized for the treatment of his dogs. There were some short-haired dogs on the trail, but men were always careful to let them sleep in their tents. (7)

• • •

The town was the most unsanitary place imaginable. I know a man who made a bet that he could go down the main street and travel the whole way jumping from one dead horse to another or to a dead dog, and he won his bet. (145)

THE FATE OF HORSES IN THE YUKON

Of the stories of animals sacrificed to man's insane scramble for oil, furs, and gold in the Yukon, the fate of the horses and other pack animals on White Pass in 1897 is one of the most senseless and heartbreaking. Note that Haskell lays blame for the loss of so many animals not just on the terrain, but on the general ignorance and stupidity of their owners—people on whom London seems to have patterned Mercedes, Charles, and Hal.

FROM WILLIAM B. HASKELL, *TWO YEARS IN THE KLONDIKE AND ALASKAN GOLD-FIELDS*
(Hartford, CT: Hartford Publishing Co., 1898)

The trail was constructed something on the principle of a huge trap. For the first three or four miles it looked very easy and attractive. For this distance there was a wagon road over which horses and wagons would meet with little difficulty. Then the Skagway, which is a shallow stream, though very swift, had to be crossed. Some of the first pilgrims had constructed a rude bridge of logs over which but one horse could pass at a time. Wagons had to be unloaded, horses led carefully over, then the wagons drawn over and reloaded. From this bridge wagons could be used three miles further, when what was quite appropriately dubbed Devil's Hill was encountered. Here the trouble began. The trail was not over two feet wide, and at the top of the hill horses were compelled to make a jump of two feet high and alight on a slippery rock. At one place there was a path up a steep incline on which logs had been laid, forming a sort of ladder.

"When you get to the top of it you are five hundred feet above sea level," said one of the few who came through safely. "The hill is very rocky, but I was careful to make notes of its condition, and there is no reason why a mountain climber should not put his horse over there with comparative ease. Notwithstanding that fact, I found a dead horse on the pass. I examined it and found that it had broken one of its legs. The owner had no more use for it and killed it. After leaving the first hill you descend, entering a cañon, when another hill is encountered with a rise of eight hundred feet.

"The path over it, or, rather, around it, should not be dignified by the name of trail. It is less than two feet wide at many places, and the walking, especially for horses, is the worst imaginable. The formation on the surface is a soft, slippery, slate rock. The path winds its crooked way around the mountain, while below it drops off sheer five hundred feet to the river. This is the place where so many horses and packs have been lost.

"One pack train of seventeen horses lost eight of them down this slide on the first trip over. The footing is all that a clear-minded, strong-nerved man would care to encounter, and it is practically impossible for such horses as are there to pack any considerable amount of supplies around this bluff.

"On the farther side of Porcupine Hill is a place where one must be very cautious. Boulders from four to ten feet square are met with. One must work around the corners of these boulders to get down in safety. It took me about one hour and a half. I went slowly, picking my way, as one accustomed to mountain climbing will do, and had no difficulty in reaching the foot of the hill. I was careful to note the dangers that a horse would encounter, and I say that a horse can go over Porcupine Hill all right if the person handling the animal knows his business. Inquiry satisfied me that the death of many horses was due solely to the inexperience of those in charge. The packs are put on the backs of the horses with gross carelessness, and what is the result? It is up hill and down hill, and around boulders, and before the journey is accomplished the packs begin to slide, and the horse's burden is thus increased threefold. A slip is made, the pack gives way, and the animal goes down to its death, or breaks a leg and is killed by the owner, who curses his luck and starts back for another horse.

"Following this place is what is known as First Bridge Hill, which covers a distance of three miles. Then comes the hill called Summit Hill, four miles of as tough climbing as one ever saw. It was on this hill that the great loss of horses occurred. The trail runs along the side of a rocky mountain, where a misstep will send an animal from five hundred to one thousand feet below. On the side of nearly all these hills the liquid mud was two feet deep, and in some places it ran like a stream. There were sharp rocks and round rocks, and great slabs of granite down which the horses slid into mud holes.

"Half the people are greenhorns and don't know how to pack a horse. They pile on the load, and when the horse gets to a bad place, the pack hits against the rocks, and, of course, makes the horse step out to keep his balance. Down go his feet, and over goes the horse. I saw one mule turn three complete somersaults, and the owner never went after either the mule or the packs. You can see dead horses and lost packs all along down the precipice, and all mixed up together. 'Why don't they go after them?' Well, it would take them a week to go down there and bring up a pack. It's two thousand feet down there in some places. Some men, after packing heavy outfits over seventeen miles of this trail, sold out for enough to pay their fare back to the United States.

"It was a sight such as one would not care to see more than once in a lifetime. Horses, tents, feed, supplies, and men were piled together is [*sic*] an apparently hopeless tangle. A drizzling rain was falling most of the time. Stubborn fires were smouldering and sputtering, and men were standing or wandering about as though they were dazed by the obstacles ahead. I couldn't help noticing the tired, haggard look on almost every face that I saw, as though the load of anxiety and care was more than they could endure."

Summit Lake is about a mile wide and six miles long, and near the middle is a tall, rocky inlet which, in rough weather, is noted for the breakers which dash upon its shores. One foggy morning, shortly after a party had started on its journey, a squall sprang up, and not being able to make out their bearings in the fog, their little boat was driven straight upon the rocks. She capsized and threw the three men into the icy water. One of them immediately sank and was never seen again. The other two struck out for the shore and finally reached it, though one was so exhausted that he had to be dragged out of the water. (463–66)

• • •

After a time the stench from dead horses became so offensive in Skagway that a mass-meeting was held to plan for the abatement of the nuisance. As a result a great number of bodies were gathered together and cremated. (467)

• • •

When this sort of thing had been going on for a little time, horse feed became scarce and horses were at a discount. Early in September a man could pick up a good horse for ten dollars. A party which, during the season of high prices had rushed back to the United States and secured a few horses, found, when they returned, that they could not be sold. So they loaded their horses with fodder, which was at a great premium, and started for the summit. Reaching there they sold the feed for eighteen dollars a sack and threw the horses in, so they got out of the dilemma very well. But by the time the hay was brought up to the hungry animals waiting for it, the other animals met on the trail, by each taking a passing nip, had reduced the quantity by about fifty per cent. The horses are fond of birch leaves, but they soon contracted mud fever, and, as they were insufficiently fed and not sheltered at all, they soon became worthless. They really died from lack of care. Horses were a good deal better on the Skagway trail than burros, although the best thing of all was an ox, which was very good for muddy traveling, and could carry a big load. The burros taken up were almost a failure. They were good over rocks, but no good at all in the swamp, which forms about two-thirds of the entire distance.

Those who succeeded in working their way past these obstacles found themselves finally at the big marsh. Of this no adequate description is possible. It is a terror for packers. A horse flounders and rolls in the mud, until he either gives up from exhaustion, or else tears his pack loose, or breaks a leg. Many of the miners were camped on this bog, which is a mile and a half long, waiting till the freeze of winter covers the ground so that they could get across. The ground was soft and springy, and very muddy even before it was trampled up. A man went to his knees in the mud, and a horse wallowed to his belly. After crossing the marsh the trail is much the same as in the earlier stages, up and down over a continuous chain of hills and mountains.

At times the gold-seekers were encouraged to believe that there was a betterment, owing to the men's efforts to corduroy the bad places, and the occasional glimpse of sun, but a night's rain would undo it all, and the morning would show it worse than ever. The horses floundered over the boulders and through the mud, which is nothing more than decomposed vegetation, and broke their legs. Then they were shot or knocked on the head. Lack of animals, and particularly the fact that it is impossible to move supplies, led many to split up their outfits and hurry on with barely enough to last them until they reached the river camps. (468–69)

A DOG OWNER'S TREATMENT OF HIS DOGS

The final selection on the treatment of the arctic sled dog is written by dog lover and missionary Egerton Young. The passage shows that brutality toward animals was not solely the province of "uncivilized" Native Americans or young, ill-prepared miners who had little or no knowledge of dogs and the Arctic. The selection, which some critics believe was the inspiration for Jack London's scene of the beating of Buck by the man in red, is all the more puzzling in light of Young's earlier account of Jack, the dog who idolized his master and risked his own life for his master.

FROM EGERTON YOUNG, *MY DOGS IN THE NORTHLAND*
(New York: Fleming H. Revell Co., 1902)

The only battles that I recall having had with Jack, were on Cuffy's account, and battles royal they were. They came about in this way. The principal food for all my dogs was fish. During the winter months the fish are frozen so hard that they have to be thawed out ere they are fed to the dogs. When the dogs were at home the fish were thawed out at the hot kitchen fire and distributed among the hungry animals in the yard outside. Cuffy could not, or would not understand that she was not to take her large, oily fish into the house and there leisurely devour it on the study or dining-room floor. A big grease-spot on the floor or carpet seemed a trifling affair in comparison with her having to eat her supper in the bitter cold. Several times had I sternly reproved her, and put her outside, to finish her fish with the other dogs. Finding at length that scoldings were of no avail, and some protests coming in from other quarters about carpets being ruined, I was at length obliged to resort to stern measures, and so one evening, when her actions had been unusually provoking, I took her out and gave her a real good whipping. As she had never before been whipped, she did not at first realize what it meant. However, I was resolved that she should know, and know so thoroughly, that the whipping would not have to be repeated, and so I continued the use of the lash until she began to vigourously cry out under its infliction.

Anticipating trouble from yet another quarter, I had prepared for the emergency. I had placed near at hand a large heavy oak axe handle, and it turned out fortunate enough for me that I had such a formidable weapon. Just as I had expected, Jack's blood was up as soon as he heard Cuffy's cries. He was on the opposite side of the large yard and busily engaged in eating his second fish. Suddenly springing up, he was a splendid sight as there he stood for an instant, head up, ears alert, and with his foot on his coveted, half-devoured fish. As Cuffy's cries continued, with a rush and a roar the enormous fellow came for me.

I knew, from some exciting experiences I had had with angry dogs in the past, that my dog-whip was of but little avail in the battle before me, and so I quickly exchanged it for the heavy axe-handle. And I had to be quick about it, for it did not take the now thoroughly angry dog long to dash across the yard and plunge recklessly at me for the rescue of his beloved mate. However, I was ready for him; and so, as he sprang viciously at me I was able to strike him such a blow that I knocked him completely over. In an instant he was up again, and once more he sprang at me just as viciously as before. However, I was on my guard, and again, with all my might, I struck him on the side of his head. He went down all in a heap, and at first I thought I had killed him.

But this was only for a few seconds. Then he was up, and again he charged me. My third blow completely dazed him, so much so that when he rallied from it he skulked off to the kennels. Next day he was distant and sulky, and it was evident that we were to have another battle ere the question as to which was master would be settled. The decisive battle came off a few days after. As I had been obliged so abruptly to leave off punishing Cuffy and fight for my life against Jack, her ladyship had become possessed with the idea that the victory had been on their side, and that she could do as she liked. The result was that one evening shortly after, she marched into the dining-room with a large fish, and there on the carpet began leisurely to devour it. And, furthermore, when requested to take up her fish and go outside she most decidedly, with ruffled curls and angry growls, refused to do anything of the kind.

It was quite evident that things were coming to a crisis in the dog kingdom. Had Jack encouraged her to thus act, and were other dogs in sympathy with her and also getting ready to go on strike against authority?

No matter, whatever it is it must be met and settled, and settled in such a manner that it will not be repeated. The first thing I did was to shut Jack up in the fish house. Then I went for Cuffy. I gave her a most thorough trouncing. Before I was through with her, she found out who was master, and never did she growl at me again.

During her castigation she had cried bitterly. These cries had terribly excited Jack. Like a caged lion, he had growled and raged in his prison abode, out of which he had made the most desperate attempts to escape. He smashed the few panes of glass in the window of the fish house, but the window was too small and high for him to struggle through.

When I had thoroughly conquered Cuffy, and we were good friends again, I armed myself with the same axe handle I had used before, and then went to have it out with Jack. The instant I unlocked the door, I sprang back on my guard. Without any hesitancy and just as viciously as before he sprang at my throat. I am confident that if I had slipped or missed him, he would have killed me. But I did not miss him. My muscles were strong and hardened by the vigourous exercise of that wild North-land, and so it was possible for me to strike a blow like a blacksmith. Big as he was and weighing nearly two hundred pounds, he went down under that blow as though shot. His recuperative power seemed marvellous. Again and again he came for me, but in every instance I was thus able to throw him over. At length he began to lose heart in his rushes, and then, after receiving a specially ugly clip on the jaw, his opposition ceased and all the fight seemed suddenly to go out of him, and there the great big fellow lay sprawled out on the ground and coolly looking at me. (129–34)

CRUELTY TO ANIMALS IN THE NAME OF FASHION

In the following passage from Anna Sewell's *Black Beauty*, Beauty is having a talk in the orchard with two other horses, one called Ginger, who has been mistreated by a former master, and Sir Oliver, an older horse, who is revealing some of the senseless and inhumane former practices in the treatment of horses, like tail docking, which prevents horses from whisking off flies. Sir Oliver turns the conversation to dogs and what they suffer in the name of fashion, illustrated by an account of a dog named Skye and her pups.

FROM ANNA SEWELL, *BLACK BEAUTY*
(New York: The H. M. Caldwell Co., 1894)

"Of course it is," said he; "to my mind, fashion is one of the wickedest things in the world. Now look, for instance, at the way they serve dogs, cutting off their tails to make them look plucky, and shearing up their pretty little ears to a point to make them look sharp, forsooth. I had a dear friend once, a brown terrier—'Skye,' they called her; she was so fond of me that she never would sleep out of my stall; she made her bed under the manger, and there she had a litter of five as pretty little puppies as need be; none were drowned, for they were a valuable kind, and how pleased she was with them! and when they got their eyes open and crawled about, it was a real pretty sight; but one day the man came and took them all away; I thought he might be afraid I should tread upon them. But it was not so; in the evening poor Skye brought them back again, one by one in her mouth; not the happy little things that they were, but bleeding and crying pitifully; they had all had a piece of their tails cut off, and the soft flap of their pretty little ears was cut quite off. How their mother licked them, and how troubled she was, poor thing! I never forgot it. They healed in time, and they forgot the pain, but the nice soft flap that of course was intended to protect the delicate part of their ears from dust and injury, was gone for ever. Why don't they cut their own children's ears into points to make them look sharp? why don't they cut the end off their noses to make them look plucky? One would be just as sensible as the other. What right have they to torment and disfigure God's creatures?" (40–41)

WORKING FOR ANIMAL RIGHTS: PETA TAKES A STEP FURTHER

The Humane Society of the United States, the first national and most prominent of the animal welfare societies, was formed in 1954 to prevent the misuse of animals. This organization describes in its statement of principles that its major crusades are in the interests of humane treatment of wildlife, farm animals, laboratory animals, and companion animals. The Humane Society works within the legal system for protection of animals against cruel treatment. Its interests are in seeing that animals are humanely treated in any situation rather than in ending all meat consumption or experimentation. Thus the Humane Society of the United States, while it would have tolerated the use of sled dogs in the Yukon gold fields, would have objected to beatings and clubbings, overloaded sleds, inadequate feeding, and the failure to provide shelter from the arctic cold.

Another of the most prominent associations for the prevention of cruelty to animals is People for the Ethical Treatment of Animals (PETA), which is best described as an animal rights organization. While PETA is also concerned with working within the legal system for improvements in the way animals are treated and would certainly embrace the principles of the Humane Society, it is one of a number of organizations that take the remedy for cruelty to animals to a radical new plane well beyond that proposed by the Humane Society of the United States. PETA does not concede that animals can be used by humans in traditional ways if humans treat them as humanely as possible. Note the very clear statement in bold letters: **"Animals are not ours to eat, wear, experiment on, or use for entertainment."**

"OUR MISSION," PETA WEB SITE
(www.peta-online.org/about/index)

People for the Ethical Treatment of Animals (PETA), with more than six hundred thousand members, is the largest animal rights organization in the world. Founded in 1980, PETA is dedicated to establishing and protecting the rights of all animals. PETA operates under the simple principle that **animals are not ours to eat, wear, experiment on, or use for entertainment**.

PETA focuses its attention on the four areas in which the largest numbers of animals suffer the most intensely for the longest periods of time: on factory farms, in laboratories, in the fur trade, and in the entertainment industry. We also work on a variety of other issues, including the cruel killing of beavers, birds and other "pests," and the abuse of backyard dogs.

PETA works through public education, cruelty investigations, research, animal rescue, legislation, special events, celebrity involvement, and direct action.

PROJECTS FOR ORAL OR WRITTEN EXPLORATION

1. What difference might the principles of the Humane Society have made in the Yukon in the lives of Buck and his mates had laws following from such principles been enforced?

2. From examining the attitudes implied by Jack London in *The Call of the Wild*, can you argue that he was in the camp of the animal welfare supporters or the animal rights supporters? Formulate a question to debate.

3. Examine closely the idea of animal consciousness and intelligence in the novel. Include in your consideration presentation of the story through the eyes of a dog and, in *Black Beauty* and *Beautiful Joe*, the first-person animal narrator. Why, given Saunders's and Sewell's objectives, was theirs a wise choice? Write a paper on the effectiveness of telling the story from the animal's point of view.

4. Look carefully at the additional excerpt from Egerton Young's memoir. This is one of the passages that led some readers to say that London had plagiarized Young's work. What is your conclusion, based on a comparison of this passage with Buck's encounter with the man in red? Consider tone and attitude as well as action.

5. Because they reject the idea of an animal as property, some animal rights activists object to the word "pet" to refer to animals, preferring instead the term "animal companion." Explore your own attitudes about an animal as property and how the idea surfaces in *The Call of the Wild*. Conduct a class debate on the issue of animals as pets.

6. Write an essay on cruelty to animals in the Yukon, using these and other documents. Also do some research on the American Society for the Prevention of Cruelty to Animals and laws that protect animals in your county.

7. Discuss the possible interpretations of the excerpt from Genesis regarding man's role vis-à-vis animals.

SUGGESTIONS FOR FURTHER READING

Arluke, A., and C. R. Sanders. *Regarding Animals*. Philadelphia: Temple University Press, 1996.

Bckoff, Marc, ed. *Encyclopedia of Animal Rights and Animal Welfare*. Westport, CT: Greenwood Press, 1998.

Carson, G. *Men, Beasts, and Gods: A History of Cruelty and Kindness to Animals*. New York: Scribner's, 1972.

Dawkins, M. S. *Through Our Eyes Only? The Search for Animal Consciousness*. San Francisco: W. H. Freeman, 1993.

Francione, G. L. *Animals, Property, and the Law*. Philadelphia: Temple University Press, 1995.

Hoage, R. J., ed. *Perceptions of Animals in American Culture*. Washington, DC: Smithsonian Institution Press, 1989.

Morris, Richard Knowles, and Michael W. Fox, eds. *On the Fifth Day: Animal Rights and Human Ethics*. Washington, D.C.: Acropolis Books, 1978.

Newkirk, Ingrid. *Free the Animals!* Chicago: Noble Press, 1992.

Rachels, J. *Created from Animals: The Moral Implications of Darwinism*. New York: Oxford University Press, 1990.

Saunders, Margaret Marshall. *Beautiful Joe: An Autobiography*. Philadelphia: C. H. Darnes, 1896.

Serpell, James. *In the Company of Animals*. Oxford: Basil Blackwell, 1986.

Sewell, Anna. *Black Beauty*. New York: The H. M. Caldwell Co., 1894.

Singer, Peter. *Animal Liberation*. New York: Avon Books, 1975.

6

The Wolf: Symbol, Myth, and Issue

At the narrative and metaphoric center of Jack London's *Call of the Wild* is the figure of the wolf, that wild progenitor of dogs, including the novel's main character Buck. This chapter on the wolf examines its place in the novel's narrative, its symbolism, and its currency as a representative of an exploited and decimated wilderness that encompasses many subarctic animals, notably whales, coyotes, bears, seals, and beavers.

CHARACTER OF WOLVES

The known predecessors of the wolf, called creodonts, are believed to have roamed arctic regions one hundred million years ago. From creodonts came not only wolves, but bears, cats, weasels, raccoons, civets, hyenas, foxes, and wild dogs.

The primary characteristics of wolf behavior, acknowledged in *The Call of the Wild*, are its organization into highly hierarchical packs (despite the tradition of the "lone wolf") led by an "alpha male" and an "alpha female," and its habit of being constantly on the move, sometimes covering large areas, in search of prey—the moose being a favorite object of arctic wolves. They are also known for their howling and marking off of territory with urine.

THE PLACE OF THE WOLF IN THE NARRATIVE

After Buck reaches the Yukon, some form of the word "wolf" appears throughout the rest of the novel with marked consistency. One explanation of this is the widely held conviction that the huskies native to the north country were the dogs on earth most closely related to wolves. The novel is rich in its literal references to wolves, first in the descriptions of the wolves' husky descendants, then in the wolflike call within Buck, and finally in Buck's joining of a pack of wolves. Tracing these literal references to wolves is an instructive way to see how London weaves wolves and the idea of wolves into his narrative.

The first of these references appears when Buck lands in Dyea and is exposed to the huskies who predominate there. In Buck's eyes, these dogs are "wolfish creatures" (8). The husky who initially attacks the innocently friendly Curly is a big dog, "the size of a full-grown wolf" (9). As all the huskies circle Curly, they assume "the wolf manner of fighting, to strike and leap away" (9).

As Buck travels in the Yukon, not only are most of his companions the "wolfish" huskies, but he himself adopts wolfish habits. He learns their method of fighting, "to cut and slash and the quick wolf snap" (14). He also learns to point his nose in the air and howl "long and wolflike" (14).

The wolfish howling and fighting connect him with his ancestors in what the narrator calls a decivilization or retrogression: "And when, on the still cold nights, he pointed his nose at a star and howled long and wolflike, it was his ancestors, dead and dust, pointing nose at star and howling down through the centuries and through him" (14). The implication is that Buck's ancestry traces ultimately back to the wolf.

When Buck and the other dogs reach Lake Laberge, they are attacked by semiwild dogs who are the closest animals to wolves that Buck has ever encountered. In them we sense that there are devastating effects of the ancient contract forged between men and wolves, for these animals have relinquished their hunting skills and have become dependent on man for food and shelter, as we discussed in Chapter Four. Yet in many months of the year, man seems to ignore the contract, and the dogs are turned out to fend for themselves. When food is low around the Lake Laberge tribal communities, the dogs are not fed at all. Their hunger, in large measure a result of their dependence, makes them brutal.

There is another reference to wolves in the account of Dolly's madness, which is shown in her "long heart-breaking wolf howl" (18). The connection between the arctic huskies and wolves is also made in Buck's encounters with dogs on the streets of Dawson: "in the main they were the wild wolf husky breed" (21).

On the way back to Skagway, when the rabbit hunt ends the rivalry between Spitz and Buck with Spitz's death, Buck is described as going after the rabbit, "leading the pack, sounding the old wolf cry" (22). The dogs chasing the rabbit are called "ill-tamed wolves" (23). When the chase culminates in the fight to the death between Spitz and Buck, the other dogs form "a silent and wolfish circle" around them, waiting to complete the kill (24).

Ironically, references to wolves proliferate after Buck joins John Thornton in the most intimate dog-man domestic relationship in the novel. Sitting around the fire with Thornton summons up visions of wild wolves and intensifies Buck's kinship to them:

> He sat by John Thornton's fire, a broad-breasted dog, white-fanged and long-furred; but behind him were the shades of all manner of dogs, half-wolves, urgent and prompting, tasting the savor of the meat he ate . . . dictating his moods, directing his actions, lying down to sleep with him when he lay down, and dreaming with him and beyond him and becoming themselves the stuff of dreams. (44)

Finally, after reaching the remote valley where they make camp, he hears the "call" again and then spies "a long lean, timber wolf" (54). A ritual begins and is repeated twice more: the wolf runs from Buck, Buck pursues, the wolf pivots on hind legs, snarling at Buck, then runs again. After they sniff noses and become friends, the wolf leads Buck away from the valley, and Buck realizes that "the call of the wild" is narratively the wolf itself: "He knew he was at last answering the call, running by the side of his wood brother toward the place from where the call surely came" (55). From this time forward, the wolf is referred to as Buck's "wild brother."

As Buck prepares to answer the call and join the wild, he takes down larger and larger animals, as a wolf would, scattering "wolverines" who come to feed on his kills. Soon, the narrator observes, "he might well have been mistaken for a gigantic wolf" (56) and becomes transformed from dog to wolf: "His muzzle was the long wolf muzzle, save that it was larger than the muzzle of any wolf" (56). His head, somewhat broader, was the wolf head on a massive scale, and "his cunning was wolf cunning" (56).

Buck is ready to join the pack, having already proven his kinship to his "brother" wolf and his ability to live the life of a wolf in the wild. The death of John Thornton releases Buck from his ties to humanity and provides the final impetus for his change of allegiance. After Thornton's death, a pack of wolves crosses into the valley, where, one after another, they attack Buck. But he vanquishes them all one by one, finally facing the entire pack for half an hour. After he has sent them all away, "one wolf, long and lean and gray, advanced cautiously" toward Buck (61). This is his wild brother, joined by "an old wolf" (62) who begins "the long wolf howl," leading others in the pack. "And now the call came to Buck in unmistakable accents" (62).

Buck's story concludes with his very physical impact on the wolves with whom he breeds, altering the characteristics of the pack. His physical presence is also manifested in his leadership of the wolf pack when he leaves his huge paw prints around the men whose throats he has slashed. He has become a wolf both physically and spiritually, "a great, gloriously coated wolf, like, and yet unlike, all the other wolves" (62).

THE WOLF AS SYMBOL

The idea of the wolf assumes a symbolic function in the novel as well. The wolf embodies that basic, ancient element from which creatures have sprung. It is the true "Self," independent of civilization. In the dog, the wolf is that quintessential being that was bargained away when the dog traded its self-sufficiency for a slavish life with men. The result is a perversion of a noble wild nature by human society. The dogs' wolflike fury shines through, but their wolfish independence as followers and killers of their own game has been lost. They seem confused about their own identity, as if they are doomed permanently to a state of transition between being dogs and being wolves, unable to reconcile the tame and wild elements within. Perhaps this is why the wolflike huskies so often turned on their own kind. Thus the husky condition, between wolf and dog, is portrayed as a dangerous one.

To state the meaning of the wolf in another way, the wolf to Buck is the real truth of his nature, from which he has been removed by centuries of domestication. In the end, through the rituals of fighting and hunting, he recovers that self, symbolized by his joining of the pack. For Buck, the wolf means the union of body and spirit.

LONDON'S FICTIONAL FASCINATION WITH WOLVES

London reveals his persistent interest in—one might even say obsession with—wolves in fiction other than *The Call of the Wild*. The list of his fictional works dealing with the subject of wolves is extensive. *White Fang* is the story of a female wolf's cub, variously described as "the fighting wolf," "the sleeping wolf," and "the blessed wolf," in which wolves devour a trapper. In a story collection entitled *The Son of the Wolf*, the title story concerns the physical and spiritual power of an Indian associated with the wolf. "Where the Trail Ends" relates the story of a dog who, like Buck, alters the strain of wolves by breeding with them. "A Daughter of Aurora" tells the tale of a highly prized lead dog named Wolf Fang. Others include "Bâtard," about a dog whose father is a gray timber wolf, and "The Law of Life," in which wolves trample over the weak in nature—the sick moose, the weak wolf in the pack, and an old man. "The Story of Jees Uck" is about a domesticated wolf driven out of camp. In "Hearts of Three," the main character is called the wolf of Wall Street. Finally, *The Sea Wolf* presents a ship's captain named Wolf Larsen who lives by a brutal code in which the strong are given leave to destroy the weak. Not surprisingly, one of the most frequent adjectives in London's fiction is "wolfish," usually suggesting the most brutal side of nature.

THE WOLF AS SYMBOL IN LONDON'S LIFE

The name of the wolf reverberates in Jack London's personal life as well as in his fiction. He named one of his favorite dogs Brown Wolf, chose as a trademark to place on his stationery and bookmarks the head of a wolf, and named his last house in Glen Ellen, California, Wolf House.

He also liked to refer to himself as "Wolf" and encouraged his wife and his best friend, George Sterling, to call him Wolf. A number of students of Jack London, including Barry Lopez (a naturalist who writes about wolves) and John Perry (a literary critic), have pointed out that London seems to associate wolves with super machismo and brute force. (Note the use of the term "wolf" to describe a menacing man who preys upon women.) Wolves in London's work and life, while they command our admiration and respect and even love, also represent what is cruel and powerful in nature—the survival of the fittest.

D. H. Lawrence, a famous British novelist, in a book of essays entitled *Classics of American Literature*, wrote that the typical American is a loner, self-sufficient, and a killer. Could London have also intended his wolf as representative of American character?

REPUTATION OF THE WOLF IN FOLKLORE

In literature and folklore, the wolf is almost always the villain, a menacing, brutal killer—a view perpetuated in the popular Grimm's fairy tales. Typically, the big, bad wolf blows down the houses of two of the three little pigs in order to gobble them up. He is the enemy of the innocent lamb, the symbol of purity. The wolf is never averse to gobbling up children and grandmothers, as he does in "Little Red Riding Hood," and presenting a formidable enemy for a little boy in "Peter and the Wolf." In *Aesop's Fables* and in the medieval *Reynard the Fox*, wolves usually represent a kind of vicious brute force as compared with the more intelligent, cunning fox. In the Middle Ages, the wolf was also associated with the devil, and in related imagery in the nineteenth century, possessed and damned humans became transformed into wolves, as werewolves, and were associated with the evil world of the vampire. In essence, the wolf represented the dark, usually repressed evil in man.

There are recurrent myths in Western culture of children being reared by wolves, but the prevailing image connecting wolves and children is a negative one: the wolf as child devourer rather than child nurturer. The English language is replete with metaphors and phrases in which the wolf is represented as low and evil. The wolf at the door, the wolf in sheep's clothing, and crying wolf all portray the wolf as the brutal and dangerous predator.

THE WOLF SPIRIT AND THE NATIVE AMERICAN

Ironically, as we discussed in Chapter Four, wild dogs and wolves were initially humankind's partners at the dawn of civilization, protecting human beings and helping them in the hunt. This situation is reflected in *The Call of the Wild* when Buck remembers his ancestors sitting around the fire with the caveman.

The wolf continued to be admired and cherished in Native American culture at a time when wolves were feared and hated by whites. Each tribe had a slightly different view of the wolf, but all seemed to regard the wolf as representative of all the variety and complexity, the strength and the weakness, of nature itself. Native peoples studied the behavior of the wolf to learn how to survive and used stories of the wolf in their ceremonies and stories. Some tribes, like the Ojibwas, focused on the wolf's family structure and faithfulness. Others, like the Oneidas, especially admired the wolf's endurance and courage. The Navajos believed that the wolf had magical powers. To the Inuits, the relationship between the predator wolf and its prey illustrated the oneness of all nature.

The revered place of the wolf in Native American culture can be seen in their initiation ceremonies in which the wolf is the central figure. Though the ceremonial story changes somewhat from tribe to tribe, the core story is basically the same: a young uninitiated man finds himself alone in the company of wolves who first threaten him and then teach him all the wolflike virtues of courage, strength, and endurance. He, in turn, goes back to his village and brings to the tribe the lessons he has learned from the wolves.

EXTERMINATION

Despite the almost spiritual bond and interdependent partner ship enjoyed by humans and wolves while humans were still basically hunters, cooperation between wolf and man dissolved when humans began keeping cows and sheep. Wolves were now seen as the enemy. In Christianity, the wolf was the devil itself—the enemy of innocence and purity, represented by the lamb, which was also a symbol of Christ himself.

So-called science and imperfect observation as well as folklore perpetuated the view of the wolf as an aggressive and fearless devourer of sheep, cows, defenseless men, women, and, especially, children and a grave robber who craved the flesh of dead humans. In Europe, this resulted in the wholesale slaughter of wolves.

The long-standing negative attitude in Europe toward wolves was intensified in the New World, where the Puritans and other religious settlers regarded the wilderness itself as the literal domain of the devil and wolves as the devil's helpers, evil incarnate. Wolves were falsely blamed for the decimating slaughter of cows and sheep, first in the colonial East and then on the frontier. As early as 1630, wolves became the targets of extermination in the New World. By wholesale extermination, the religious settler was protecting not only the kingdom of God but his own worldly profits. In an action typical of those that prevailed throughout the Americas, the Puritan Massachusetts Bay Colony offered cash to anyone who brought in a dead wolf, a practice that was formalized by anti-wolf legislation.

While the main reason alleged for the killing of wolves continued to be the protection of livestock, fashion in furs also contributed to the wolf's demise. For example, in 1850, the demand for beaver fur was replaced by the demand for wolf fur, so bounties for wolves increased. By the end of the nineteenth century, few states were without wolf-regulating legislation, and few countries in the Americas placed any limits on the killing of wolves.

In 1914, the annual bounties paid by the U.S. government and private businesses for the killing of wolves totaled over $1,000,000. Yet farmers and hunters were convinced that the wolf was still a dangerous threat to the commerce of the nation, so in 1915, the Department of Agriculture created the U.S. Bureau of Biological Survey to deal further with the problem of predators like the wolf. In that year, Congress voted a budget of $125,000 to the agency for the extermination of wolves, a trend that would continue for well over five decades. On March 2, 1931, the U.S. Congress passed legislation directing the secretary of agriculture (and later the secretary of the interior) to "conduct campaigns for the destruction or control of (predatory) animals," especially on both public and private lands in the western United States.

As recently as 1972, many states still had laws awarding bounties for the killing of wolves: Alaska, Arizona, Arkansas, Colorado, Idaho, Indiana, Iowa, Missouri, Montana, Oklahoma, Oregon, South Dakota, Texas, Utah, Wisconsin, and Wyoming. Ontario,

Quebec, and the Northwest Territories were still paying bounties for wolf hides, and other areas of both Canada and the United States maintained plans for wolf extermination by poison. Eastern Europe and Russia still maintained policies of wolf extermination.

METHODS OF EXTERMINATION

The methods used to exterminate wolves in the western United States as late as the 1970s were cruel beyond imagination. Professional trappers who made their livings by bringing wolf hides to both public agencies and private businesses for bounties quickly found that they could not secure sufficient bounty money by simply shooting wolves, so wolves were trapped and then bludgeoned to death, poisoned, caught in game pits, dynamited, flooded out of and drowned in their dens, or caught and infected with mange before being released to infect other wolves. They were burned alive and tied to two horses to be pulled apart. In perfecting ways to poison wolves, experiments were conducted by the U.S. government on dogs.

The favored method of one bounty hunter named Ben Corbin, who operated in the far west, was to bait spring hooks, attached to steel lines, with chunks of chicken and place them outside wolf dens. When wolf pups, coming out of the den at night, ate the chicken, the springs would snap, propelling the hooks into the pup's stomach or throat and securing them to the steel lines. The next time Corbin checked on his traps, he had only to club the wolves over the head in order to harvest the skins to sell.

To secure wolf urine with which to trap more wolves, the penises of captured wolves were wired shut. When it was likely that their bladders were filled, they were killed, the bladders were removed, and the urine was used to trap other wolves.

Nor were the descendants of European settlers the only peoples cruel to wolves. In order to kill wolves that they believed were taking too much game or to secure the fur of wolves, Eskimos heated and coiled and then froze long pieces of whale bone. They then coated the coiled bones with fat and set them where wolves would devour them. Once the wolves had swallowed them, the bones would thaw, uncoil, and puncture the wolves' intestines, killing them slowly and painfully.

RESULTS OF THE EXTERMINATION POLICIES

As a result of governmental and private crusades for extinction of the wolf, the species had disappeared completely in the eastern United States by the time of the Civil War. To have some sense of the enormity and impact of extermination policies, consider that even after three centuries of planned extermination, there were in 1901 some 1 million wolves in North Dakota alone. Yet by the mid-1970s there were only 1,300 gray wolves in the entire United States, excepting Alaska, only 10,000 in Alaska, and only 50,000 in all of Canada. By this time, the red wolf was extinct.

REVISIONS OF THE VIEW OF WOLVES

Fortunately for the species, however, the work of naturalists in the last three decades of the twentieth century has slowly begun changing society's view of the wolf and how it should be treated. Certainly, corrective information about wolves was in order, for few animals have been so maligned, so despised, and so misunderstood as the wolf. For all Jack London's fascination with wolves, it has been pointed out that he, as well, perpetuated gross misconceptions about wolves in his fiction, especially in those instances in which wolves kill human beings and devour them.

Two widely held and long-standing misconceptions were finally challenged by modern science: the idea that the wolf is an aggressive attacker of human beings and the idea that the wolf has actually killed hundreds of human beings. Every field biologist who has worked with wolves in the last three decades of the twentieth century has established without a shadow of a doubt that wolves, far from aggressively attacking human beings, are extraordinarily shy and will invariably run from human beings. Some biologists have been able to hold down unprotesting wolves long enough to perform examinations of them. Others report that single human beings can invariably frighten away whole packs of wolves, even from fresh kills.

L. David Mech in *The Wolf: The Ecology and Behavior of an Endangered Species* (Minnesota: University of Minnesota Press, 1970), summarizes the results of scrutiny of respectable scientific reports that healthy wolves have slaughtered human beings. Accounts of wolves terrorizing villages in France in the 1760s were, upon further study, found to be attacks by dog-wolf mixes. Investigations of reported multiple killings by wolves in northern European areas have invariably emerged with the same conclusion: there have been no authenticated cases of nonrabid wolves killing human beings and no authenticated reports of nonrabid wolves attacking human beings.

Mech, who did his own investigation of wolves in North America, states the following:

> In North America, no scientifically acceptable evidence is available to support the claim that healthy wild wolves are dangerous to man. In fact, I could find only one documented report in a scientific journal of a wolf attack on a human being. (291)

Furthermore, in areas of heavy wolf population, like parks in Ontario, Canada, thousands of children camp in the wild each year. Despite this, there have been no reports of wolf attacks.

Another claim by livestock ranchers was that wolves, if left alone, would decimate their herds of cattle and sheep. Yet researchers, in examining the stomach contents of dead wolves, found that only a small percentage had remains of domestic cattle in their stomachs. Their findings failed to convince ranchers that the number of herd animals killed by wolves was insignificant.

ENDANGERED SPECIES ACT

In the 1960s, legislation began to be discussed and introduced to reverse some of the damage done to wild populations of wolves. The reasons for this reexamination were complex: the results of competent studies of the wolf, a greater awareness of the extent to which the wolf and other wild creatures had been obliterated, many irreversibly, and a greater awareness of the critical interdependence of all creatures, including human beings.

The first great turning point in the fate of wolves came in 1967 when the federal government placed them on the endangered-species list. Yet wolves continued to be killed for sport until 1974. Positive action came with the legislation that had the greatest impact on the preservation of wildlife, including wolves: the Endangered Species Act of 1973. Attempts were continued throughout the rest of the twentieth century to modify the 1973 act to either make it more effective or to weaken it.

Those with the greater interest in preserving wildlife argued (and still argue) that the lives of all animals threatened with extinction in areas that were once their natural habitats should be protected. They maintained that predators like wolves and mountain lions should be protected even if it meant that farmers had to develop alternate ways of protecting their livestock and even lost an occasional cow or sheep. They also argued that vanishing seals and otters had to be protected even if it meant that fishermen had fewer fish for their nets. If the species at issue was a rare and lowly toad or fish and would be threatened with extinction by lucrative construction like a dam or building project, environmentalists contended that the construction should be prohibited in the interest of the natural environment and the future of the species.

On the other hand, farmers, especially, argued (and argue) that wolves, coyotes, and other predators were a threat to their sheep, cows, and livelihoods. Those who made their livings from the fur business mounted similar arguments. Those who invested in construction that was held up because of protection laws contended that their projects benefited people. They asserted that when the needs of humans conflict with those of lower creatures, the decision should always be to the advantage of people.

Resistance to wolf protection is strong in some areas even at the close of the twentieth century. The state of Minnesota, for example, continued openly to trap and kill wolves after 1974 despite the federal government's warnings of sanctions. Finally, in 1978, to cool off tensions about the wolf, the federal government removed the wolf from the list of endangered species in Minnesota, and Minnesota's policy of thinning out wolves resumed with impunity. But in 1983 and 1984, the state tried to open the way for the sport hunting of wolves. This time, however, the courts intervened to stop the hunting. Still, the fight over wolves continues in Minnesota, Wyoming, and other areas. Sometimes farmers are reduced to alarmist tactics, as in Texas during June 1999, when the wounding of one calf (which survived) sent up such an alarm of a possible wolf attack that the story made national news. That the account received such attention would suggest that it is an isolated instance, and that, in fact, wolves are not decimating cattle and sheep herds, despite protection of wolves.

In providing a future in the United States for the nearly extinct wolves, plans were approved to reintroduce wolves into key areas where they had once been numerous. Wolves "reappeared" in Yellowstone Park, which had once been a key native area for them. (Whether they came back into the park naturally after a period of protection or whether park rangers themselves quietly introduced them into the park is still a matter of debate.) But the issue of the wolf is still controversial and far from being amicably resolved. Objections continue to be raised by cattlemen and sheep farmers and by hunters who claim that wolves kill too much of their wild game.

OTHER WILDLIFE

The wolf is only one of many animals that became extinct or were killed to the verge of extinction in the Americas. The devastation of wildlife other than wolves in the Yukon, Alaska, and the Northwest Territories in general began as early as the late eighteenth century and continued well into the nineteenth century, long before the Yukon gold rush occurred. There had been little control of the hunting of beavers, otters, and seals for their pelts or of whales for their oil. Their numbers were dangerously reduced in the arctic and subarctic regions of North America even before the end of the nineteenth century. Buffalo and many kinds of whales, otters, beavers, seals, birds (including the bald eagle), and fish had already been hunted to the verge of extinction. Some creatures had been killed for their fur, for oil, or for food, but the motive for killing many others, like the wolf, coyote, mountain lion, otter, and hawk, for example, was to protect the profits of farmers and fishermen who were in competition with these animals or thought that certain animals were threatening their livelihoods. In 1915, the Bureau of Biological Survey targeted several predators for deliberate extinction in the lower United States—not only wolves, but mountain lions, coyotes, and bears.

Getting rid of animals natural to certain areas produced a disastrous domino effect. People failed to learn quickly enough that elements of the wild could be gone forever and that eliminating any species, however small, could upset the ecological balance of the environment and create new problems for humankind. In some areas, for example, hunting the wolf and coyote to extinction caused serious repercussions. The mice and rabbits that had been the main diet of the predators overran the fields and destroyed crops. This mass destruction of plants needed to retain the soil and moisture led, in turn, to soil erosion.

The following excerpts from documents illustrate the attitudes toward wolves and the environmental issues involving control of wolves. The earliest documents are the Massachusetts Bay Colony laws that placed a bounty on wolves. An excerpt from H. Perry Robinson's 1911 book *Of Distinguished Animals* shows the public fear of wolves. Other documents include evidence and testimony before the subcommittee on Fisheries and Wildlife Conservation of the House of Representatives in 1972: a letter from the secretary of the interior and excerpts from an article by Araby Colton in *The Howl: The Monthly Newsletter of Canadian and American Wolf Defenders* (entered in evidence). From congressional hearings held in 1987, there is an excerpt from the testimony of a congressman from Montana who objected to the relocation of wolves to Yellowstone Park and an excerpt from the testimony in support of such a measure by Frank Dunkle, director of the Fish and Wildlife Service.

BOUNTIES ON WOLVES IN COLONIAL MASSACHUSETTS

The theology that the Puritans brought with them to the New World from Europe did not kindly predispose them to wolves. Wolves were usually used in Scripture as metaphors for evil and overpowering cruelty. Tradition associated them with werewolves and witches. So when wolves attacked the cattle and sheep and other domestic animals of these New England settlers, they scarcely hesitated before enacting laws to rid their communities of these indigenous creatures.

As soon as the Puritans began raising livestock in significant numbers, they placed bounties on wolves. The first law that formalized these bounties was enacted in 1645. Because problems associated with wolves were perceived to continue, tougher laws were enacted in 1661 for the "destruction of wolves," and more lucrative bounties were made available for those bringing in the ears of killed wolves.

FROM "WOLVES," IN *THE COLONIAL LAWS OF MASSACHUSETTS,* REPRINTED FROM THE EDITION OF 1672, WITH THE SUPPLEMENTS THROUGH 1686, PUBLISHED BY ORDER OF THE CITY COUNCIL OF BOSTON
(Boston: Samuel Green, 1887)

WOLVES

Whereas great Loss and Damage doth befall this Commonwealth by reason of Wolves, which destroy great numbers of our Cattle, notwithstanding provision formerly made by this Court for Suppressing of them: therefore for the better encouragement of any to set about a work of so great concernment,

It is Ordered by this Court and the Authority thereof, that any person either English or Indian that shall kill any *Wolfe* or *Wolves*, within ten miles of any Plantation in this Jurisdiction, shall have for every *Wolfe* by him or them so killed *ten shillings*, paid out of the Treasury of the Country; Provided that due proof be made thereof unto the Plantation next adjoining where such *Wolfe* or *Wolves* were killed. (159)

• • •

Besides all other Considerations and Provisions for the destruction of Wolves; It is Ordered by this Court and the Authority thereof; That every such Indian or Indians, as shall any way destroy any *Wolfe* or *Wolves*, and deliver the Heads of such Wolves unto the Select men of any Township in this Jurisdiction; shall receive of such Select men, either two pounds of Powder, and eight pounds of Shot, or one pound of powder, and four pounds of shot, and five shillings in Corne or other pay, or else they shall receive of the Country Treasurer, Ten shillings a head, and no powder and shot, which such Indian shall chuse; and such Select men as shall pay any Indian according to their order, shall rebate it out of their next Country Rate with the Treasurer; any Law or Custome to the contrary notwithstanding, and all Select men or other that by virtue of this Order or any other, shall make payment for any Wolves, shall cut off the Eares of all such Wolves heads, and cause them to be buried, that so none may be twice paid for. [1661]

This Court doth Order, as an Encouragement to persons to destroy Wolves; That henceforth every person killing any Wolfe, shall be allowed out of the Treasury of that County where such Wolfe was Slain, *Twenty shillings*, and by the Town *Ten Shillings*, and by the Country Treasurer *Ten shillings*; which the Constable of each Town (on the sight of the ears of such Wolves being cut off) shall pay out of the next Country Rate, which the Treasurer shall allow. [1662] (160)

FEAR AND HATRED OF THE WOLF

Robinson speculates on why the wolf is so universally feared and hated. The "evidence" that he gives—resting on folk wisdom, wrongly interpreted observations, and rumor—has been repeatedly refuted by modern naturalists as unsupportable and undocumented.

FROM H. PERRY ROBINSON, *OF DISTINGUISHED ANIMALS*
(Philadelphia: J. B. Lippincott, 1911)

Provided the wolf were big enough, there is nothing that it could not swallow whole and instantaneously.

Yet the chief horror of being torn to pieces by wolves lies perhaps in the thought that death comes, as it were piecemeal. . . . There is something of the same terror, as in the case of a bound man eaten alive by rats, in the mental image of death at the jaws of a pack of wolves. . . . [T]he wolf can deal no killing blow with its paws, and it attacks first with the teeth and kills by biting, or rather by snapping and tearing; and where a pack pulls down some large animal, like stag or horse or ox, one may well believe that before the thing is dead it is already partly eaten, many pieces having already been torn from it and immediately swallowed.

But the universal human hatred of the wolf has rested not so much on the fact that, "assiduous in the shepherd's harms," it kills other animals, or on its method of killing them, nor even upon its occasional waylaying, when "fierce descending" in the pack, of men and women. In the folklore and legend of almost all countries it is invested with the two awful attributes of being an eater of babies and a spoiler of graves. (63)

• • •

More than one writer has defended the wolf against the accusation of grave-robbery, and certainly its paws are ill-adapted to digging; but the indictment turns up in too many places, among peoples too wide-sundered, to encourage a belief that is without foundation. . . .

That the wolf eats children, not only in myth, as the fearsome wer-wolf or *loup-garou*, but in actual life, is only too well authenticated in other countries besides India. . . .

Thus it is, by destruction of children, that in India every year the wolf is responsible for the deaths of more human beings than the tiger. Not that it does not, especially when in company, sometimes attack adults; and horrid tales are told of how in famine times, when the natives are too weak to defend themselves, the wolves grow bold and come out in daylight to kill and feast on men and women. (63–65)

LEGISLATION TO PROTECT ENDANGERED SPECIES

In the prepared testimony of Nathaniel Reed, an assistant secretary of the interior, we find proposed legislation to protect endangered species. Such legislation would prohibit the use of poisons to kill wildlife and would rescind earlier bills like that of March 2, 1931, which called for the elimination of predatory animals, including bears, wolves, and coyotes. The sentiments expressed in Reed's letter formed the basis of the first effective Endangered Species Act.

FROM NATHANIEL REED, "LETTER TO EDWARD A. GARMATZ, CHAIRMAN, COMMITTEE ON MERCHANT MARINE AND FISHERIES, HOUSE OF REPRESENTATIVES, 1972," IN *PREDATORY MAMMALS AND ENDANGERED SPECIES. HEARINGS BEFORE THE SUBCOMMITTEE ON FISHERIES AND WILDLIFE CONSERVATION,* 92ND CONGRESS, 2ND SESSION, MARCH 20, 21 AND APRIL 10, 11, 1972, SERIAL NO. 92–22
(Washington, DC: U.S. Government Printing Office, 1972)

U.S. Department of the Interior,
Office of the Secretary,
Washington, D.C., March 20, 1972.

Hon. Edward A. Garmatz,
Chairman, Committee on Merchant Marine and Fisheries, House of Representatives, Washington, D.C.

Dear Mr. Chairman: We respond to your request for comment on H.R. 689, H.R. 1081, H.R. 3561, H.R. 7260, H.R. 8256, H.R. 8673 and H.R. 9668, similar bills "To establish a national policy and program with respect to wild predatory mammals and for other purposes."

This Department strongly recommends enactment of H.R. 13152, H.R. 13153 or H.R. 13261, the Administration's proposed "Federal Animal Damage Control Act of 1972", in lieu of the aforementioned bills.

Each of the bills to which this report is addressed would recognize as a policy of Congress that predatory mammals "are among the wildlife resources of interest and value to the people of the United States", and would authorize the Secretary of the Interior to engage in the conservation of such predatory mammals. H.R. 689, H.R. 1081, H.R. 3561 and H.R. 8256 would further authorize the employment, in each regional office of the Bureau of Sport Fisheries and Wildlife, of an "extension mammal control agent" whose responsibility it would be to demonstrate techniques of preventing depredations by wildlife predatory mammals and methods by which to trap individual mammals causing such depredations. The number of such agents and of persons otherwise concerned with control of predatory mammals, except those employed to investigate the biology or ecology of predatory mammals, would be limited to six.

H.R. 9668 contains similar provisions, but provides in addition that no person shall be authorized to use poisons on public lands for animal control except when, because of "unusual and extraordinary circumstances", such use is determined by the Secretary of the Interior and the Administrator of the Environmental Protection Agency to be imperative. H.R. 7260 would prohibit the demonstration of animal control methods which entail the use of poisons or chemosterilants in rural and suburban areas. H.R. 8673 would direct that neither the Secretary of the Interior nor any other officer or agency of the United States "may participate with or assist any State agency, or any other person, in the killing or control of predatory mammals". The Secretary would be required, rather, to establish a program "for compensating persons whose domestic animals are killed or injured by predatory mammals".

The number and scope of these bills demonstrate a growing public concern for the fate of those wildlife species generally described as predatory animals. Until recently, the prevailing attitude had been reflected by the Act of March 2, 1931 (7 U.S.C. 426–426 (b)), which directed the Secretary of Agriculture and later, the Secretary of the Interior "to conduct campaigns for the destruction or control of (predatory) animals". Pursuant to this mandate, the Bureau of Sport Fisheries and Wildlife has provided predatory animal control services on public and private lands in many western states. These services are funded jointly by the Federal Government and interested agencies, public and private, at the State and local levels. In recognition that the objectives of this program had become subject to public criticism, Secretary Morton announced on July 9, 1971 the appointment of an expert study team "to initiate a complete review of predator control activities to identify problem areas and seek their resolution". "I personally pledge", the Secretary said in making this announcement, "that performance will follow program so that our imperiled predators will not perish in a sea of platitudes".

On February 8, President Nixon proposed enactment of the "Federal Animal Damage Control Act of 1972" now pending before your Committee, and issued on [*sic*] Executive Order which directed that heads of Federal agencies "take such action as is necessary to prevent on any Federal lands under their jurisdiction . . . (1) the field use of any chemical toxicant for the purpose of killing a predatory mammal or bird; or (2) the field use of any chemical toxicant which causes any secondary poisoning effect for the purpose of killing mammals, birds, or reptiles". In taking these actions, the President endorsed the conclusion of the Advisory Committee on Predator Control that necessary control of coyotes and other predators can be accomplished by methods other than poisons, and recommended that the Congress act to "shift the emphasis of the current direct Federal predator control program to one of research and technical and financial assistance to the States to help them control predator populations by means other than poisons".

Thus, H.R. 13152, H.R. 13153, and H.R. 13261, which together have been sponsored by 30 members of your Committee, incorporates several recommendations made to this Department and the Council on Environmental Quality by the Advisory Committee on Predatory Control in its report, "Predatory Control—1971". Briefly, the Administration proposal would (1) authorize an expanded Federal program of research concerning the control and conservation of predatory animals; (2) prohibit on Federal lands the field use of chemical toxicants for the purpose of killing predatory animals, except when such use may be required to cope with an emergency; (3) authorize Federal grants-in-aid to States for implementation of predatory control programs; and (4) repeal in its entirety the Act of March 2, 1931. A full discussion of its provisions is contained in Secretary Morton's letter to the Speaker of the House, dated February 8, 1972.

We believe that the "Federal Animal Damage Control Act of 1972" is responsive both to the judgment that direct Federal participation in predator control activity should be curtailed, and to the need for selective control by the States of those species which constitute a substantial threat to human health or safety, domestic livestock and other property, or to the effective management of other natural resources. Its enactment would again affirm the belief, expressed last month by President Nixon, that "Americans today set high value on the preservation of wildlife".

The Office of Management and Budget has advised that enactment of H.R. 13152, H.R. 13153 and H.R. 13261 would be in accord with the program of the President.

Sincerely yours,

NATHANIEL REED,
Assistant Secretary of the Interior. (6)

DEFENSE OF WOLVES

During consideration of the adoption of the 1972 Endangered Species Act, testimony was entered on the subject of aerial wolf hunting in Alaska. The following excerpt is from a newsletter devoted to the defense of wolves. The practices to which the writer, Araby Colton, testifies bring the wolf closer to extinction in one of the few areas where it still exists. Permits are issued for the killing by one individual of thirty to forty wolves a year. The inexact shooting from airplanes means that many more wolves than those actually harvested are wounded and die painful deaths in the wilderness.

FROM ARABY COLTON, "LETTER TO WOLF DEFENDERS," IN
*PREDATORY MAMMALS AND ENDANGERED SPECIES. HEARINGS
BEFORE THE SUBCOMMITTEE ON FISHERIES AND WILDLIFE
CONSERVATION*, 92ND CONGRESS, 2ND SESSION, MARCH 20, 21
AND APRIL 10, 11, 1972, SERIAL NO. 92–22
(Washington, DC: U.S. Government Printing Office, 1972)

Dear Wolf Defenders: This HOWL is late, because the first news out of Alaska was so shocking we took time to gather data from several sources, to bring you the facts. We are tempted to indulge in purple prose, but we restrain ourselves. There's no time for rhetoric.

On the inside page we print excerpts from letters and articles which substantiate the following:

1. Some arrogant barbarians in Alaska are striking back; they seem determined to show that no one, not even the United States Congress nor the President of the United States shall tell them how to run their affairs.

2. They have decided that the words "to administer" in Public Law 92-159 (H.R. 5060) give them the right to massacre and torture wolves, without limit.

3. The Alaska Department of Fish and Game is issuing permits to anyone who asks—each permit gives the right to kill 10 wolves.

4. Many hunters are getting 3 and 4 permits, thus being able to kill 30 or 40 wolves—they sell the furs for $200.

5. This hunting is all aerial, the most unsporting, inhumane, nonselective massacre of wildlife ever conceived.

6. For every wolf killed many are fatally wounded, to die lingering, agonizing deaths.

7. The killing is statewide, without excuse of "predator control", threat to ungulates, or threat to domestic stock or private property; it is "blood sport", no more, no less.

8. The Alaska Department of Fish and Game is shamelessly ignoring its own pious claims to being the protector of wolves; it is aiding and abetting the extermination of wolves.

9. The weapon used is the 12 gauge shotgun, an illegal weapon, with which it is impossible to make a clean, humane kill.

10. The aerial massacre of Alaska's wolves bears no resemblance to "big game hunting", with seasons, bag limits, and restrictions as to sex, age, etc.—it is butchery, state-wide and unlimited.

* * * * * * *

First contributor to the wolf sanctuary—Mildred Schuchard, of Medford, Oregon.

Public Law 92–159 (H.R. 5060) prohibits airborne hunting except if it is "to administer or protect or aid in the administration or protection of land, water, wildlife, livestock, domesticated animals, human life, or crops . . ."

But according to Ed Martley, *Fairbanks Daily News-Miner*, January 15, 1972, "Bob Hinman, chief of the department's (Alaska Fish and Game) game division in Fairbanks, explained the department's views on aerial wolf hunting. This hunting is definitely not for predator control, he said. Rather, it is allowed to make use of a resource that, without aerial hunting, would be largely unavailable."

In other words, the only way wolves can be killed in quantity is if they are given no chance at all, if they are butchered, and the Alaska Department of Fish and Game is making the crime possible, is encouraging it. (311)

OPPOSITION TO DESIGNATION OF THE WOLF AS AN ENDANGERED SPECIES

In 1987, congressional hearings were held to reaffirm the Endangered Species Act and to protect wolves further by reintroducing them into areas in the lower forty-eight states where they had once thrived. The key area in question was Yellowstone Park. In his testimony, Representative Ron Marlenee of Montana objects to such a plan, arguing that since the wolf is not endangered throughout the world, it should not be on the endangered-species list. Furthermore, he thinks that consideration should be given to the killing of game by wolves, which lessens the wild game available to hunters. If the government introduces wolves to Yellowstone Park, he argues, there is no guarantee that wolves will not wander out of the park's boundaries to threaten livestock and wild game and interfere with other business endeavors.

FROM "STATEMENT OF HON. RON MARLENEE, U.S. REPRESENTATIVE FROM MONTANA," IN *ENDANGERED SPECIES ACT REAUTHORIZATION. HEARING BEFORE THE SUBCOMMITTEE ON FISHERIES AND WILDLIFE CONSERVATION AND THE ENVIRONMENT*, 100TH CONGRESS, 1ST SESSION, MARCH 17, 1987, SERIAL NO. 100–8
(Washington DC: U.S. Government Printing Office, 1987)

MR. MARLENEE. Thank you, Mr. Chairman, for the opportunity to testify today before your subcommittee as you begin reauthorization of the Endangered Species Act. Mr. Chairman, as ranking member on the National Parks and Public Lands Subcommittee of the Committee on the Interior, I have several concerns about the Endangered Species Act particularly as it relates to the recovery of the Rocky Mountain wolf and the grizzly bear. (4)

• • •

What happens when the wolf pack consumes deer and elk and moose that would have been available for sportsmen? Will the State be able to control the wolf to protect our big-game hunting seasons, or will it be forced to close areas for hunting?

Mr. Chairman, there are those who claim the wolf will not have an effect on big-game populations, but I want to point out that a single wolf pack, which is a female and male and four wolf pups, can kill 23 elk or 88 deer in one winter. The wolves kill more than just the sick and the lame animals. Montana has recognized [*sic*] as one of the last opportunities to hunt big game, and the State cannot continue to successfully manage these populations when it has no control over a Federally protected species or has no protection from the lawsuits by the obstructionists or the environmentalists or the organizations like the Defenders of Wildlife.

An even bigger management problem occurs in those areas outside of the experimental zone where the wolf is protected by the Endangered Species Act. The 1985 court decision in Minnesota held there could be virtually no taking of an endangered species. Now, in Montana we have the ridiculous situation—and I would point out how ridiculous this is— where the wolf is a predator, with a bounty in Canada, until it crosses that imaginary line called a boundary, and then it magically becomes endangered or threatened.

Now, the wolf is not globally endangered and should not be listed as such, and we should have the flexibility to take those things into consideration under our act. I have passed out to members of the committee an article that appeared in Sports Afield called "Wolves at my Door." There is some humor in this article. It is written tongue-in-cheek, and I would suggest it as fun reading for the members of the committee when you are considering this act. Over the years I have written articles about the wolves, their increasing predation on wildlife and domestic animals. It tells about the wolves on the outskirts of White Horse in the Yukon, and it certainly points out how the wolf is not an endangered or threatened species, but that the children and pets on the outskirts of this, one of the major towns of Canada, are the threatened ones. (5–6)

• • •

Now, we are told not to worry about conflicts between predator control programs and the wolf. We are told that there are few conflicts between the wolf and livestock because in Minnesota the livestock producers have learned to change their management and to minimize conflicts.

Now, I keep hearing over and over again this rhetoric about, "Well, we can handle this endangered and threatened species; they do it in Minnesota. That's fine; there's no problems there. There is no predation," et cetera, et cetera, et cetera. I am getting sick and tired of hearing it. (6)

• • •

Closing, Mr. Chairman, States which are burdened—and I emphasize burdened—by endangered species and threatened species need more flexibility in managing these species. In respect to the wolf, we do not need any experimental population transplanted into the greater Yellowstone area or the northern ecosystems. Where the wolf is recovering naturally, Congress should legislatively delist the wolf so that wildlife agencies can properly manage it in conjunction with the big-game populations, allowing it to be trapped, hunted, and harvested.

Those who say that, well, we can reintroduce the wolf into selected areas like Yellowstone Park or some selected wilderness areas don't realize that as soon as that happens and the wolf ranges for 300 miles or 400 miles or 150 miles even, he is out of that experimental zone and he is into the areas of livestock management, big-game harvests, and that that wolf will then be used even though the promise is there of harvesting that wolf and keeping it under control, the threat is there then of stopping timber harvests, stopping road building, stopping oil exploration on public lands, and even hunting seasons. (6–7)

PROTECTION OF THE WOLF

In tentative support of additional protections for predators, especially wolves and bears, Frank Dunkle, director of the Fish and Wildlife Service, tries to consider the pros and cons of reintroducing wildlife to areas where they once flourished but have now disappeared. Dunkle asks the subcommittee to reexamine the old views of the wolf and to look more carefully at the old imperative to eliminate predators at all costs to protect livestock and game. Dunkle's timidity in declaring his views illustrates the heated politics involved in the question. As a result of these hearings, wolves were reintroduced into Yellowstone Park, but the controversy over the matter has never died.

FROM "TESTIMONY OF FRANK DUNKLE, DIRECTOR OF FISH
AND WILDLIFE SERVICE," IN *ENDANGERED SPECIES ACT
REAUTHORIZATION. HEARING BEFORE THE SUBCOMMITTEE ON
FISHERIES AND WILDLIFE CONSERVATION AND THE
ENVIRONMENT*, 100TH CONGRESS, 1ST SESSION, MARCH 17,
1987, SERIAL NO. 100–8
(Washington, DC: U.S. Government Printing Office, 1987)

Your other question was: should we take a species that is seemingly in good shape in some other part of the Nation or the world or the continent and go ahead and try to establish or to keep it as endangered in another place; that is, Canada, and then putting a population into the United States, namely, Montana, Idaho, or Wyoming?

It has been the recommendation of a number of people that the gray wolf was a recognized part of the ecosystem in the United States. One of the areas of large public land holdings is in the Idaho-Wyoming-Montana area, and there the gray wolf was a real and accepted part of that ecosystem.

There are those people who would like to see us establish a population back into that area. We have tried to address that kind of thinking, but also to address the idea that if we do establish a species that seems to be doing well somewhere else that once was an inhabitant of another area, that we should do so in close consultation and with understanding of the uses of that area now and the requirements, needs, and desires of the people in the area.

We are far from putting a wolf into the Yellowstone ecosystem, and the folks there are far from allowing us to at this point. I think it has to be done with discretion and understanding. So I would say that the species is endangered and/or threatened, and we are looking at that area in the United States as a possible location for reintroduction of a species that was once there, I guess I am not discussing whether or not we should or shouldn't keep it listed as endangered, because it is not threatened or endangered in another area. We are talking about putting it back into an area where it once was. (46)

• • •

and so all wolves are bad as we have been taught. Thus, wolves take livestock, and we so we [*sic*] reduce them.

As we moved into a hunter or sportsman era, the predator was seen as an adversary to the hunter who wanted those populations of game animals for a sport hunt, and then anything that a coyote, a wolf, a grizzly bear, or others took was then taking from the hunter's bag. So you have that sort of thing that will be developing. And the panel brought that out this morning.

So we will have several conflicts. But basically we are a Nation that has told ourselves that predation is bad and it takes away from us, and that is what it is based on. We are introducing a large carnivore into an area where we have in the past carefully tried to eliminate it, as was brought out by the panel, and folks are just not ready to jump up and say, "Isn't this wonderful to bring him back."

There are, you know, few, if any, real documented cases of wolves eating up people on an established basis. (47–48)

PROJECTS FOR ORAL OR WRITTEN EXPLORATION

1. Conduct a debate on whether the view of the wolf in *The Call of the Wild* is primarily positive or negative.

2. Contrast the novel's pictures of the true wolf with those of the wolf-dog. What do the similarities and differences tell us about London's view of nature and civilization?

3. Write a paper on the wolf as a symbol of the American or as a symbol of the Native American.

4. Present a book report on one of the recent studies of wolves cited in the bibliography. Conclude your report with an assessment of London's understanding of wolves as measured by recent scientific studies.

5. Interview a farmer or a hunter on the issue of predator control and the Endangered Species Act. Present your findings to the class.

6. Invite a speaker from an animal protection organization such as the Sierra Club to present that organization's position on the Endangered Species Act.

7. After thoroughly investigating the matter, conduct a class debate on the issue of protecting predatory animals.

8. Make a list of as many figures of speech as you can find involving wolves. Write a report on the wolf as it has become rooted in our language.

SUGGESTIONS FOR FURTHER READING

Allen, Durward. *Our Wildlife Legacy.* New York: Funk & Wagnalls, 1954.

Bass, Rick. *The Ninemile Wolves.* Livingston, MT: Chase City Press, 1992.

Chase, Alston. *Playing God in Yellowstone.* Boston: Atlantic Monthly Press, 1986.

Crisler, Lois. *Arctic Wild.* New York: Harper & Bros., 1958.

Daniels, Edwin. *Wolf Walking.* New York: Stewart, Tabori & Chang, 1997.

Fox, Michael. *The Soul of the Wolf.* Boston: Little, Brown & Co., 1980.

Lopez, Barry. *Of Wolves and Men.* New York: Charles Scribner's Sons, 1978.

McIntyre, Rick. *A Society of Wolves.* Stillwater, MN: Voyageur Press, 1993.

Mech, L. David. *The Wolf: The Ecology and Behavior of an Endangered Species.* Minneapolis: University of Minnesota Press, 1970.

Mowat, Farley. *Never Cry Wolf.* New York: Dell Publishing Company, 1968.

Murie, Adolph. *The Wolves of Mount McKinley*. Washington, DC: U.S. Government Printing Office, 1944.

Steinhart, Peter. *The Company of Wolves*. New York: Random House, 1995.

Turbak, Gary. *Twilight Hunters*. Flagstaff, AZ: Northland Press, 1987.

Young, Stanley, and Edward Goldman. *The Wolves of North America*. New York: Dover Publications, 1964.

Index

About the Author

CLAUDIA DURST JOHNSON is Professor Emeritus at the University of Alabama, where she served as chair of the English Department for twelve years. She is series editor of the Greenwood Press "Literature in Context" series, for which she has authored numerous works including *Understanding* To Kill a Mockingbird (1994), *Understanding* The Scarlet Letter (1995), *Understanding* Adventures of Huckleberry Finn (1996), *Understanding* The Crucible (1998), and most recently *Understanding* The Grapes of Wrath (1999).